ONE
BLOOD

SUNY Series, The Body in Culture, History, and Religion
Howard Eilberg-Schwartz, editor

ONE
BLOOD

The Jamaican Body

by

Elisa Janine Sobo

STATE UNIVERSITY OF NEW YORK PRESS

Published by
State University of New York Press, Albany

For information, address State University of New York
Press, State University Plaza, Albany, NY 12246

Production by Marilyn P. Semerad
Marketing by Fran Keneston

Library of Congress Cataloging-in-Publication Data

Sobo, Elisa Janine, 1963–
        One blood: the Jamaican body / Elisa Janine Sobo.
            p.   cm. — (SUNY series, the body in culture, history, and
    religion)
        Includes bibliographical references and index.
        ISBN 0–7914–1429–9 (hardcover). — ISBN 0–7914–1430–2 (paper)
        1. Folk medicine—Jamaica. 2. Body, Human—Social aspects–
    –Jamaica. 3. Jamaicans—Kinship. 4. Jamaicans—Health and hygiene.
    5. Jamaicans—Social conditions. I. Title. II. Series.
    GR121.J2S63   1993
    398'.353—dc20
                                                                    92–22887
                                                                    CIP

10 9 8 7 6 5 4 3 2 1

Contents

ONE BLOOD

Acknowledgments

This book is the culmination of the efforts of many people; I cannot name them all. I am especially grateful and indebted to Professor F. G. Bailey for the guidance, support, and training that he provided. I owe William Wedenoja many thanks for sharing with me his theoretical, ethnographic, and practical knowledge of Jamaica.

For comments on various sections of the manuscript or for suggestions concerning the work leading up to it, I also thank Alice Schlegel, Atwood Gaines, Barbara Rylko-Bauer, Fitz John P. Poole, Janis Jenkins, Jill Korbin, Lynn Morgan, Mark Nichter, Nicole Sault, Patricia Antoniello, Theodore Schwartz, Thomas Csordas, and Yosella Moyle. Honorary field assistants Naomi and D. J. deserve special mention for their insight, fortitude, and temerity.

Thanks also go to the Jamaican people who offered kind help and hospitality. Confidentiality bars me from acknowledging key informants by name, but this book would not exist without their friendship and participation.

Introduction

This book discusses the conceptions of embodied health and sickness held by impoverished rural Jamaicans of African descent.[1] Sicknesses, in Jamaica and elsewhere, are more than physical symptoms indicating diseased bodily states. Sicknesses may also indicate problems with and within a group's social and moral system, and individuals may use concepts of health and sickness to express these problems. Some culturally constructed sicknesses or syndromes have emerged especially for this purpose.

When people are distressed by features in their social lives, the body can serve as a symbolic arena. Those who challenge the social system may become sick with symptoms grouped together into culturally recognized syndromes. With their bodies and through the metaphorical use of the language of health and sickness, people indirectly (but sometimes strategically and consciously) argue their positions.

Comments made about a state of bodily affairs involve observations about the social and moral order.[2] Ideas about health and sickness do not always undermine the received order; often they support it. The moral order is made up of rules and expectations about what is considered as right and good, and ideally it upholds the social system. Individual immorality undermines the social system because self-interest or egoism is placed ahead of the group's interest. Egoistic acts (and sometimes even thoughts), which deny the primacy of the group or assert nontraditional values, can result in (or are the result of) sickness. From sickness, people can infer antisocial, immoral goings on: sick people are people who

1

have made waves, whether these be small (such as rejecting received wisdom about standing in the rain) or large (sodomy performed in a Catholic churchyard).

So sickness may be viewed as a punishment, whether retroactive or timely, symbolic or direct, for transgressions against society and the moral order. Sickness may also serve a positive personal function: by focusing on the somatic dimension of their complaints, sufferers can address or escape problems inherent in the social and moral order that cannot be directly confronted.

This study explores sickness and health as a social arena. It focuses on gender relations because here many of the tensions that characterize Jamaican culture, such as that between attaining secure interpersonal relationships and maintaining a protective layer of privacy and isolation, gain prominence. Ideas about kin and children are explored along the way because of their connections to beliefs about the body—especially in its gendered dimension.

Social causes are credited and sickness is deemed "created" and extraordinary only after asocial causes and "natural" sicknesses are ruled out or (and this is important) where blaming another, blaming the victim, and/or airing grievances are seen as expedient. In such a case, which always involves an animate outside agent, circumstantial evidence indicating a social and moral breach is pointed out.

Although an attacker could be wholly responsible for all wrongdoing, a victim accusing another of witchcraft takes the chance of being cast as a culpable participant in a socially disruptive relationship. S/he faces the possible shame and embarrassment of having private business made public, of being accused of having an overly suspicious mind, and of being blamed for provoking his or her misfortunes with "sin," whether this means an action that led to a transgressor's justifiable ire and reaction or the willful neglect of traditionally respected behavioral precautions. Still, social explanations for sicknesses often take precedence over asocial ones.

Chapter 1 provides background information and depicts the setting in which the sickness discourses described in this book take place. Chapter 2 provides a detailed description of the Jamaican ethnophysiological belief system. In brief, the body is seen as a necessarily permeable system that must be maintained in equilibrium. As Chapter 3 explains, the reproductive system and the body both follow the same ethnophysiological model and work according to the same principles.

Chapters 4, 5, and 6 describe the social and moral order by which Jamaicans attempt to live. The ideal social world is divided between egoistic strangers and altruistic kin, but the real world, Jamaicans believe, consists of only egoistic individuals. This engenders resentment, expressed in concern over being attacked by others. Attacks on health are seen as most efficacious, and people believe that poisons are often hidden in food. Knowledge of this affects eating habits. Men generally fear poison more than women, because men do not cook for themselves.

Chapters 7 and 8 explore the relations between parents and children, and Chapters 9, 10, and 11 focus on those between men and women. Children are valued and social adulthood depends on caring for them well; those who do not produce and raise children, like those who do not establish interdependent heterosexual relations and those who avoid kin obligations, are branded as being antisocial. But gender relations, like social relations in general, are full of wariness and distrust.

Chapter 12 explores "tying," in which women bind men to them by adding menstrual blood to men's food. This can lead to a type of "bad belly" sickness. Chapter 13 focuses on the "bad belly" of unwanted pregnancy, which aids in an understanding of the subject of Chapter 14: the "false belly," "witchcraft baby," or spirit impregnation.

These syndromes involve the incorporation of a disagreeable and therefore sickening substance that, when taken in through an orifice that symbolizes for each gender the trusting fashion in which they must accept offerings from others if they are to be a part of society, announces its presence in a form of "bad belly." As Farmer notes, "Suffering strains cultural norms and brings them into sharp relief" (1988, 80). In Jamaican beliefs about their bodies, we find access to Jamaican beliefs about their world as a whole and their problematic place within it.

Carrying water back to the yard

PART
ONE

Traditional Health
Beliefs

Chapter 1

The Research Setting

Jamaica, an independent nation since 1962, is the third largest of the Greater Antilles, an arc of islands located in the western Caribbean Sea. A tropical island 4,230.5 square miles in area and with a population of almost 2.4 million people, Jamaica has flat but narrow coastal plains. Slaveholding colonizers found these attractive and established sugar plantations and cattle ranches. They also greatly depleted the once densely forested island's stock of timber, as their fellow citizens valued "exotic" hardwoods. Still verdant, Jamaica's interior has over 120 streams and rivers and countless steep valleys and mountains, which reach as high as 7,400 feet in the east. The island's original name was probably *Xaymaca*, a word used by some of its first inhabitants, Arawak Indians, perhaps to mean "land of wood and water."[1]

"TOWN" AND "COUNTRY": MY ARRIVAL

Jamaica's present capital, Kingston, which I first saw in the summer of 1988, sometimes seems about to be overrun by goats and street vendors. The apparent disorganization and raucous color of this hot, dusty city, called "town" by Jamaicans, can be quite intimidating. Downtown, at a place

7

called "parade," a rainbow of cars and vans with monikers
like The Exterminator painted across their windshields
speed by, radios blaring, and stuffed to near-bursting with
uncomfortable people whose heads and arms often protrude
from the windows. Drivers dodging crowds impervious to
traffic laws must keep a special lookout for young boys pushing handmade wooden carts heavy with goods belonging to
"higglers," or market women.

Off the street, hawkers with cardboard boxes or baskets
full of fruit, candy, or sundries such as toilet paper, cheap
watches, or the daily tabloid push their wares. Idle men lean
against crumbling colonial storefronts with cigarettes dan-
gling from their lips and caps pulled low, harassing passing
women with superficially sweet entreaties and pleas for
attention. "Town" (Kingston) is known by all Jamaicans as a
place in which "everybody looking something from you."
While the same holds true for "country," most say that only
necessity or "compulsion" makes country people journey into
town: they fear its hustlers and thieves. They also find the
pace too quick, dress and customs foreign, and the crowds of
strangers unnerving. The stress of travel is another factor
that keeps rural folk "in country."

Jamaican's sometimes liken their busses to the slave
ships that brought West Africans to the island. My first
minibus ride was, like each subsequent venture, a lesson in
discomfort. After taking care of business in town, I found "a
transport" to the area in which I would live. "Packed so til it
can't take message," the old van full of sweating people sat in
the heat for over one half-hour before we moved. "Driver like
to kill us all," passengers mumbled to themselves. No one left
for a breath of air because to do so would mean giving up a
hard-won space. Commanded by a man in an unbuttoned,
untucked long-sleeved shirt who sported several gold-toned
chains with big medallions and a pair of dark glasses, the bus
finally pulled out honking, left the city limits with speed, and
careened over the narrow, potholed junction road through
mountains overgrown with greenery to Port Antonio in the
north.

I settled myself in a northeastern coastal "district," or village, of about eight hundred people just off the single-lane, rutted main highway. It was in this village, where I lived for a year between 1988 and 1989, that I learned about most of the beliefs and practices discussed in this book.

Except in sections of this chapter describing the national context of the study, I often use the term *Jamaicans* in reference to the people whose lives and thoughts I describe. I do so because most Jamaicans are members of the group that this book specifically concerns: poor, rural people of African descent.[2] I tested the representativeness of my findings for this group during the final month of research when I worked with William Wedenoja in two of his fieldsites, one a central mountain village near Mandeville and the other a southwestern fishing village near Savanna la Mar. Media accounts and data gathered during several short trips to Kingston indicate that my findings also apply to impoverished city dwellers but I have not confirmed this.

The village that I lived in, like most others, consists of a conglomeration of people brought together only by geography and ancestry: they share a postal agency, patronize the same shops, and have many relatives in common. No one has any more legitimate authority than the next person except insofar as others allow it to them. In general, respect accompanies certain occupations or riches; class is important, and those desiring of respect strive to adopt the lifestyle of the Jamaican elite, which includes certain appliances, hairstyles, vocabularies, and so on.

"In country," life's pace is slow. Unemployment and underemployment rates run high. When not working in their yards or farming, people willingly sit for hours on verandas watching others amble past on errands. Some wait time out at the shop on "the main," or the coastal road that passes below the village. The shop is a typical one-room structure with the usual scant stock of soap, tinned mackerel, biscuits, cornmeal, and matches. Generally, all stock is stored behind a counter, with chicken-wire separating customers from shopkeepers and their wares. Out front, under the corru-

gated zinc overhang, mostly men but also idle youths and a
few women gather, chatting or sitting silently on wooden
stools worn smooth, watching for the sagging country bus to
pull by to see who gets on and who comes off, noting just
what each fellow villager wears and carries. Such information can have great strategic importance.

PERSONAL APPEARANCE

In one's "yard," that is, within the bounds of the land on
which one has a home, ragged "judging" (shabby, threadbare,
and unpresentable) clothes get worn. But to "walk out," even
if only to a local shop for salt pork, requires attention to
appearance. "We are young ladies," a ten-year-old informed
me as she and her sister prepared to fetch bread for their
caretaker by changing clothes and replaiting their hair. On
major or social outings, such as when going out of the district,
to church, or "up street" to see "what a go on" at the pub,
clothing—even shoes—must be fresh and clean no matter
how old. Holes must be mended and clothes well pressed,
even if this means the use of a charcoal-heated iron on a
scorching hot day. New clothes are reduced to yard-wear in a
short time because of the vigor with which Jamaicans wash.

Young men and women love to affect a stylish appearance, and to "shock out," or impress, with their dress. They
are especially keen to meet Easter, Independence Day in
August, and Christmas with "new brand" clothing "suits,"
even when money "runnings" are tight. At Christmas, the
words of one carol are sung as: "Don we now our *new*
apparel." No one openly admits to wearing "old broke," or the
castoffs of others. Clothes relatives send as gifts from "foreign" (anywhere overseas; usually England or the U.S.A.) are
frequently passed off as new when they are not.

Modesty and a concern about the effects of the skin-dark-
ening, health-endangering rays of the sun lead most
Jamaicans to cover themselves with clothing. Although
"rebels" and some city women "walk street" in shorts, pants,

and miniskirts, the more conservative majority stick with skirts and dresses that cover the knees and half-sleeved blouses or T-shirts. Most women feel strange without a belt to keep things "together." They always "lap frock tail" when sitting down on low stools or logs, bringing their rear skirt hems up through their legs like a diaper, guarding their crotches from male eyes and other irritants.

Men wear long pants (rarely dungarees) and long-sleeved shirts or "ganzies" (knit T-shirts or jerseys). Like the women, they do not tuck their shirts in but smooth them down over their waists. Bare feet for males as for females are all right in the yard but not on the street, and socks are necessary for trips to town. People like to don caps, and many have nice hats for special occasions, when men wear suitcoats.

Jamaicans take pride in their appearance and all but the most deeply impoverished have one outfit for church and funerals. Each Sunday a parade of girls in lacy frocks and hats, boys with white dress shirts, a few older men in mismatched slacks and jackets, and "plenty" women in high-heeled shoes carrying umbrellas to ward off the sun makes its way down mule paths and along the roads to church. People openly carry Bibles, but nothing more; purses, totes, and opaque plastic bags conceal personal goods from the eyes of others, whom Jamaicans always cast as "too beg," "red eye," and "too bad mind and grudgeful" (too envious and too quick to cast aspersions).

"WALKING OUT"

On weekdays and Saturdays, women may leave their yards and walk with loads atop their heads, whether laundry being taken to the river to wash or stones being carried for construction or road work. Men with machetes and tall boots head to their fields and gardens or to those of others for whom they work. Now and again, they ride donkeys. Many children go off to school, dressed in tidy, mandatory uniforms. Young unemployed men saunter off to sit and smoke or chat with others, while young women "care" children and do other domestic work in their own yards. Those cooking send children "up shop" for ingredients as needed, since storage, refrigeration, and bulk purchases are generally a problem. Unless haste is absolutely mandatory, and especially in the heat of the day, everyone walks slowly.

Children often cluster in large groups, but adults do not. With the exception of courting teens who chance their caretakers' wrath, men and women rarely socialize as couples or even walk together. Men almost always "walk out" alone. Women more often meet up and walk in twos or threesomes. This is partly because many women do not feel safe alone and also because, while it is acceptable for men to cluster at rum shops to chat, women (who are expected to keep to their yards) can only exchange news and advice when a "mission" such as taking washing to the river brings them out. Even so, they usually walk with related females, such as daughters or the girlfriends or wives of their brothers.

No one, male or female, wishes to be seen talking with others too often lest s/he be labeled a gossip, and walking with kin helps lessen this risk. Avoiding strangers also helps keep "business" more private, in theory. People know, however, that even their closest kin can turn around and harm them by sharing with other villagers even the tiniest bit of incriminating evidence about "what really a go on" in their lives.

SEEING, SMELLING, HEARING

People with "roadside" yards know "plenty" because, being adjacent to the road, they see things happen. They see people pass from here to there and draw their own conclusions. But even those who must walk over narrow tracks through "bush" or untended vegetation to reach their yards know others' "business," because "they will hear." The surest way to learn is to watch and "study a thing," and all Jamaicans know how to "pick sense out of nonsense."

Knowing who has wealth of any kind is of the utmost

importance in this world of grinding impoverishment because then strategic alliances can be sought. So also is knowing about others' antics, such as hoarding or "sleeping out" (with a lover, away from home), because this knowledge can be used to stop them from gaining command of resources. People try to cover their tracks and guard their positions while, at the same time, undermining those of others. When inept, manipulations to these ends are laughed at. When unjust and uncovered, they also bring shame. Almost every person must "try a thing" to get by, and in one context or another this can be cast to "look bad."

In addition to things seen, certain odors characterize daily life in the village I lived in. These include the stench of dirty hog pens and the smell of stale sweat. Often, the sweet scent of marijuana percolates out from under the big mango tree where idle young men sit and "reason." "Later on up in the day," one notices the floral freshness of those who have recently bathed. On weekends, the smell of chicken being "jerked" or barbecued for sale to pub-goers fills the air by the shop. Certain people, mostly women, regularly sell treats, such as sweet oranges or peanuts (which they pack in small plastic bags and then tie to a bent wire hanger), to hungry or "peckish" revelers. These small-scale vendors appear at funerals and other gatherings as well. Special occasions are always accompanied by the strong "renk" odor of simmering curried goat, a necessary dish at any large gathering.

Weekends are always noisy. The village has two pubs; they face each other from opposite sides of the road. Each of the pub owners has installed a gigantic "set" or sound system with speakers six feet tall. People come from outside as well as inside the village to dance and look for a sex partner or to gamble and drink with usually good-natured belligerence. Each pub has an ill-lit "lawn," or covered patio, for dancing; a terrace for milling about, conversing, and surveying others; a small backroom for serious gambling; and a bar. Like most pubs, these are brightly decorated but rather dilapidated establishments in which no two glasses match and customers chip their own ice.

During the week, the district is normally filled only with peaceful rural sounds. These begin in the early morning with cocks crowing and people beginning to stir, chopping wood or running water at one of the public spigots. Barking puppies, bleating goats, braying donkeys, and twittering birds also make themselves heard. Sometimes, a pig being slaughtered cries out, squealing for quite some time before it dies.

The late afternoon brings the laughter of children returning from school and the "lick" of the domino tiles men slap down onto wooden tables at the pub. Often, during the evening hours, all village radios broadcast the favorite station, and one hears it continuously and softly when passing others' yards as, for example, on the way down from one's garden in the bush "up top," at the end of the road. Now and again, a loudly played tape or a quarrel bespeaking the tensions that lie beneath the seeming calm of rural life disrupts this peace. On Wednesday nights and Sundays, gospel and redemption hymns float out through open church windows.

THE NATION'S ECONOMY

Poverty exacerbates the tensions of daily life. The present economy has its historical roots in the slave-based plantation system of the British colonial regime. Large landholdings were controlled by colonizers and sugar was produced for export. Slave labor was used until the practice was abolished in 1834; then, the "discipline of hunger" replaced the "discipline of slavery" (Mintz 1986, 70). Only a portion of freed slaves remained on the plantations; indentured East Indians provided much of the postemancipation tenant labor. Ex-slaves preferred to work for wages, however small (Kaplan et al. 1976, 63).

Many freed men and women cultivated their own plots, sometimes selling from what they produced. A marketing system was already intact, because slaves (especially women) often had to raise much of their own food and were allowed off of the plantation to sell surpluses at Sunday markets

(Mintz 1974; Patterson 1969, 224). Plantation owners monop-
olized the fertile coastal plains, so ex-slaves were driven
inland to the highlands, where they established small subsistence gardens among the rocky slopes. A number of churches
founded "free villages" by buying up ruined estates and selling small parcels to church-going ex-slaves (Mintz 1987;
Black 1983). Still, many ex-slaves remained landless. The
land settlement programs of the early 1940s have not helped:
the eventual subdivision of parcels by kin groups led to plots
too small to profitably till. Many lie fallow today (Brodber
1989, 68). Only about half of all rural Jamaicans own the
land they live on (Barrett 1988, 11).

In the late 1800s, after sugar profits had declined, a few
entrepreneurs established a trade in bananas, and the economy turned upward again. Much of the capital involved was
American; the Jamaican economy remained (and remains)
dependent on foreign investors. The attention paid to foreign
markets underlies Jamaica's weak internal intersectoral and
interindustry links. A reliance on foreign goods (and a concomitant disinterest in consuming local products) complicates the nation's economic woes (Davies and Witter 1989).

A well-educated professional administrative class emerged
to manage foreign interests. The ruling class that replaced the
colonial regime came out of this service sector. Partly owing to
this and also because good land has been hard for peasants to
secure, education (despite its elitist nature and the system's
financial woes) has slowly replaced agricultural pursuits as
the preferred route to social advancement (Austin 1984; Brodber 1989).

After World War II, large numbers of Jamaicans moved to
cities seeking work. The nation is becoming increasingly
urban: while in 1970, 41 percent of Jamaicans were classified
as urban dwellers, by 1982, 48 percent were (STATIN 1988a,
10). Agricultural enterprise has dwindled in importance. In
1950, agriculture contributed over 36 percent to Jamaica's
gross domestic product (Kaplan et al. 1976, 232). By the
1980s, agriculture's contribution to the GDP hovered at only
about 6 percent (STATIN 1989, 314).

Nonetheless, a peasant class does persist. Jamaican communities form a continuum that runs from subsistence and cash-crop farming to pure wage labor (and unemployment). Generally speaking, reliance on wage labor increases with population density and proximity to a town, plantation, or mining operation. Pure farming is rare, and most rural communities, including the one in which I lived, are made up of people who rely on a fluctuating mixture of strategies for economic survival. But "occupational multiplicity" can have deleterious effects in the long run. People who do not specialize do not build guilds or other bases for power (Brodber 1989; Comitas 1973).

As a nation, Jamaica now looks toward free-market tourism, manufacturing, and bauxite mining for its income. Mining, which contributed almost nothing to the GDP during the 1950s (Kaplan et al. 1976, 232) now accounts for 7.5 percent of GDP (STATIN 1988a, 314). Manufacturing, too, has shown great increase, from 6.5 percent of the GDP in 1950 (Kaplan et al. 1976, 232) to 22.2 percent in 1988 (STATIN 1988a, 314). As for tourism, in 1988 Jamaica had over one million visitors and received over $500 million U.S. in foreign travel (STATIN 1989, 318–19).

But much of the profit from these sectors gets returned to foreign investors. Bauxite mining (which may decrease in importance because of recycling) is not labor-intensive and uses only 0.7 percent of the nation's employed labor force (STATIN 1989, 218). Tourism relies on imported foods and amenities. Manufacturing often involves sweatshop-like export-processing operations carried out in free production zones for foreign corporations. The majority of Jamaica's citizens gain little from these industries. Jamaica has one of the greatest disparities in income levels in the world (Pariser 1985, 24), and if anything, tourism, mining, and manufacturing exacerbate the gap between rich and poor.

According to M. G. Smith, 85 percent of all Jamaicans belong to the impoverished lower class—the group that this book is about. They remain unemployed or find menial and often seasonal jobs as hotel maids, banana packers, sugarcane cutters, and sweatshop seamstresses. Only 12 percent of Jamaicans hold skilled positions and only 3 percent are classified as professionals (M. G. Smith, 1989).

In 1987 the per capita yearly income was about $1,000 U.S. (STATIN 1988b, 126) and 20.8 percent of the labor force was unemployed, with a rate of 13.6 percent for males and 29.5 percent for females (64). Underemployment is not represented in these figures. Where I lived fully one-third of the population was unemployed. Two-thirds of these were between the ages of fourteen and thirty-four (STATIN 1982). For comparison, the unemployment rate in the U.S. now hovers between 7 and 8 percent.

The majority of Jamaicans rely on a "gray-market" or informal economy, one rich with "entrepreneurship, technological creativity and innovativeness, and highly motivated work effort, all of which are in short supply in the formal economy" (Davies and Witter 1989, 99). Trade for the masses is handled by higglers, mostly women, who form the infrastructure of the distribution system on which people have come to rely over the past centuries. The existence of an internal market system is an outgrowth of the market system developed by slaves (Bush 1990; Mintz 1974).

Higglers are middle merchants who buy wholesale and sell retail, whether their stock is tomatoes, cabbage, and scallions or cheap clothing and hair oil brought in from Miami or Panama. Some work from their verandas, selling eggs, ice, bread, or any other commodity. A true higgler is a feisty traveling woman who carts produce from the countryside into town every weekend on an overloaded bus or a cooperatively hired and similarly packed truck. The cost of transportation is high, and profits are low, but by wisely investing pennies some higglers have been able to "uplift" themselves.[3]

A few other ways to make a living exist. Goats and garden vegetables may be raised. Women—whose occupational and survival strategies are discussed in Barrow (1988), Massiah (1988), and Senior (1991)—may take in washing when it is available and some do "day work," helping in others' homes or yards when needed, usually for about $4 or $5 U.S. plus lunch. Small farmers sometimes employ helpers, especially when planting or harvesting. Men may find construction work, building houses from cement blocks for people wealthier than themselves. Like the women, they usually work for those who receive "foreign" money, whether pensions from jobs held abroad or gifts from relatives who have managed to emigrate despite recent tightening of policies. Only those with aid from overseas can hire help or build large houses.

The foreign exchange that pays wages is not limited to capitalist investments or pensions and relatives' remittances: much of it comes through the black market from *ganja*[4] (marijuana) sales. This brings in an estimated $200 million U.S. each year (Pariser 1985, 29), which equals the Jamaican food import bill (28). In 1988, Jamaica was the United States' third biggest marijuana supplier. If money that ends up outside the island is taken into account, the *ganja* trade could be worth as much as $1 billion U.S. (De Cordoba 1988). For comparison, tourism, one of the island's most important industries, brought in $525 million U.S. in 1988 (STATIN 1989, 319).

GEOGRAPHY

Most of the plants Jamaica has gained fame for, such as *ganja*, bananas, and sugarcane, as well as breadfruit, mangoes, passion fruit, and other tropical produce, are not indigenous. My Jamaican friends often boasted that even a dropped seed—any kind of seed—will sprout and develop into a thriving plant. In general, this is true, and each group of settlers that reached the island added something to Jamaica's stock of flora. Ackee, a fruit brought from west Africa by slave ships, and breadfruit, probably introduced by Captain Bligh, are both "country" staples when in season. The Spaniards brought bananas, coconut, sugarcane, and citrus. The Arawak Indians brought sweet potatoes and maize, and the East Indians brought *ganja*.

Much Jamaican soil is receptive and productive. But rocky ground, steep grades, and constant erosion pose problems in the mountainous interior, where so many ex-slaves were forced to settle. Additionally, some small farmers have trouble because many commercially available seeds are designed to grow in conjunction with specific types of expensive fertilizer.

Much of the earth in Jamaica is reddish in color because of the large amount of bauxite and other minerals in the soil. However, except where bauxite mining is underway and along the roadside or rural paths, most of the earth is covered with foliage and dotted with clearings on which stand one- and two-room homes made of boards, little sheds that house cooking hearths or pit toilets, or large residences of cement blocks. The red earth is hidden on the plains of the south and northwest with rows of sugarcane and other crops and, especially in the south, with meadows and low scrub brush. The interior and the east coast are jungly. In general, Jamaica presents itself in green against a blue, blue sky. Jamaicans have capitalized on the variety of plants grown here: many are believed to have pharmacological applications and are used frequently.

While Jamaica's mountains are steeper and higher in the east where the Blue Mountains rise into damp fog, the smaller western chains are more rugged owing to the karst topography, particularly in the "cockpit country." This section of the western highlands appears from a plane as if it had been hit by a shower of giant meteors. It is full of pits and peaks, valleys and cones because, over time, many of the underground caves that lace this countryside have collapsed, dropping the earth on top of them down to form the cockpits. The topography looks like the inside of an egg carton. The whole area is covered in greenery and resembles a pool table on which the pocket-maker has gone mad. Although largely unoccupied the area used to provide sanctuary for Maroons, or runaway slaves, who banded together as rebels.

A variety of animals inhabit Jamaica. There are many kinds of hummingbirds and butterflies. Toads and frogs, which whistle at night, abound. Huge "John Crow" turkey buzzards often circle low in the afternoon sky. It is said that they signal an impending funeral. Many types of lizards also thrive. Jamaicans fear these almost as much as they fear the nonpoisonous snakes found in the island. Ghosts, it is said, often take the form of these reptiles. Pests such as mosquitoes, rats, and giant winged cockroaches are plentiful.

Domestic animals include the pig and goat; dogs and cats are kept to guard yards and catch rats. Large landholders may raise cattle or have horses, but only a few peasants can afford even a donkey or a mule. Wild hogs roam the interior, and mongeese often steal and devour chickens. The sea is rich with (but quickly being depleted of) fish.

WEATHER

Jamaica is always warm, with an average temperature of about 80 degrees. Working in the sun or riding on packed buses can make it seem much hotter. People always carry a "rag" (a kerchief or washcloth) with which to wipe away the sweat that rolls from their brows, and they often wear hats because "sun will junk you" (make you sick). Hats also offer protection from dampness and breezes (and allow wearers to express their sense of style). Rainfall is heavy in the east and happens at least once a day in autumn. The national average yearly rainfall is 195 cm. or 77 inches.

The weather cycle joins with other cycles and the year can be seen in terms of what crops are in, what trees are bearing, or what activities children are pursuing. For example, someone thinking of September might refer to the time pimento trees bear. December is, in the east, kite-making season because of the constant breeze. People know May as the time when children hunt land crabs, July as the season of "plenty mango," and August as the month in which Independence holidays are held and as "[avocado] pear time." October and November are generally rainy, followed by "Christmas breeze," then a dry spell from January until March when the rain resumes. Breezes characterize Easter, summer comes, and then hurricane season arrives. As Pariser says, "hurricanes represent the one outstanding negative in an otherwise impeccably hospitable climate" (1985, 10).

The last hurricane to devastate the island hit on 12 September 1988, barely three weeks after I arrived, foisting upon me a painfully close view of crisis behavior. "Mister Gilbert," as the Jamaicans respectfully called this menace, was the fiercest hurricane to hit the western Caribbean this century. The clichés about trees felled like so many toothpicks and zinc sheet roofs lifted like lids from tin cans aptly describe the scenes Gilbert's force wrought. Many homes were completely "dashed away," some left "all mash up" and others wholly carried off, with only bare red-painted cement foundations proving that they once existed (ruined homes with dirt floors often left no evidence). Driving rains and giant waves soaked everything, and livestock not killed was set free by the hurricane. Crops and roads were damaged, water supplies tainted, and power lines downed. To top things off, a grain elevator in the island's only flour mill exploded one week later.

POPULATION

Despite Hurricane Gilbert, I got to know Jamaica, an island in which appearances and managed presentations of self—and of one's racial and cultural backgrounds—are of prime importance. The prevalence of dark skin notwithstanding, whiteness is a valued characteristic here and most Jamaicans consider it insulting to be called black by fellow islanders. African heritage is often denied or submerged. Although attitudes are changing and black pride movements have met with some success, Brodber (1989) shows that color prejudice, which she identifies as a variant of racism, is still prevalent. This is especially true in rural areas (Kaplan et al. 1976, 96). The effects this color prejudice has on self-esteem and opportunities cannot be underestimated.

Power in Jamaica is concentrated in the hands of the light-skinned European and Middle Eastern minority. At the time of the 1982 census, only 0.3 percent of all Jamaicans were identified as white: two-thirds of these individuals were of European descent and the rest were Syrian or Lebanese (STATIN 1989, 102). Less conservative figures indicate that about 2 percent of all Jamaicans are European or Middle Eastern in origin. Nearly 3 percent are of unmixed Chinese or East Indian descent. But 95 percent of Jamaica's 2.4 million people have African ancestors (Hudson and Seyler 1989, 45).

The Jamaican social system has been characterized as a color and class system in which people rank each other, both conceptually and practically (as in hiring practices and marriage preferences), according to skin color. This system grew out of slavery and colonialism. The social structure can be visualized as a pyramid in which a small white elite at the top is supported by a large base of blacks. Brown-skinned individuals of mixed European and African ancestry are generally in the middle. Although a few light-skinned and more than a few brown-skinned people are members of the lower class, darkness of color, "African" traditions, and low status are positively correlated and assigned a place at society's base (Brodber 1989; Henriques 1958; Hoetink 1985; M. G. Smith 1984).

A number of blacks have moved into top positions, but the elite are still largely light-skinned, which perpetuates the link people make between color and status. People scrutinize their complexions in photos and destroy those in which they "show" too dark. Faces that come out light, or "bright," are favored. For example, one woman congratulating a bride remarked that she could not have chosen finer bridesmaids, for they were not black but "nice brown ladies." I was often complimented by young girls for having "good" hair, a "straight" nose, and a "clear" (i.e., light) complexion. But people also pointed out that my olive skin and wavy dark hair marked me as not being fully white.

Jamaicans of whatever color are deeply religious. Even political meetings begin with prayers. Although Jamaican spirituality is not confined to institutional settings, churches abound. For example, there were four (and later five) churches in the village where I (and 800 others) lived: one Methodist, two Pentecostal, and one (and then two) Revivalist churches. In total, only about 100 villagers attended church regularly (although some did belong to churches in different districts). Membership was heavily female, and individuals with higher status preferred Methodist gatherings.

The majority of Jamaicans identify themselves as Christians. This is, in part, due to the influence of the color and class system in which European traditions are venerated. For example, despite its growing national and international popularity (Barrett 1988), Rastafarianism (an indigenous messianic movement that, using mostly the Old Testament, celebrates blackness and reveres deceased Ethiopian emperor Haile Selassie as God) is not accorded enough respect to be included as a census category. Rastafarians are often targets for abuse, being cast as thieves and scoundrels. Many who profess to be Rasta men are, indeed, outlaws; however, true Rastafarians are peaceful and hardworking folk, usually living isolated lives as far away from "Babylon" ("the system") as they can.

Christians are part of "the system," and certain churches (especially Anglican and Methodist) are said to be more Christian and, consequently, more "civilized" than others. Just as they often discount their blackness, most Jamaicans would cringe to think that their Christianity involves African religious holdovers, and people belonging to the less European-style churches are often defensive. Nonetheless, especially for the lower-status rural poor, church does involve many African-based traditions (Barrett 1988; Hogg 1964; Simpson 1970). Even in more European-style church services, hymn lyrics of English origin are often sung and accompanied by instruments in an African fashion (Brodber 1989, 73).

Actually, many who consider themselves Christian for census purposes live what "true" Christians call "worldlian" lives, being unable to resist the pull toward recreations like gambling and dance. But those who wish to maintain the respect of other villagers must belong to a church and must stay away from the pubs and street life.

MEALS

While most Jamaicans stay in their yards each Sunday, reserving that day for the family and a big dinner of "rice and peas" (rice made with coconut milk and red beans) and chicken, all other days are workdays. People generally rise with the sun, boil a little tea from "bush" (herbs), and fill their mornings with work. Tea simply means any hot drink, always sweetened and whitened with condensed milk, if possible. Without sugar, drinks of any kind taste "too fresh" for the Jamaican palate.

Breakfast, generally eaten at about nine o'clock, usually consists of belly-filling deep-fried flour dumplings or porridge made from rice or cornmeal and sweetened and "whitened" with condensed milk. When in season, people have ackee and saltfish. Ackee is a yellow fruit, poisonous if not properly prepared, which comes in a red pod with black seeds. It is similar to an avocado in nutritional content and looks like greasy scrambled eggs when cooked. Another typical breakfast, for those who can get it, is calaloo (a type of spinach) "steamed" in coconut oil and served with thick slices of dense white bread. Generally, anything can be eaten at breakfast, but flesh foods, with the exception of fish, are more often dinner fare.

Those who "work out," or away from the yard, often miss cooked breakfast and usually have to eat dinner later than normal. Because cooking with one-pot coal stoves or wood fires takes time, they eat things like tinned, corned "bully" beef or sardines on white bread before setting out. Often they have lunch, which may mean a small packet of sugarcream-filled cookies and a soda pop or perhaps "bun and cheese," a spice bun with a cut of processed, canned orange cheese. Many Jamaicans are reluctant to eat away from their yards but most will resort to these sorts of packaged foods when "hunger bites" (if they have money to do so). Lunch is seen as a snack which "holds" people until they can get dinner. With the exception of those who "work out," snacking is uncommon among adults.

Jamaicans generally eat dinner in the "evening," between

three and five o'clock. The fuller the plate, the better; people like to eat and to see others eat large portions. Typical meals consist of boiled rice or "food," a class that consists of starchy things like yams, boiled dumplings, sweet potatoes, or roasted breadfruit. Meals must also contain "salting" or some sort of "meat kind" (animal flesh) if at all possible. For some, the "salting" or "salt thing" consists of a teaspoon of canned mackerel placed in the center of however much rice they can buy to cook that day. Those who can afford it serve chicken, pork, beef, or fish, and portions increase with income. Mutton or goat is a treat. Some people cook soup once a week.

Black pepper, salt, scallions, and thyme are typical seasonings, and coconut oil and "plenty" salt is used. Sometimes, people cook with curry powder; curried chicken backs are a typical dish. Gravy or drippings are necessary to "moisten" the "food" or rice, and "drinks" (such as sugar-laced water or fruit punch from powder) must be served to wash things down. Jamaicans rarely eat vegetables other than starchy "foods," boiled pumpkin (which sometimes serves as "food"), and a little calaloo. Many people carefully pick out and discard the bits of scallion and tomato they see in their gravy.

Most people complain of a perceived lack of variety in their diets. Many suffer anemia and other deficiency diseases—one-third of all households surveyed in a 1979 Tropical Metabolism Research Unit project could not satisfy even 80 percent of their energy needs (McLeod 1982). Some simply do not get enough food to eat, while others do not eat enough nutritious food. The Jamaican diet is not unhealthy in general but the increasing tendency to rely on white flour and processed sugar has caused problems by detracting from the nutritional value of the traditional diet, which included more tubers and legumes and less processed sweeteners and bleached flours.

TABLOID TALES

Those who do not "work out" often rest during the late morning hours after tending to their home chores. A person might sleep or read a borrowed, tattered copy of one of the two Jamaican tabloids. While U.S. tabloids dwell on space aliens and magical slimming regimens, Jamaican ones are packed with stories about homosexuality, incest, bestial acts, and strife between women and men. Rape, adultery, jealousy, and irresponsible fathers are all common topics. People meeting on the street often offer opinions on stories carried in the tabloids, share similar tales, and pass judgment on those involved. People make claims about their own morals in the process, just as they do when gossiping about real and immediate affairs.

Often, the ultimate reason for disapproving of a deed concerns the harm it can bring the body. Through talk of the body, whether in the context of tabloid scandals or of day-to-day living, and through gossip about the health and sickness of fellow villagers, ideas about the social and moral order and accompanying fears gain expression. Notions held about the body's workings affect health-related behaviors. They promote moral and sociable behavior because the things that most adversely affect health are immoral and antisocial. Sickness discourse rhetorically supports and/or subverts the social and moral order.

AVOIDING SICKNESS

The traditional precautions against sickness, whether it is willfully caused by another or taken up asocially in the course of daily life, are based on traditional notions concerning how the body works. Most of these notions come from common-sense observations and are metaphorical transformations or extensions of easily seen workings of the physical, social, and cultural environment. This is explained in the next chapter.

RESEARCH METHODS

Before going on, let me briefly explain how data were collected. I obtained much of my data through the traditional anthropological technique of participant-observation. Family-style living arrangements provided me with a way to quickly gain exposure to all aspects of rural Jamaican life, both public and private. At first, I had a room in the yard of a very low-status and quarrelsome group of ten people representing four generations. I joined a more "respectable," two-generation household after four months. My move, a response to hurricane-related housing problems, allowed me easier access to a representative selection of villagers because the second household was better integrated into the village social system.

Much material emerged during the conversations and interactions of the people I was surrounded by; in this sense, the study was naturalistic. Most of the data collection was done in villagers' yards as people saw to chores or we rested at day's end; some was done in community settings as, for example, on the front porch of the main shop. I also collected data in two clinics and at two religious healing centers. I supplemented my observations and the lessons friends and protectors gave me with intensive interviews, group discussions, the collection of informants' drawings of the body and its inner workings, and the use of questionnaires and census-taking.

I talked with children and adults, strangers, and casual friends, as well as to those with whom deep trust had been established; I gained data from people from all over the island as well as from the villagers. As noted, this book concerns poor rural Jamaicans, but I did talk with health service providers and members of the elite and middle classes to broaden my understanding of lower-class life. Over 120 villagers, half men and half women, acted as friends and instructors. Their stories and my interactions with them provided a context for (and gave me a way to check) the in-depth information that I obtained from forty key informants, two-thirds of whom were women. Most of these women were either between twenty and thirty-five or over fifty years old; most of the men were between the ages of twenty and fifty. While three of these men and two of these women lived well by Jamaican standards, the other thirty-five key informants were as impoverished as most of their fellow citizens.

   The nature of the study did not deter many from formally
participating: matters pertaining to sexuality are topics of
everyday discussion in Jamaica. While some declined to do
body drawings (many Jamaicans, particularly older ones, feel
shy about drawing as they have had little experience with it),
I encountered significant degrees of resistance and fabrication only in the clinics, when certain clients—and certain
practitioners—sought to impress me as sharing what they
imagined to be my values. But under most conditions, hon-
esty and openness prevailed. The connection Jamaicans draw
between sex and health makes the topic amenable to conversation, as is shown in the chapters that follow.

Chapter 2

The Jamaican Body

Farmer argues that the "increasingly fine-grained analyses" of medical anthropologists are "fragmentary," failing to engage in any "emic" or subject-centered study of indigenous health models (1988, 62–63). He promotes "eliciting informants' explanatory models.... Such an approach takes informants' discourse seriously" (68). In addition to discourse concerning and explaining sickness, health, and physiological functioning, the following description is based on informants' body drawings and an analysis of actions taken with regard to it. Later chapters describe the links between the indigenous model explained below and the social and moral order in which it is actualized.

Basically, impoverished rural Jamaicans see the body as an open system that must stay "equalized." Ideally, the body maintains itself at a certain warm temperature. But, because it has pores and is permeable, the body's temperature may be thrown off by thermal changes in the external world. Although dangerous, especially for the "tender" or those not "fit" (the physically vulnerable or the infirm), permeability is necessary for proper heat exchange and for the elimination of wastes. Keeping the system clean and thermally regulated is required for maintaining health.

"BUILDING" THE BODY
AND FILLING THE "BELLY"

Permeability is also necessary because the body must take in food to build the components of its structure and replenish those lost through work and other aspects of living. Food goes from the mouth through a tube to the "belly," the large inner cavity, which resembles a big bag and holds (among other things) a "maw" or "grinder." Different foods turn into different bodily components as needed, and the purity of these depends upon the nature of what gets ingested.

People eat to "build up" their bodies and also to "fill belly": to satiate hunger. People know that drinks and warm, moist, cooked food can "fat" them and bring fullness while cold rice, "overnight food" (leftovers), and "dryers" such as store-bought crackers usually cannot. "Real" food settles down in the belly in a hunger-satisfying way, filling nooks and working into spaces; "dryers" tend to float around. That which makes one fullest is called "food," which in common Jamaican usage means only tubers—"belly"-filling starches not seen as otherwise nutritious. Things like milk, vegetables, and herb teas and tonics do not so much "fill belly" as serve to build bodily components.

Blood, the most vital and meaning-invested component of all, comes in several types. When unqualified by an adjective or the context in which it is used, the word *blood* means the red kind, built from thick, dark liquids such as soup, stout, and porridge, and from reddish edibles such as tomatoes. Some feel the blood of "meat kind" such as pork or "mutton" (goat meat) is directly incorporated into human blood; others say that its juices "build" blood. While differences of opinion sometimes indicate divergent levels of biomedical under-standing (and so reveal peoples' educational achievements and, often, their socioeconomic backgrounds), here they merely signify two different strategies for explaining bodily processes that are not highly elaborated in the culture.

Wild hog meat, redder than regular meat, is seen as

supernutritious and vitality-boosting because wild hogs feed on characteristically pure, red-colored roots, considered to be beneficial blood builders. People point out that flesh foods not used "soon" and those from which all vital fluid has drained (such as beef cooked too long in soup) lose their nutritive value and only serve as "food" to "fill belly."

"Sinews," another form of blood, comes from okra, fish eyes, and other slimy foods with light-colored, gelatinous ooze, such as egg whites and cow "foot." "Sinews" includes but is not limited to synovial fluid, which resembles egg whites and lubricates, making joints "sipple." The eyes are filled with "sinews" and glide in their sockets with its aid. "Sinews" is also associated with procreation and with the nervous system. Many call it "white" blood in contrast to the red.

People have less elaborate ideas about what edibles other bodily components are made of. They know that vitamins, contained in strengthening tablets and tonics available at pharmacies and also, they believe, in water, "build" and fatten. Some contend that animal flesh builds muscles. Most say that corn meal builds flesh. A few propose that milk builds bones, at least in children but not necessarily in adults whose bones have already developed. People generally take the regeneration of flesh, bones, and other bodily components for granted. Knowledge of the body focuses on the blood and the workings of the "belly."

ENERGY AND LIFE "CONDITIONS"

While different foods "fill belly" and "build," energy levels depend upon one's mental state. Living where "the conditions" (that is, the society one must deal with) are harmonious and agreeable ensures vitality. Tradition emphasizes the concordance of the two states fat and happy. A fat body is an attractive, healthy one, but it takes more than food to gain or maintain size and a sense of vigor. However well-fed, unhappy people lack energy and "draw down" as fat "melts off."

A Jamaican seeing someone grow thin would wonder at

"the conditions" and life stresses that might spur such weight loss (rather than offering congratulations for it, as we do in the United States). When a young unemployed woman named Martha lost weight and grew sluggish, villagers knew that she and her live-in boyfriend, who spent many nights away from home, "must have something." Indeed, the young man had "taken up with" his sister's boyfriend's sister. Martha now had no lover and no source of money. Her declining physical state denoted this change in "the conditions." Even if she had plenty to eat, she would still have lacked energy and "pulled down mauger" (grown meager), as people with "worries" "can't fat."

FATNESS, THINNESS, AND OVERRIPE FRUIT

Fatness at its best is associated with the qualities of moistness, fertility, and "kindness" (a sociable and giving nature) as well as with happiness, vitality, and bodily health in general. Fatness connotes fullness and juicy ripeness, like that of fruit "well sweet" and soon to burst. Young girls grow fat in late adolescence as a prelude to childbearing; young men fill out when they "come onto" adulthood.

Jamaicans call pleasing things "sweet." When someone laughs or smiles, they are commonly asked, "Is what sweet you so?" People associate sweet goodness with fatness, too. Men describing plump women they find attractive often use the adjective *sweet*. MayVee, who used to "share out" dinner for me, once made the best pork dish I have ever tasted. The succulent meat literally melted in our mouths, and MayVee announced as we ate, "Pork sweet, eee?"

Something sweet is ready to eat or ripe for enjoyment. Generally, when a Jamaican dreams of green-colored things or "well green," unripe fruit, the time is considered premature for whatever s/he has been thinking about doing. But a dream of fruit at its fullest, sweetest stage of development means that the time is ripe. The dreamer must seize the moment, or like overripe fruit, the plan will burst and begin its decay. Ripeness means readiness. It can also mean rude precociousness, just as "green" can describe naïveté. Children who "go on like they big" are denigrated: "You too ripe!"

Too much ripeness can be unwelcome. Overripe fruit rots and its sweetness sours. Like people and other living things, fruit has a life cycle. As it approaches maturity it swells and grows sweet. But after fruit ripens it declines, coming to resemble feces: soft, dark, fetid, and maggot-infested. Overripe fruit never gets eaten. By picking fruit just as it "turns" from green Jamaicans avoid contamination with rot, which they fear greatly. The expletive *rhatid* expresses, as a homonym, the connection between rotted matter and problems worthy of wrath, which is pronounced "rhat" (Cassidy 1982, 175).

Ideas about decay are used in discourse. While playing bingo in the backroom of a shop "on the main [road]," something only the more rebellious characters do as it brings disapproval, one rowdy woman denounced another boisterous player for not having bathed. The accused, who had bathed, retorted: "You stink like ripe banana" (in other words, you stink like feces). The first woman turned this accusation of foulness around by taking power from it, warning that most of the "bellyful a ripe mango" on which she had lately gorged now sat decomposing in her lower "tripe," or rectum, ready for gaseous expulsion.

All that gets taken into the body, whether to "build" or "fill belly," must get used or expelled as "filth" or "dirt" because unincorporated excess begins to swell and decay. Knowledge of this leads people to associate superfluous or unutilized food, fat, health, and such with filth and the inevitable process of decomposition. Some Jamaicans speak of "good fat" and "bad fat," the good being firm like a "fit" mango and the bad being "soft," hanging "slack," and denoting declining "fitness" as if a person was an overripe fruit, beginning to break down or rot. Unused food or fat that stays in the body for too long decays in place and can sicken or kill. Defecation must occur.

In his study of the meanings ascribed to the numbers used in the lottery-style gambling game "drop pan," played illegally throughout Jamaica, Chevannes lists "shit," "money," "ripe fruit," and "beggar" as meanings assigned to one of the numbers (1989, 48). Villagers where I lived mentioned "gold." Chevannes attends to the inverse association between feces and money or gold. Accidental contact with feces and dreams in which it figures foretell fortuitous contact with money or something else good. But the links between "money," "shit," and "ripe fruit" need further explication.

Ripe fruit is something sweet and good, but unused or stored too long, ripe fruit rots quickly, coming to resemble feces. Picture the flesh of an overripe banana; consider the mango rotting in the bingo player's "tripe." Feces are only good when passed, as health depends on proper digestive flow. This process has a parallel on the social level. Resources must flow through a network of kin if the group is to persist. This is why an antisocial, "mean" person, who guards his or her money (or fruit trees, etc.) and denies others who would "beg" some the chance to benefit, is seen as a decadent force. An overabundance of perishable resources not passed on will rot. Only when passed on are resources transformed from potential feces or socially useless "shit" into "money" or "gold" that can benefit others.

Unshared riches turn to "shit" in a more obvious fashion when a "mean" person's investment fails or when greed leads to problems for him or her. This can happen through overindulgence or when "mean" actions provoke magical attacks. Then, even the richest "turn beggar." "Meanness" causes bodily and social decay.

A body that does not efficiently rid itself of excess and rotting waste can turn septic inside as feces begin to fester. The inevitable cycle of life means that sweet things turn bad and sour; those that decay in the body and stay too long bring sickness. The "belly" might even "burst" from buildup. So even fat and fullness, normally associated with health and vitality, carry suggestions of death when contextual variations (such as life-cycle stages or flouted behavioral expectations) lead people to logical extrapolations inverting the meaning of fat.

The concept of thinness goes hand in hand with ideas antithetical to those associated with "good fat." Thinness and fatness are to each other as lean, dry white chicken meat is to fatty, moist dark chicken meat—the part most Jamaicans prefer. Ideas about overwork, infertility, and a lack of "kindness" are linked with the notion of thinness. People taunt that others will "dry up" from antisocial "meanness." Store-bought snack food, which is uncooked, is also associated with thinness. Its preparation and ingestion does not rely on the regular division of labor and tradition of sharing; it represents the antisocial.

Not enough fat, as well as too much fat, indicates imbalance, and things located on either side of the fatness continuum, whether toward "bad fat" or thinness, carry negative, antisocial, antilife connotations. The dry, light nature of thinness precludes the association with dank, steamy, septic decay that can accompany other logically inverted or extended meanings for fat gone bad. Nonetheless, thin people are understood to lack the vitality associated with moist "good fat." This makes sense because low levels of bodily fluids and fat impair life-affirming fertility: underweight women often do not ovulate regularly and have trouble conceiving.

Like an erect penis or breasts plumped with milk, the body seems more vital when full of blood and large in size. While too much blood or food overburdens the body and can rot and cause sickness, as noted above, "dry" bodies have no vital nature at all. Skinny, childless, and docile, Mistress Greene was treated poorly by her husband. People shook their heads and said, "Look how she mauger so." A slim person, especially a slim woman, is called "mauger": meager and powerless—as if not alive at all and, like a mummy or an empty husk, far beyond that powerfully dangerous state of decay.

WASTE

Good health depends upon fatness but a balance between intake and outflow must be maintained. In a "normalized" body, extra liquids become urine, and unutilized solid "food" turns to "didi" (feces), which move from the "belly" cavity through the "tripe" (intestines) until expelled. Urine and feces "must stink" because they are wastes, a young girl explained. People who do not use the toilet often enough literally fill up with waste: a mother asked her five-year-old daughter why the white missionaries always had such soft and overfat bellies, and the little girl offered that "the tripe them fulla didi." The mother responded, with delight, "They fulla shit."

Some substances are not recognized as waste until incorporated into the body. Usually, they work their way out in sweat, called "bad water" when supersaturated with toxins. Some say that sweat forms from water drunk, and it carries toxins from the flesh, picking up waste as it makes its way to the skin for expulsion through the "pulps" (pores). Curry, for example, comes out in the sweat, people say, turning it yellow. Working hard is good because it makes the body sweat, but "pulps" clogged with dirt cannot serve as passages. Keeping skin clean aids the expulsion of toxins in sweat. Because it carries waste, sweat can be redolent; bathing serves to "freshen."

Most blood-borne toxins are purged with bowel movements and urination, but people can take special preventative steps to ensure blood cleanliness. Health-related concern over the state of one's blood is typical among descendents of the African Diaspora. So is the practice of cleansing it: "bush" (herbal) teas commonly serve as blood purifiers (Laguerre 1987; Snow 1974). For Jamaicans, a brew's bitterness indicates its effectiveness. Cerasee (*Mimordica charontia*) tea is an island favorite. Tea of ground bissy (*Cola acuminata*) also is said to remove strong toxins. Most tea brewed for breakfast has preventative blood-purifying action.[1]

"Dirty" blood might result from eating something disagreeable, such as soured food or "fertilizer [laced] food." It might come from breathing in poison, such as insecticide; many say that this causes cancer in the chest (milk drunk daily will absorb the dust and "lift it off" the chest). By referring to insecticides and fertilizers, opinions about certain aspects of modernization are expressed.

While "dirty" blood might simply indicate abnormal bodily inefficiency, it can also signal "slackness" in "caring the body" and a failure to follow preventative measures, "bush" tea drinking included. The sickness called "bad blood" (any venereal disease) involves taking in blood-fouling poisons from another person's genitals.

"SUGAR"

"Sugar" refers to diabetes and conditions with diabetes-like symptoms. It occurs when a person eats too much sugar, when the blood "sieve" (supposed to sit at the "belly bottom," fanning the blood so it passes over foods and incorporates those it can) fails to limit the amount of sugar allowed to pass into the blood, and when the "sieve" cannot properly dredge excess sugar from the blood. Sores that fail to heal (a true diabetic symptom) signal "sugar." Their fetid and septic nature is reminiscent of overripe, rotting fruit; they can stink and run and larvae can infest them. Sugar-free items like diet soda, not often seen in rural Jamaica, are understood to be for diabetics or those suffering from "sugar." Certain bitter or acidic teas, such as those brewed from rice bitters (*Andrographis paniculata*) or ginger, "cut" sugar and "freshen" blood, returning it to its natural state.

"PRESSURE"

For some, concern about blood centers on controlling the volume or amount rather than (but not to the exclusion of) altering its sweetness or maintaining its purity. Again, equilibrium is essential. Too little blood is linked with fatigue and remedied with liquid foods that build blood and increase its volume. "Punch" made with dark molasses and red "tonic" wine are recommended. Those who listen to advice on anemia given by public health workers advise people low on blood to eat liver and green vegetables. Solid foods known to "build" and fatten (like oil-laden raw peanuts), leaving people strong and ready for work, are also good.

People would rather have too little blood than too much, because it is nicer to add things to the diet than to take them away. Blood-building comestibles promote the invigorating, empowering flow of fortified blood. But too much blood leads to "pressure." This causes headaches, weakness, and often death. "Pressure" usually refers to hypertension but can also describe hypertension-like symptoms. In any case, individuals have different "pressure" thresholds. Jamaicans know that people who "carry too much weight" and use too much salt are often sick with "pressure," the value of fatness and the distaste for "fresh" (unsalted or "natural") foods notwithstanding. Garlic tea "cuts pressure," and certain broad leaves tied about the head, such as those of the breadfruit tree (*Artocarpis aldilis*) or trumpet tree (*Cecropia petata*), relieve "pressure" headaches.

INNER ANATOMY AND INNER FLOW

Blood is the primary and most thought about bodily component, but the most important part of the inner body is the "belly." This big cavity or bag extends from just below the breast to the pelvis, with tubes leading out at its bottom. The "belly" is full of bags and tubes, such as the "urine bag" and "blood tubes." A main conduit leads from the top of the body through the "belly" to the bottom (not from bottom to top), with tributary bags and tubes along its length. Sometimes, tube and bag connections are not thought of as tightly coupled. A substance improperly propelled can meander off course, slide into an unsuitable tube or bag, lodge, and cause problems.

Inside the body, things are "sipple" or slippery and loosely held with "strings." Otherwise, they would glide out of place. Some of the "strings," like the aorta or "heartstring," not only hold up the organs, flesh or muscles, and bags such as the bladder, but also serve as conduits for blood, pumped by the heart. Blood washes out, over, and through the internal body in "strings."

Normally, foods moving through the network of tubes and bags flow down and out, from top to bottom. The "stomach," which is a cavity and not a food bag, is located just above the "belly" at the chest or breast—the area where the heart and "mind" are. The "mind" is the seat of volition, agency, and intention. A person often says s/he will go somewhere or do a thing "if my mind tell me." The brain or "marrow," located in the head, is simply a computational tool and a storage space for facts.

Things that do not move down into the "belly" properly can "sit on the stomach" and aggravate it. So can "acid" food like oranges. "Ashes water" (water mixed with ashes taken from a fire) eases "stomach" trouble. Some recommend eating a roast ripe banana, burnt peel and all.

"BELLY" TROUBLE

Most sickness gets started in the "belly" because of its central role in the incorporation of substances taken in (that is, their conversion into bodily components such as blood) and the concomitant expurgation of foreign matter, whether the wasted part of food or drink, toxins, or even another's bodily substance (such as sexual effluvia). When health maintenance measures are ignored, "belly" functions are disturbed and sickness results.

Gas is usually produced in manageable amounts in the "belly"; some say that it is made in the "gas bag" or appendix located there. "Tea" (any hot drink) must be taken every morning to "ease off" the gas that builds up overnight as food is digested and the "belly" empties out. Hot drinks "take off the pressure," allowing the person to belch. But when "tea" is not taken, excess gas accumulates, creating problems.

Warm carbonated beverages, especially ginger beer, and certain types of "bush" tea provide relief when gas gets bad. For example, some mint teas "turn it down" (into flatulence) while others "ease it off" (helping one to belch). Moreover, because an empty "belly" is hot from gas and therefore sensitive to cold, cold refreshments—especially liquids—are considered too much of a shock. Things such as ice cream and watermelon "twist the tripe" in an empty "belly."

Normally, small belches signal hunger. However, if one does not eat "on time" (people generally eat in the morning and again between three and five o'clock) and if one does not eat "plenty," extra gas forms. It fills the space food should have occupied, causing a full feeling and a lost appetite. Gas can rise to the head, causing headaches (as well as intense belching). It can enter the blood in bubbles, increasing "pressure," or lodge in other parts of the body, causing pain and swelling. One woman, explaining gas to me, says that the "frothy froth" sometimes seen in just-butchered meat is "cause from gas."

One morning, Florence left for the river to do wash without "taking tea." At noon, she sent her small daughter for a soda: her "belly" had filled with gas, which she needed to "belch off." By dinner time, however, Florence's appetite had gone. Her "belly" had ballooned and she could put nothing in however she tried. "Gas take me up," she complained, lamenting her morning "carelessness." A different woman—one known for breaking with tradition—argued that morning tea makes no difference. She pointed out that those who stridently claim it does are those who belch the loudest. The loudest belchers, in turn, blame their conditions on eating lightly (although they are stout) or eating irritating foods. Their traditional understandings about gas persist.

Another "belly" complaint, biliousness, is a nauseous, sour-stomach feeling most common in "pickney" (children) who overindulge in sugary snacks of "pickney food," such as sweet potato pudding or mangoes (as opposed to cooked meals). Eating too much of these, or of foods with opposing characteristics that do not mix well or that simply "disagree" with one's body, causes production of "boil," a yellow-green substance. "Boil" (probably bile) can be seen in the vomit biliousness produces (or which mothers induce as a cure).

External boils, people say, share only a name with internally produced "boil." They are not filled with it. However, boils do stink, and they "burst when well ripe," so they contain a similarly decaying substance. "Burst" carries specific meaning: overstressed elastic objects such as an overfull "belly," a boil, or an overripe fruit's skin—all overtly likened by Jamaicans—"burst" but never "break." The association between "boil" and rotting ripe fruit, then, extends to include boils, which ripen and burst, letting off fetid fluid, much like sweet fruit that decomposes in the "belly" to make "boil."

A "belly" problem also common to children is worms. All people, like all animals, are said to have worms. If they grow too big or too numerous, worms can take up too much room in the child's small "belly" and limit the appetite. In addition, these parasites "eat off" the food the child consumes. Sometimes, they even bite the "tripe" (intestines) or "belly," causing pain. A body infested with and overtaxed by worms cannot develop properly or be kept "fit." "Bush" teas like vervine (*Stachytarpheta jamaicensis*) and store-bought medicines, which "operate" a child and cause diarrhea, can purge the body of worms by sending them out in the feces. Offending substances "operated" out are "cut" from the system; the link between the usage of these words and the idea that surgeons operate, cut, and remove things to restore proper health is clear.

"WASHOUT"

When Jamaicans say "belly working," they mean it is laboring to wash an excess of disagreeable things down and out. The class of teas and medicines that "work" the "belly" through purgative action is known, generically, as "washout." "Washout," the Jamaican cure-all, ensures proper "belly" function and enhances the purity of the individual and his or her blood and system as a whole. Understandings about maintaining clear "bellies" explain the frequency with which "washouts" are taken: once a month, just like menstruation, is advised.

"Washout" is practiced by most African-Caribbean peoples (Laguerre 1987) and it is also common among African-Americans (Snow 1974). Cathartic purges also figured prominently in the health practices of the British colonizers (Hanna 1988; Payer 1988; 116–17), which encouraged the elaboration and persistence of the cleansing tradition among the descendants of Jamaica's West African slaves. Today, every household medicinal supply includes, if nothing more, a purgative of some sort, such as epsom salts, cathartic herbs, or castor oil. "Washout's" ethnomedicinal importance in Jamaica leads many to mistake medical life-support devices seen in hospitals, such as nasogastric tubes, as mechanical "washout" cures.

BLOCKAGE

Food should pass down and out of the "belly" unless it is incorporated as a bodily component. However, the hardness and density of some foods (such as coco tubers and bone) makes their expulsion difficult. "Hard food" tends to clog the area at the bottom of the "belly" cavity through which waste would enter the exit tube; it can also lodge in and block the "tripe" itself. "Drogs" (dregs) can clog the "urine tube" so people carefully strain all drinks to remove particles such as coffee grounds and undissolved sugar. Carelessness can lead to a "stoppage of water." This is commoner in men because their "urine tubes" are narrow. It requires the attention of a biomedical doctor because accretions of "drogs" take hold very firmly. Biomedical explanations for this syndrome include urinary tract tumors and kidney failure.

Although Jamaicans cannot treat "stoppage of water" without biomedical aid, they can do something about problems too much "hard" food causes. "Washouts" break down and clear out logjams of "hard" foods or other things, unclogging that blocked drain so a free flow of waste can resume. When food has no exit, the "belly" fills up and the appetite decreases. Sometimes, the backup of food leads to a swelling of the "belly" or vomiting. Things sitting in the "belly" and waiting for a way out can become rotten, as noted before, causing pain like indigestion and even graver sicknesses like cancers. The early signs of pregnancy can mimic the symptoms of "hard" food blockage, and "washouts" are often taken as women attempt to "ease themselves."

TEMPERATURE

Temperature can also affect the flow of substances through the body. Because of this, "carrying too much weight" can be as detrimental as carrying too little: when things get too heavy they begin to "cool down" or "sleep up" and flow slowly, sometimes coming to a halt, as if "froze." Similarly, thin things can flow heatedly and freely—sometimes too freely, flowing right out. Blood too warm and thin might run out through a cut too fast and bring death or sickness.

Observation of physical events in the environment shows Jamaicans that hot things are thin and quick while cool ones are thick and slow. For example, a cool pen does not write because its ink "sleep up" (a neighbor showed me how to take a match to the tip of a clogged pen to thin the ink and ease its flow). Inactivity makes a thing cold as opposed to hot. Activity is associated with heat and vigor; a working body is "hot," whether thin or fat.

In a warm state, whether from hot weather, physical labor, or both, viscous fluids thin out and "come runny." In a cool state, they coagulate. One man surmised that first-hand knowledge of the firming effect of coolness underlies foreigners' distaste for "grease," which many Jamaicans love. A chilly climate, which he attributed to all places "foreign," makes ingested "grease" "sleep" in the blood of foreigners, causing "blockage." He concluded that foreigners should avoid butter and oils to keep "fit" within the constraints of their environment.

"COLD"

One woman told of a friend who died of thrombosis after moving to England. Before emigrating, the friend had sustained serious injuries in a car accident in Jamaica. "Bruise blood," the blood from internal injuries that fails to dissolve, can block blood vessels. So too can "cold" (mucous), which is a constant threat to the free flow of fluids throughout the body. The frigid English weather not only chilled and further thickened the friend's undissolved "bruise blood" but also caused the overproduction of "cold." The combination blocked circulation and killed the friend.

"Cold" is manufactured by the body, usually in the "belly." Generally, the reaction between the opposites of hot (it is warm inside the body) and cold (as, for example, when one takes a cold drink) creates small amounts of this mucous. A little always exists, another reason for taking a hot drink each morning: besides "easing" gas, hot beverages can "melt out" the "slime" which coats the "chest" overnight. When "fresh" and new, "cold" is clear or whitish; as it "ripens" it yellows. In cases of overexposure, as when ice water is drunk to excess or a person gets caught in a draft, extra "cold" is made. It is significant that Jamaicans speak of "catching draft," alluding to the belief that drafts enter through the "pulps" (pores) and get caught within the body.

"Cold" can also be made in specific parts of the body if they come in contact with chilly surfaces; rain on a bare head brings a head cold, and sitting directly on cool concrete can lead to "cold" forming up in the "batty" (bottom), which causes constipation. People sit on "stale news" (old newspapers) or banana leaves to avoid this. Going from a hot task, like ironing, to a cool one, like taking a bath (most Jamaicans have no water heaters), causes "cold" to "form up" too. Moving from a hot dance hall into the cool night air can bring on "cold" formation simply by the change in temperature encountered.

No matter where it forms, if not passed out through the bowels excess "cold" can move through the body, "sleep" (harden up), "caulk" (clog) any tube, bind any joint (as in arthritis), or wrap around the organs. If left unchecked, "cold" can grow into pneumonia, tuberculosis, or other life-threatening conditions. Besides blocking tubes, unpurged excess "cold" can lead to fever because the body attempts to melt it so it can be more easily coughed up, moved down, blown out, or expelled in urine, feces, and sweat. Sometimes, people even throw it up; one woman described a time when her daughter, then extremely ill, "vomit up pure cold."

Jasmine, unpacking a gift package from the United States, happily exclaimed that she had received two bottles of "cold medicine." Seeing milk of magnesia, I questioned her. I read her the label, which described the liquid as a laxative. She nodded in agreement, "cold medicine," explaining that purged "cold" passed out can be seen in fecal matter as strands and lumps of mucous.

Many a cleansing and prophylactic "bush" tea is referred to simply as "cold" tea because of its laxative effects. Some of these herbal remedies actually stimulate "cold" production, causing congestion as an allergic reaction does. The increased phlegm is taken as proof that the medicine has loosened "cold" for purging. Aggravated digestive disorders and skewed electrolyte balances caused by over-purging only feed the culturally constructed need for "washout" as people interpret the symptoms these cause according to the ethnophysiological model available.

FEVER: BEING "HOT" AND "OPEN"

Fever results when the body heats itself up too much in its quest to "melt out" "cold" or to dilate or "open" sufficiently to regain equilibrium and "equalize" itself. When "open" and "hot," the harbingers of sickness (whether "cold," dirty drinking water, or body-warming "acid" food) can be worked out from the "belly" or from the blood, through the flesh, and out the "pulps," or pores.

Though the normal body stays warm and permeable or "open" to a point, the feverish body is overheated and too dilated. It must be helped out if equilibrium is to be regained and serious sickness avoided. Knowledge of the effects of coolness and heat can be applied in attempts to normalize or "equalize" things and to aid the body in its efforts to purge or regain its balance and heal itself should sickness strike.

Fevered blood is abnormally "hot" with toxins and must get cleansed, which ultimately "cools" it. Normal maintenance in taking blood-"cooling" drinks and preparations follows this prophylactic principle. But when fever incapacitates, "melting," "baking," or "steaming" disagreeable things out is far more efficient than trying to "bind" or solidify them for passage with cooling treatment.

For "steaming," a person covers up with a sheet or blanket and sits on a plank over a washtub filled with steaming water in which herbs like fever grass (*Cymbopogon citratus*) have been boiled. This makes the body sweat. Feverish individuals often reek because their "bad water" sweat expurgates foul things. Once healed, a body will "close" sufficiently but not excessively; it will "get back together," or return to a normal state.

What one uses to heat (or cool) a body is neither hot or cold in itself. At times, people casually label a remedy hot or cold depending on its characteristic effects on the body. Rum might be called hot because it warms the blood, keeps it from "sleeping," causes it to flow faster, "opens" the body so that toxins can be purged, and promotes sweating. So might thyme, cinnamon, and black pepper, which "give heat" too. Lime juice and certain topical herbal preparations "draw heat [out]."

Medicinal treatments either warm or cool the body and its contents—melting and freeing things or thickening and firming them. They "open" the body further, making it sweat more and moving the heart to pump faster, or "close" it down, inducing sleep. Openness and looseness is associated with heat, impermeability and tightness with cold. But people avoid making simplistic hot or cold categorizations. And some medicinal items both heat and cool the body, their effects depending on the problem being treated and methods used.

"WORK" AND EVERYDAY "HEAT"

Hard work such as digging yams or hauling a load also causes the body to become active and "hot." Blood vessels dilate and cleansing blood flows throughout the body. Over-taxed workers are figuratively said to sweat blood. Workers' pores do open but they sweat a type of water, dissipating the heat work creates and ridding the body of toxins. Unless overtaxing, work promotes health.

Another activity that heats and thus "opens" the body and involves excretions is sexual intercourse. Jamaicans refer to sex as "work," think of it as health-promoting, and regard the postcoital stage as a "hot state" in which pores are open, blood vessels dilated, joints loose, and "sinews" flowing.

When not excessive, warmth is healthy and signals vitality; it indicates activity and "fitness." One preacher exclaimed that merciful God "doesn't attack us in our cold blood," transforming the meaning of that old phrase. A person with cold blood would be sluggish and unable to react in self-defense. But God punishes fairly, the preacher said, and would rather see us change our ways than perish.

The sleeping body, like the working one, is in an "open" or "hot state." People sleep together in closed rooms (which I find grow very warm and stuffy as night passes). The body is hot to the touch, and movement becomes fluid rather than stiff, which is the case when the body is "cold" (for instance, when arthritic). "Open," "hot" bodies have loosened "structures" or skeletons; "sinews" flows and joints are "sipple."

THE DANGER OF PERMEABILITY

A draft coming through an open window is considered very dangerous to a sleeper, and to go outside when "hot," even to answer a cry for help, can cause serious physical problems. A "hot" body is very vulnerable as it is "open" and easily penetrated. Chamber pots are kept inside at night because a trip outside through the "night dew" to the toilet could lead to dizziness and collapse. A person would surely "catch draft" through open pores and "take up cold." By the same logic, people wait for their bodies to cool before bathing after heat-generating work (like cooking or digging ditches).

Cold water would unduly chill a "hot" body. Bath houses or sheds are built not only for privacy, but also to protect bathers from chilling breezes.

A person in a "hot state" is also easily penetrated by the breath of "duppies" (ancestral ghosts) or air wafted when a "duppy" walks by. If these foreign substances enter the body, any kind of sickness can result. This is another reason for the reluctance people have to leave their warm beds to check strange sounds at night.

Pores are slightly protected by the hairs that grow out of them. Shaving leaves pores (and thus the internal body) unguarded, and exposing oneself to the elements is foolhardy since the consequences are known. Women do not shave their legs or armpits. Men who shave their faces, such as government employees and Christians, ignore this principle (many Jamaican men have little facial hair to shave in any case). People with thinning hair or hair that is brittle and prone to break off worry for their health, as drafts "caught up" through exposed scalps can lead to "madness" or other severe sicknesses. Hats or "tieheads" (scarves) are often worn out of doors for protection, especially by "old heads" (seniors) and at night.

SKIN PROBLEMS

Toxins should use pores as exits, not entrances. When the impurities in the body exceed its capacity to expel, bumps, pimples, rashes, boils, and other unusual patches can "come up" through the skin. A "funny" dark patch developed on an older man's left foot, and his wife explained it as his body's effort to expel the poisons he was exposed to while working in a lead-casting factory. "Bad water" (fever sweat) also causes skin problems as the body tries to rid itself of toxins. Some people suggest popping open pimples and "water blisters" (which look like herpes sores) to speed healing.

"Teenager bumps" or pimples are caused by a buildup of unreleased sexual fluids, a logical extension of the notion that a good thing like money or vital fat can go rancid or bad if ill-used or not spent, and of the idea that overfull, overripe fruit bursts and sours. Some say "teenager bumps" are more common among well-off youths whose caretakers "feed them up" well with "rich" foods but keep them celibate.

Sometimes skin problems result from external provocations. For example, certain plants can "scratch you" or cause rashes. Contact with stolen money, kept in her "thread bag" under her bra and on her breast, caused one woman's breast cancer: the "badness" of the money seeped in through the skin, poisoning the breast, which had to be "cut" or "operated" (removed).

People often say (sometimes jokingly, sometimes seriously) that "sin" has caused their bumps. "Sin" links the "natural," temporal body with the spiritual world from which the moral order emanates. One woman who had severely harmed another, maiming her for life, developed ugly black spots on her face after a time: her sin came out on her skin, observers said. Sin, a non-material predisposer for illness, takes on material form here and needs to be excreted from the body. Color (and race) is thus linked to moral character. This is also seen when villagers resort to name-calling: "dirty black naygur" refers to, among other things, the metaphorical "uncleanliness" and "darkness" of "sin."

Sinners often do not "care" their bodies well and, not being "fit," are susceptible to sickness. Also, God and his angels do not protect sinners, leaving them vulnerable to attacks by demons or by "duppies" (ghosts). Sinners, or "careless" people, do not follow social and moral rules and do not "live good" as their neighbors would have them, and health is the target preferred by those with "bad minds" intending retributive harm. Later chapters explore this aspect of sickness more fully.

BODY BASICS

This, then, is how Jamaicans understand their bodies to work. The body contains a mazelike assemblage of loosely connected transport tubes, storage bags, "strings" that link and support things, flesh or muscle, and the bones of the "structure." The invigorating and cleansing flow of "normalized" blood through "bloodstrings" that are neither too constricted or too dilated, in a body neither too "closed" or too "open," too tight or too loose, signals and ensures good health. The body should get washed out at least once a month. Orifices exist for the transfer of heat and waste, as well as for the incorporation of body-building nutrients and medicines that prevent and cure sickness.

Sickness results when the body's internal equilibrium is upset by the entrance of disagreeable foreign matter, which triggers stress reactions like the overproduction of otherwise normal substances, so the body's permeability must be guarded. Sickness also results when something mistakenly slips into the wrong bag or tube and lodges and rots or clogs the system. A lack of attention to proper, timely nutrition and the nature of the blood can also "bring problem."

The idea is not so much that battles for power and territory are being fought between alien germ forces and armed white blood cells (see Martin 1991 regarding metaphors used in the United States) but rather that sickness is caused by reactions that lead to the festering rot and rising gas typical of decomposition. These reactions are reminiscent of the life cycle of fruit, which like the body is at its peak or "well fit" when "full," firm, and juicy. They occur when something that can disturb the balance of the body happens or finds its way in and is not "cut," "operated," "worked," or removed efficiently enough or in a timely fashion.

Chapter 3

The Ethnophysiology
of Reproduction

The general principles behind reproduction and sex follow the ethnophysiological model described in Chapter 2. Male and female bodies differ only in that each has some unique sets of tubes and bags which the other does not and also because females must take in semen, which contains male wastes. The female body can handle the trauma of receiving semen, while the male body cannot. This belief does not mean that women are more "fit" than men. But since "normal" men do not take in semen, women are branded as less clean.

ANAL INTERCOURSE AND AIDS

Vaginas are built to take in semen. Ned, my "sister's" boyfriend, claimed that AIDS is a problem for homosexual men because semen, which normally moves from the vagina to the womb, has no natural destination when ejaculated into the anus. Moreover, the rectum does not have an easy opening (like the vagina) for draining out matter that lingers. Nor do men have a natural monthly "washout" like menstruation.

51

Semen that enters the male rectum always gets lost inside and rots, Ned explained, causing AIDS.

Ned's inventive use of traditional health beliefs to illuminate a new health threat is one example of the creative ways that traditional models get extended as people attempt to come up with plausible explanations for new problems. It is also an example of the way in which support for moral judgments is expressed in ethnophysiological terms.

Anal intercourse, with a man or a woman, harms the body. In addition to the "natural" bodily toll it takes, its immorality makes it dangerous. It constitutes a behavioral infraction against the moral order in which only sex that can lead to procreation is acceptable. It violates the understanding that humans should be responsible custodians for the bodies God lends them. Those who traumatize the body unduly are "careless" and so less deserving of divine protection. Spiritual consequences, such as being bothered by ghosts, can follow.

Anal sex shows itself on as well as in the body. One grandmother, observing the backside of a thin and not "well-shaped" woman walking on the road before her house, declared, "As I look upon the gal's batty, I know say the man trouble the gal's batty. What sin, eh? The lord God did give him [i.e., the "gal"] the batty hole to pass out the dung—didn't give it for nothing to go into." The "gal's" flat "batty" and her knock-kneed walk indicated a habit of anal sex. (The woman telling me this had reason to look for negative qualities in the passer-by. Some years ago, the two women had quarreled regarding the ownership of some fruit trees. They have never resolved their differences.)

Anal intercourse is all the more harmful and "careless" when between men. Still, the Jamaicans I talked to and media coverage indicated that most Jamaicans do not share Ned's American-influenced idea that AIDS attacks only male homosexuals (Ned was in America during the early years of the AIDS epidemic, when such was thought to be the case). In actuality, half (49 percent) of the ninety-six cases reported by March 1989 were traced to heterosexual contact (*Gleaner*

1989a). Those who have heard that most AIDS victims are black either believe this is a racist fabrication (some say to conceal a white plan to exterminate black nations) or, giving in to the color prejudice engendered by colonialism and slavery, construe it as proof that blacks are "slack" and immoral.

Because traditional ethnophysiological beliefs are applied creatively to new problems in efforts to understand and manage them, AIDS patients are believed to be covered with burst sores and pustules full of impurities being "worked out" of the blood through the skin. One woman told of a patient who, because of the extent of her suppurating sores, had to be ensconced in plastic wrap before she was transported to a Kingston hospital. AIDS is believed to be spread by contact with the decaying matter excreted in these sores as well as through sexual contact.

AIDS, like gonorrhea, is recognized as a sexually transmitted disease. Most villagers believe AIDS was introduced to human circles by people who have sex with animals. Animal effluvia that penetrates the body causes an adverse reaction, not only because it is animal (and so extremely foreign and toxic to humans) but also because it contains waste. Like ejaculated sperm that does not meet an egg, it is out of place in the human body.

"DISCHARGE"

Improperly deposited or disposed of bodily secretions constitute a significant health risk. Women "dirtied" by unused sperm's nonreproductive presence in them must expel it. A man's own sperm causes problems only when stored in his body for too long. "Germs" (sperm) "germinate" in the "seed bag" (scrotum).[1] Some compare the scrotum to avocado pears, with their large round seeds or pits. In this case, "seed" refers not just to the sperm itself but also to the testicles that store it.

When a man ejaculates, sperm (along with impurities that have collected in the groin) moves up and out from the "seed bag." "Sinews," stored above and behind the "seed bag" in a tube called the "line" in the lower back, eases its passage. Alternatively, some suggest that sperm is stored with the "sinews" itself in the spine (or in a bag behind the spine) and is propelled directly from that location, bypassing the "seed bag." For some, the only "seed" associated with the scrotum are the nutlike testicles themselves.

Sperm, "sinews," and waste matter combine to make "discharge," which leaves the body at orgasm. Another word for "discharge" is "juice." People rarely drink fruit juice without adding sweetened condensed milk. As a result, prepared juice beverages are thick, opaque, and light in color. Things called juice, including "discharge," are all milky in appearance. For example, what Northern Americans call the "milk" of the coconut most Jamaicans call "juice."

Sperm "fats" women, making them sexually appealing and attractive. Girls grow plump in their teen years as a perceived result of becoming sexually active. To support their claim for the health-enhancing value of sperm, many people say that women who work as prostitues or perform oral sex (neither of which is condoned) get fat too; names are often named.

But sperm cannot always be easily incorporated into a receptor's body to fatten. Blood types differ and those of each lover cannot always blend. Also, semen can lodge in spaces not accessible to the red blood with which it might otherwise mix. Once outcast, "discharge" quickly decomposes and, like decaying matter of any sort lodged in the body, causes sickness if not disposed of. When people are engaged in conversation and this issue is raised, instead of saying "sperm fats" they will say that the toxicity of "discharge" makes prostitutes "pull down"; they usually refer to specific thin women in making their point.

"Discharge" defiles the receptor. The waste it contains is toxic, fouling, and all the more noxious because it was already rejected by another body. But Jamaicans assume that sex itself necessitates the deposit of one's substance into another. Tradition has it that in lesbian couples one woman acts as a "man," having supposedly "stretched" her external genitalia into an insertable pseudo-penis with the aid of an oil made for this purpose (a lesbian informant agreed that this was, among some couples, the case). As long as the person receiving the fouling semen is female, all is fine.

Male justifications for frequent intercourse include the belief that without it "discharge" piles up. Overfullness with aging "sinews" and unexpelled waste has deleterious effects. The male body corrects small imbalances through wet dreams, but large excesses can harden up in the spine, causing back pain and sexual problems. Men emphasize the importance of "clearing the line" during sex. It is assumed that men will find partners and so need never masturbate to "clear the line." Women who stay celibate too long may suffer ruined nerves as "sinews" balances come undone. "Discharging" "equalizes" and cleanses the body, promoting and signaling good health. People—mostly men—use this knowledge to justify frequent sex and to coerce others into it.

"DRY SPINE"

A man who runs out of "sinews" has "dry spine." This condition involves ejaculatory dysfunction and can occur if a man involves himself with a "white liver woman," a woman with an insatiable appetite for sex. Only men, according to Jamaican constructions of gender, have insatiable sexual urges. Men use this knowledge to justify their sexual hunger.

Jamaicans do not say so directly, but the liver of an unusually lustful woman may be described as white because it is full of "sinews," because of the symbolic link between egoism and lightness, or because sex-hungry women conform to the stereotyped view of sexually ravenous white female tourists. These women are greatly feared by men who feel insecure of their ability to satisfy women sexually.

Sex taxes the male constitution because men lose so much "sinews" when "discharging." Men afraid of the physical rigors of sexual intercourse experience performance anxiety. An impotent man or one who simply "can't do the work" is vindictively called "soft," and this could harm his reputation. In addition to fear, too much sexual labor can cause impotence by "drying up" a man's store of "sinews."

Men with "dry spine" "draw down" thin as their vital "juices" are depleted. Some have trouble urinating: not a drop of "sinews" remains to help ease urine's passage. Squatting like women is said to help. April, telling me about a man so "damaged" by an overenthusiastic partner that he could hardly walk, offered a story about a cock with light, dry, stringy meat. Rooster meat should be dark, moist, fatty, and rich. Hindsight told her that this cock must have suffered a terrible case of "dry spine": she remembered that his hen "wives" demanded "plenty" sex.

"Dry spine" can reverse itself over time, but recovery demands total sexual abstinence so that the body can renew its store of "sinews." Sufferers take lime juice because, as it "draws out heat," it dissipates the libido or "nature." The Pope must drink "plenty" lime juice in order to maintain his celibacy, surmised Joy: having "nature" is only natural, and health requires expurgating it rather than simply repressing and not spending it. But any man who has gone too far in expressing his "nature" and has dried his "sinews line" must eat "plenty" slimy okra and other "sinews"-building and semen-like foods. Coconut "jelly" (the white gel-like meat of young "water" or "jelly" coconuts), milky soursop (*Annona muricata*) "juice," and drinks made from Irish moss (*Gracilaria spp.*), a seaweed that "come like a semen" (i.e., resembles "discharge") when prepared, are especially helpful to "put it back."

"ROOTS"

A healthy "nature" depends on having healthy blood and is itself a sign of vitality. "Roots tonic" energizes the body by building, cleansing, and mobilizing the blood. This increases sexual potency. "Roots tonic" is made mainly from plant roots gathered during the full moon, when they are supposedly plumpest and most powerful. Their stiff, cylindrical, swollen shapes are associated with the penis, called "the wood" or "big bamboo." Woody, natural, and the color of blood, "roots tonic" is good for building healthy blood and a strong "nature" in any man wishing to "push the wood" (and any woman wishing to express her own libido).

"Roots tonic," sometimes just called "the roots," can be made by anyone, but a specialist ("roots man") is often consulted. The specific needs of an individual, his or her palate, and the roots at hand determine the mix, but "tonic" recipes almost always include chainey root (*Smilax balbisiana*), sarsaparilla (*Smilax ornata*), and any of a number of plants called "strongback" (e.g., *Cuphea parsonia, Desmodium canum., Morinda royoc, Sauvagesia brownei*). A few villagers mentioned other plants with names like blood wiss, raw moon, and "tan deh [stand there] buddy" ("buddy" meaning penis). The properties of evenly numbered combinations cancel each other, but an extra root serves as a catalyst: only odd numbers are used.

Roots, bark, and "wiss" (woody vines; wicker) are chipped, mixed, and boiled. After about an hour, when the water has boiled down by half and looks bloody or brownish-red, it is cooled and strained. Most people sweeten their "roots juice" with honey and other strengthening ingredients before pouring it into a recycled rum bottle. Linseed oil and molasses, both believed to increase the libido directly, should not be added by those with "dry spine." But those who need no sexual rest may use these to boost the power of "the roots" (which can cause bottles to explode and lids to pop).

"Tonic" is taken in shot glasses, which Jamaicans call "wine glasses" because liquids that resemble and build the blood, itself often called "wine," get served in them. A man with "dry spine" takes "roots tonic" once every morning and night for about a year's time. Many men whose spines are fine take "the roots" regularly too, swearing by its effects on potency. But taking "tonic" is not limited to those with sexual concerns: "roots tonic" promotes good health in general because it enhances circulation, blood quality, and so the whole body. People take "tonic" whenever they like as a

health maintenance measure. Too much can dangerously
overheat the body, but it takes a lot for this to happen.

PENETRATING DANGERS

Sex is healthy. But through sex women, "hot" from "the
work" and all the more "open" because of the thrusting action
of the penis, expose themselves to certain dangers, including
impregnation. Condoms can shoot off of the penis (a "gun in a
baggie") during sex, lodge somewhere, rot, and cause sickness. If a condom clogged a woman's "tube" (unqualified,
"tube" refers to the vagina), infertility and problems caused
by a backlog of decomposing menses would ensue.

Vindictive men are said to put egg membranes on top of
their penises before intercourse, causing harm in accordance
with the principle of blocked flow. The thin translucent egg
skin comes off, rots, and sickens the female partner. The real
or imagined threat of this practice makes women wary and
gives them reason to remain faithful, as their men would
have them do.

MENSTRUATION

Heterosexually active women cannot avoid "discharge"
which, from the time it leaves a man until its incorporation into
an egg or a fetus, is potentially dangerous and defiling. If conception does not occur, gravity "runs" semen from the "tube."
Any leftovers in the womb may rot. So women menstruate,
flushing out unused semen. Men do not have sex with menstruating women because, among other reasons, they fear contact
with the decomposing semen that menstrual blood carries.

Having a baby sweeps out impurities that build up within
the reproductive bags and tube(s) even better than the
menses do. Mothers claim, "Me clean," insulting childless
others by insinuating that they are physically impure. Postmenopausal women have "closed" wombs; "discharge" cannot
lodge within them. It runs out the "tube," unused.

Some Jamaicans believe that intercourse brings on menarche (the onset of cyclic menstruation) by "opening" a girl's womb and exposing her to the danger of trapping male "discharge." However, as others observe, menarche can also occur before the girl becomes sexually active. All agree that menstruation carries out more than just semen. It releases excess blood that would otherwise accumulate and bring on "pressure." But more importantly, it cleanses the body of toxins and excess "sinews." Females, like males, "discharge" during intercourse and their "discharge" also contains impurities and "sinews" (and some believe germ cells). Nonetheless, menstruation is necessary for a full cleansing and so for good health.

Women worry when the menses are not forthcoming. They practice menstrual regulation then, using purgative teas to wash out or "bring down" the blood. Having many lovers can cause menstrual irregularity. Semen from several men tax the body much more than one man's "germs" because each man's "discharge" has its own toxicity and one man's may "disagree" with another's (like edibles that cause biliousness), speeding decay and compounding the likelihood of sicknesses. This, as well as the other physically traumatic effects of having multiple partners, keeps many women from seeking "outside sex." Husbands and boyfriends appreciate this.

Menstrual blood itself is pure and clean; it is the waste matter and semen carried down by the blood that is "unclean." The dark chunks and strings of "clotty-clotty" in menstrual blood contain the actual impurities and waste material: things being worked out of the blood, bunches of semen, and clots of "cold" which would otherwise accumulate and "block tube(s)." Menstruating is often called "seeing the health."

Men do not menstruate. People simply say their bodies are not designed to purge others' "discharge." Also, the nature of men's work causes their bodies to sweat more than women's, leaving fewer impurities inside and so no need for monthly flows. The majority of the remaining impurities are eliminated with "discharge." Additionally, male bodies do not tend to accumulate blood, which leads to "pressure," like women's do.

Nonetheless, men follow women's lead, trying to take "washout" once a month to purify the blood and cleanse the system. The ethnophysiology of menstrual purging provides the basic guideline for health maintenance and so for "washout." "Washout" is a mechanical, self-induced substitute for (or in some female cases, an augmentation of) an organic female health process. The gynocentric nature of Jamaican health beliefs—the centrality of women's ethnophysiological functioning—is, in part, a function of women's traditional role as primary healthcare provider.

Men are safe from the dangers of the "hot state" that menstruation's mechanism for bringing on "the health" entails for women. The womb, vagina, and blood vessels "open" to increase the flow of cleansing blood. A menstruating woman should not take a "washout" because it would increase the flow from her already "open" womb and "bloodstrings," cause hemorrhaging, and possibly death. Warm water is favored for bathing at this time.

Menstruating women must stay out of drafts: the chances to "catch up cold" or take in pernicious matter increase in "hot," "open" periods. During the rest of the month, wearing panties and keeping one's skirt down and tucked between one's legs when sitting is sufficient, but now extra precautions must be taken. Menstrual pads, whether "clat" (cloth) rags or store-bought sanitary napkins, do more than absorb blood. They also offer protection from drafts and other intrusions that might penetrate the vagina and get "caught" in the womb during this vulnerable period. Because so "open," menstruating women are easily impregnated; sexual intercourse should be avoided.

A body in the process of cleaning itself, as with fever, is sick. Menstruating women can therefore claim to be sick and often do so to avoid daily duties. Calling menstruation a sickness also serves to keep women from pursuing certain activities (such as cooking), and it highlights the pollution they carry.

Menopause puts an end to the menses, because when a woman "has out her lot" of children and runs out of eggs, she begins to "close." During this time, and until her body reestablishes its equilibrium, she needs a way to let off the excess "heat" that toxins in the body engender. For a while, hot blood rushes up to the chest and head, causing hot flashes. Some say that men experience this too; all bodies age and many have problems with heat dissipation. But as a group of older women assured me, men do not discuss these experiences as women do, so we do not hear of men's menopause-like symptoms.

CONCEPTION

Pregnancy begins when sperm or male "discharge" meets a "ripe" egg or female "discharge" in a woman's "tube(s)." The parallels seen between the sexes are expressed by those who call both egg and sperm "germs" or "sperm." Pregnancy can also begin when a duppy "interferes with" or "troubles" (rapes) a living woman. Then, the "fetus" usually consists of lumps of phlegm and bad, often hot, air.

Many women, usually older ones, believe they have one "tube" and one "egg sac." Younger women and those who have been exposed to biomedical models of the reproductive organs speak of two "tubes," which lead to the vagina from two ovaries. Some of those only partially knowledgeable of modern biological concepts explain that we have one male and one female "egg sac." Siblings of the same sex occur when a woman has only one ovary. A rarer claim for a dual "tube" system pits the "right tube," which leads to the womb, against the "wrong" one, on the left. Ectopic pregnancies take place here when "germs" do not "move right."

Eggs mature either monthly or upon sexual excitation, burst when overripe and no longer fertilizable (like decaying fruit breaks open), and move out through the "tube." One woman explained that a burst egg washes out in the menses: her period was late by a few days when she felt a plop in her panties that, on examination, turned out to be a drop of whitish matter with a small dark dot of a yolk in the center;

menstrual blood followed soon after. Had the egg not burst and had she had intercourse with a man with whom she "fit" just as it ripened—one whose sperm would not "melt out" because her blood agreed with it and one whose genitalia "fit" hers—she probably would have had an egg-expelling orgasm and conceived.

If a woman has an orgasm before her man, the discharged egg gets washed away before conception can begin to happen. This belief does not necessarily compete with the sometimes simultaneously held, school-taught idea that menstruation exists to wash away burst, unfertilized eggs. People who believe both ideas claim that even if one egg a month does get washed out, others can still get discharged. They highlight the role the menses play in purging toxins. Those who say women only have one fertile period a month either deny that "discharging" releases eggs or fail to see that women might have more than one orgasm monthly.

Calling orgasms "discharge" and claiming that they release male and female "sperm" bespeaks the traditionally ideal outcome of sex: procreation. Sex can be for fun, but people should never guard against conception; blood must flow freely between as well as within bodies. Should the fertile contents of male and female "discharge" meet, a "netty-netty" clot of blood forms. This moves into the womb, thought of as a small sac at the top of the vagina. It does not "devel up" or "form up" recognizably before three months' time.

A missed period can indicate that "cold caulk up" the "tube(s)" as well as the presence of a fetus. Young girls who miss their periods but who do not exhibit the symptoms of bowel blockage may wishfully mark their increasing weight as a sign of the good health that sex encourages rather than resigning themselves to pregnancy. Only those familiar with the signs of pregnancy (or those who "well want" a baby) "feel say they pregnant" from the start. Pregnancy tests are not readily available and usually it is not until the fetus becomes "active" that a woman is convinced of her pregnancy. Men can tell easily, some claim, as wombs "close" and intercourse feels different.

PREGNANCY

Early signs of gestation—altered appetite, nausea, and swelling—mimic the symptoms of blocked "tripe." Badly clogged bowels keep the menses from passing out the "belly bottom" where the tube that leads blood to the womb is. Women know from experience that missed menstruation does not always indicate conception; things may simply be running late. Spontaneous abortions (which usually look just like menstruation) and periodic amenorrhea are, in fact, more common than pregnancy. A woman experiencing a menstrual delay can "take washout" to clear out "cold" or whatever may be blocking the menstrual path.

A pregnant woman is "unclean" because all her waste backs up and because she retains a not-yet-human fetus. Would-be menses collect behind or above the fetus in a clump or "nest," which becomes the afterbirth. Some is channeled into the fetus, building it. The fetus remains a lump of blood until the second trimester when it has formed its own protective "baby bag." It now begins to move and women who previously did not connect their amenorrhea and other symptoms with pregnancy are now set straight.

Some believe the fetus now moves from the small sac of a womb to the "belly" cavity where it has more room to grow. Even those who argue that it stays in the womb agree that it gets anchored to the inside of its mother's navel with a "navel string." Problems occur when it gets anchored wrong or gets lost and lodges in one of the many internal tubes.

After three or four months the fetus begins to "form up," taking on a toadlike or froglike shape. Food reaches it through a tube that leads down from the "maw" or "[food] grinder" in its mother's "belly." Sperm reachs it after every act of intercourse. At first, sperm nourishes and "grows" it through direct accretion. When a mouth forms, sperm enters through it, as does food. These nutrients also enter through the "mole," the soft spot on the skull, which does not harden until well after birth.

Sperm from any man is accepted by a growing fetus. Gen-

erally, the impregnator is considered the father. Still, "whoso-
ever the mother names" is awarded paternity, whether or not
the original impregnator. Mothers try to name men who are
"conscious" (concerned about their actions). If unnamed, biological fathers usually do not challenge those who would
assume their duties. Generally, women press paternity
claims, not men. Although legal pressure is rarely brought to
bear, the blood tests involved are thought to work because
sperm becomes incorporated as a baby's blood.

The growing fetus still looks nothing like a child. If a
woman chooses to "wash away baby" (abort)—a frequently
taken but rarely "owned" or admitted-to step—she usually
does it by the second trimester. The "washout" that she con-
cocts for this purpose moves, as does food, through the "belly"
then down a tube to the "baby bag" and sweeps what would
later "form up" into a baby out through the vagina. Birth control pills, easy to get and promoted by the state, are frequently thought to work in much the same way. Women often
take their pills only after having had sex; if a woman thinks
she is "growing" a baby, she might swallow a whole packet at
one sitting to effect a massive "washout." In light of traditional beliefs about reproduction, this is an understandable
action. The woman can explain away her abortion as a miscarriage if questions arise.

Second trimester abortions also follow the "washout"
model, itself based on the ethnophysiology of menstruation.
But because the fetus has begun to "form up," complications
can occur. Like "hard food," the fetus must now be softened or
broken up to be "raked" out. Many women fear that the
"headskull" that forms in this period may stay inside and
hinder future pregnancies. Abortions that fail to flush out the
entire fetus can sicken or kill a woman and damage the "tender" fetus that she tried to expel. A woman's enemies may
point to her handicapped child as evidence of her attempt to
abort and so of her immorality.

Women who will become mothers must watch themselves
when they become convinced of pregnancies. A baby with a
lot of hair can cause feelings like indigestion if it rises and its

head rubs up against its mother's "stomach," or worse occurs if the fetus accidentally slips out of place in the "belly" and lodges in an unfortunate space (such as in the "chest," blocking air intake). To protect against these kinds of scenarios, women bind their unborn babies in place by tying a cloth sash about the waist. Much like the child's own "navel string," this cloth serves to anchor it.

The fetus is "tender" and vulnerable during this time. Its position in the body follows the mother's. It lies on its side when she does and sits when she sits. Drinking a bottle with her head arched back might suffocate it. A mother's cravings must be met or her child's body will be marked. But she must not eat too much of any one thing or her child's body will reflect an oversupply. One woman's baby came out with big red blotches because she ate too many tomatoes. A fetus needs nutritious food (but "nothing special") if it is to "form up" well, but women must be careful with their food because people or spirits may interfere with it and so harm the unborn child, perhaps altering its shape or causing a miscarriage. Yet because a mother's eyes watch the front and her unborn child's watch the back, duppies that could "give trouble" directly (and easily, as she is extrapermeable) pose little threat during pregnancy.

A mother's attitudes also affect her unborn child. A sad mother produces a depressed child; an "active" one, a productive child. In light of this, most women prefer to work until delivery (and because of economic need, most have to). A woman "sorry for" a person she sees, such as a paraplegic, creates a similar handicap in her unborn child, and one who takes fright upon seeing a frog creates a permanently frog-shaped baby in her "belly."

Women must not walk over ropes or vines, which can cause a baby to entwine and perhaps strangle in the "navel string." Washwater must also be sidestepped because effluvia left in the dirty water can drift up and penetrate through the vagina to harm an unborn child. This is especially true in later pregnancy when the "passage" starts "opening." A fetus becomes "firmer" over time, offsetting this danger.

BIRTH

In the final stages of pregnancy, a mother should drink certain teas to gently cleanse her baby's skin; they wash over it as they pass through the body. She should eat "plenty" okra and other slippery foods to "build" "sinews," which lubricate her inner tubes in preparation for an easy delivery. For its part, the baby begins creating "slime" to ease its passage. People liken the baby, in its bag, to a ripening fruit. If it stays inside (on the "tree") too long, the "headwater" grows "over-ripe" and "thick with corruption."

Intercourse makes a woman more "open" and is encouraged during her last trimester. Midwives used to advise their clients to have sex when labor was delayed or after a problematic pregnancy. The physical trauma of sex was thought to help induce labor. The prostaglandins contained in the sweat expelled by men during intercourse may also induce delivery (Kitzinger 1982, 192).

Thyme (*Thymus vulgaris*) tea and castor oil were regularly used to speed delivery after the onset of labor when home birth was the norm, but now, a woman caught drinking "bush" tea is severely reprimanded by hospital personnel. Natural labor is not always awaited and doctors often "push start" women electrically or intentionally open their amniotic sacs to induce labor, if convenient. One woman's doctor turned away after a wordless examination only to come back at her with scissors and "burst" her bag. He neither asked permission nor explained himself. This type of behavior is said to be typical; people often complain that clinicians act too "rough."

No matter what, "pain must come." It is an integral part of the childbirth experience. A "first time" (old-time) midwife felt that modern government midwives are wrong to attempt to quell the normal pain of labor, which signifies the body's effort to expel the baby and tells the mother when to push. The old midwife used to set clients on a bed, preferably a hard one, lined with newspaper. She washed each client's genital area with warm soapy water and rum. In case of fatigue or intense pains, she had the mother blow into a pint bottle during contractions. She placed one of the mother's feet on the floor and had the mother sit with her back against the wall or headboard. She sometimes gave hot stout with grated nutmeg to ease a difficult labor.

After birth as after a miscarriage, mild purgatives like broom weed (*Corchorus siliquosus*) tea can be drunk to induce the quick delivery of the placenta. Ideas about easing it out, as in labor, delivery, and for a bowel blockage, follow the purgative menstrual model. "Washout" concoctions traverse and cleanse the "belly" and inner sacs and tubes, sweeping the placenta and other pregnancy-related leftovers out through the vagina below. This is imperative: retained afterbirth causes "bad belly" as it rots in the body and blocks regular flow. It can even turn into a tumor. Traditionally, the disposed placenta had magical contraceptive effects if properly buried with money by a midwife (many suspected that the midwives pocketed the cash).

Squatting over a pot of hot water ensures the ejection of all waste. The steam enters the body and "melts" all recalcitrant matter which then slides out. Washing out is especially important after a miscarriage (or abortion) and when a pregnancy is false and the "baby" is made up of objects or matter such as phlegm lumps, "bad" air, or "cold." Evildoers can "set" a "false belly" in a woman; the means to do so are explored in Chapter 14. Many report having seen these "witchcraft babies," and almost all have tales of them. They take the shapes of lizards, cow heads, and other disgusting things. Often, "witchcraft babies" stay in the "belly" longer than nine months, which is how they are discovered; other times, they are exposed at birth. Women's bodies must be thoroughly purged of such disagreeable matter.

POSTPARTUM PRECAUTIONS

Birth, like menstruation and sex, puts women into "hot," "open" states, so similar precautions are taken. The back and pelvis have "opened" and "come sipple" or "loose" and the "belly" is distended. A woman must refrain from sexual intercourse for a time if she is to "get herself together." Many suggest that nine weeks of celibacy suffices but others claim one full year of abstinence is best. Sex just after birth not only stresses the body but is also very liable to result in conception because of the "open" state of the female partner. It "looks bad" if a man impregnates a woman before a year has passed because, in not letting her regain fitness, he looks "too aggressive."

New mothers should replace the fluid lost at and just after parturition with soup, porridge, and other blood-building foods. They should belt or "bind" their waists to help their bodies "knit" back together or "harden" and also to keep their flaccid wombs from filling with gas or other potentially dangerous airs that can enter through the vagina. Calico cloths used to be fashioned expressly for this purpose. Maternity pads or "clat" keep things from entering through the open vagina and soak up the postpartum drippings that bear witness to the new mother's temporary "uncleanliness." Men worried about contamination do not "trouble" recently pregnant women for sex.

"Babycold," a potentially crippling and sometimes fatal disease involving the overproduction of "cold," can easily affect the lower torso and legs of new, "open" mothers. Until recently, most only bathed in warm water and stayed indoors for nine days and nights to protect themselves. Houses were dark because heavy cloths were hung over windows and doors to block drafts (and ghosts—I return to this in Chapter 14) that might enter through cracks.

PROTECTING THE NEWBORN

Newborn babies are very "tender": a baby's pores and "mole" remain "open" for three to four months. If shaken when still very young and "soft," the blood just forming in a baby's "belly" can "turn down" and come out through the genitals. One young girl cautioned that this can happen when a newborn's older siblings jump on the bed where it is lying. A "likkle [little] tik" of water with bleachlike laundry bluing given orally stops the bleeding.

It takes time for babies to completely "harden up." But "tenderness" has its good points: still "soft," a baby's features can be modeled (for instance, the nose may be manipulated in an effort to make it "straight"). Its body can be "stretched" to promote "good shape" and well-functioning limbs. Children escape the perils of "that tender age" as they grow increasingly "firm" with each passing month and year.

Good feeding helps "grow" and strengthen a baby. A mother should not nurse when hungry. When her "belly" is empty, the baby sucks mostly gas and gains no food-borne nutrients. Cow's milk and other foods that "build" "sinews" increases a woman's store of breast milk. So too does sperm, but it is important that a woman only have intercourse with lovers whose sperm helped "grow" the child. Otherwise, the child will suffer crippling "brukfoot" (literally, broken feet: the child will have trouble walking) from drinking "bad" breast milk—milk containing sperm that is alien to its body—and from contact with or the ingestion of foreign sweat that may remain on the mother's breast.

As Farmer found for Haiti, bodily fluids like breast milk serve as "moral barometers" in rural Jamaica—their effects "submit 'private' problems...to public scrutiny" (1988, 62). Women with small, slow children risk being accused by regular mates or malevolent neighbors of having an "outside man." They also risk having the economic instability that forced them into a liaison so soon after childbirth shamefully publicized. A woman involved with a man who had nothing to do with her child's development must wean her baby or it will get sick. This leaves the man with a monopoly on her body and succor. It helps the woman maintain attractive breasts that "stand up," and so helps her to keep the man. Men with money prefer to spend it on "a healthy somebody," and a sagging bosom indicates a declining physical condition.

Letting a menstruating woman hold one's child also

endangers its health. The decaying waste menstruating women release causes a sickness reaction in a baby's body. Although not openly declared to me, the association of menstruation with the state of nonpregnancy and the fact that one's cast off substances can be used to control others may increase the importance of minding this taboo. As we will see, women have a reputation for "trickify" thinking and a menstruating woman who wants to hold another's baby might, in Jamaica where children are highly valued, have "commanding" that child in mind.

THE POWER OF EFFLUVIA

Effluvia free of toxins and expelled from a "clean" person (one pure both physically and morally, such as a churchyard healer who practices when "fresh" or just-bathed and when spiritually clean from a period of fasting, praying, and celibacy) is, in its purity, health-promoting. Healers often rub patients' bodies with their own sweat because of this, one man explained. The cleansing action of the blood of Jesus is expounded in churches throughout the island (indeed, a North American visiting me during my fieldwork noted, "They seem a little preoccupied with blood"). One's urine can cure one's own pink eye, and one's saliva can "well" one's own cuts, but only the truly pure can, as Jesus did, share effluvia without endangering recipients, whose bodies would otherwise reject these fluids as foreign matter.

When contaminated, as they normally are, the fluids that transport waste out of the body can "sick." They can also compel, by altering the "minds" of others into whose bodies they get incorporated. But if too much of what is essentially decomposing matter, and thus noxious poison, is given, the targeted person could become sick and could even die. As one might expect, this sickness begins in the "belly." It is but one form of the generic Jamaican complaint called "bad belly."

"Bad belly" occurs when the physiological principles outlined in this and the preceding chapter are violated. It can happen "naturally" but the violation of principles governing morality and social relations can also instigate "bad belly." Farmer calls a disorder like this a "disorder of experience" because it can be traced to unsanctioned and disorderly social and moral experiences, and "the stories told by sufferers, and by their consociates, play a key role in the shaping of that experience" (1988, 62).

A deeper understanding of the functions and symbolism of specific forms of "bad belly" and the principles underlying them can only be had after traditional social and moral ideals are discussed. The next three chapters describe the social setting in which health beliefs are put into play, expanded upon, manipulated, and made sense of.

Family portrait, one week after the hurricane

PART TWO

Patterns of Social
Interaction

Chapter 4

"Family" and "Strangers"

A full understanding of how ideas about the body are used in discourse concerning the social and moral order presupposes a full understanding of that order. The following three chapters describe Jamaican social interaction, focusing on attitudes toward trusting others. Jamaicans describe themselves in ways that are often self-deprecating (and full of the color prejudice and classism engendered by and supportive of colonialism's legacy, the color and class system); the chapters reflect this.

Traditional intragroup expectations of solidarity, support, and cooperation are strong in Jamaica but so is the anticipation of competition, sabotage, and coercion. Insecurities are manifest in the knowledge and fear people have of poisons, especially those that act on the body to alter dispositions and compel action.

GREETINGS AND THE COMMON THEME OF SHARING

In rural Jamaica, relatives and friends greet each other with good-natured requests for whatever a person may happen to carry. "A what inna the bag fe me?" and "A what fe

75

lunch?" are as commonly heard as "Beg you a dollar now man" when people greet those they know at the local shop or in passing on back roads. Salutations express expectations concerning the mutual obligations that exist between friends and family members, who form noncompetitive reciprocity networks for support through sharing and exchange.

"Yes, Auntie! Save some dinner fe we!" calls Reggie, passing Bee who sits on a low stump, washing her small granddaughter's clothes in front of their house, a tiny structure of zinc sheets and wood. "Dinner done finish—share out and eat long time [ago]!" she chides as she scrubs an old blouse white and clean. The man, nearly sixty, sinewy but "well fit" for his age, carries on his head a stalk of plantain cut from his garden or "ground," located over a mile up the road, in "the bush." "Gimme some of the plantain them, brother Reggie!" she begs, laughing "fe you and fe me, no?"

KINSHIP MYTHS

Reggie and Bee share no real family ties, but like most Jamaicans they cloak their relationship in congenial kinship terms. Nonkin have no obligations to each other and are generally competitive. But biologically defined kin groups may not have sufficient membership to provide all that the family needs. Even if a kin group is large enough to be able to make and grow most everything they need, the procurement of money and modern material goods demands nonkin interaction. The idiom of kinship implies an altruistic basis for exchanges between nonkin.

Not being Jamaican, I had no "backative" of true kin to automatically and un-self-consciously come to my aid and defense. The woman I lived with knew this. She considered her fellow villagers' penchant for exploiting others and quickly concluded that I was at a disadvantage. Having "neither leaf, nor branch, nor tree," as a "stranger" in Jamaica, she explained, everyone could respond "You are nothing to me" should I request support of any kind. So she brought me into her kin group, calling me "daughter" to imply that we shared blood. The vertical inequalities contained in the mother-daughter relation—however important in other contexts—were overshadowed by the equality mother and daughter are endowed with by virtue of their unification in the us : them : : kin : nonkin equation. Her statement moved me from the category of "stranger" into the category of "family."

Since nonkin are "nothing" to each other, unrelated people who would rely on each other and spend time in each other's company become fictive kin. This maintains the simple binary kin-nonkin opposition. It releases nonkin who maintain relations from the interstice between these categories by removing their anomalous status. It involves both parties in a superficially equal relationship in which they share "one blood" and "one love" and are of "one accord" instead of being divided "strangers."

Kin relations depend on blood and are idealized as inalienable and enduring, no matter what the economic conditions may be. Even after death, they persist: ancestors survive as ghosts ("duppies"). This makes for large kin groups. Ideally, the dead should "rest" and leave the living alone, but duppies often call on kinship rights and obligations. This expresses ideas about the tenacity with which some cling to thier relatives and gives vent to the feeling that some kin wrongfully insist on making others fulfill outrageous demands (see Goldberg 1979).

BLOOD AND RELATIONS

Kinship is concrete and consubstantial: it is based on sharing bodily substances. It is consanguineal in that the main substances shared are all considered by Jamaicans as blood. Male and female sexual fluids ("white" blood) mix for conception. Some sperm gets transformed into red blood inside the female body. The fetus "feeds" on this. Females contribute red blood too, both in the form of blood itself and in the form of food, which gets transformed into blood after the fetus eats it. Kinship bonds are "tied" with blood incorporated into the body of a growing fetus. Blood ties physically compel children to behave altruistically in relation to their parents.

The creation of real kinship is not always seen as fixed or finished at birth. Older, more traditional Jamaicans say that babies continue the consubstantiation process that creates kin even after birth by drinking their mothers' milk: since breast milk is made of bodily substance, its ingestion can create a kinship tie between a baby and an otherwise unrelated wet nurse. While biological motherhood is central in establishing maternity rights when they are in question, extremely traditional Jamaicans subscribe to an attenuated form of what Watson (cited in Meigs 1987, 120) refers to as "nurture kinship": kinship that can be altered after birth by what Meigs calls "postnatal acts."

A child not related by virtue of received blood can become as if related to someone by virtue of that person's caretaking efforts. A woman who feeds a child after it is born can claim motherhood: she "grows" it, as the genetic mother did when she fed it in her womb. Likewise, a man who spends his money on food for a child can claim fatherhood. Following the ethnophysiological model of parenthood, kinship can be established and claimed by a caretaker who puts great amounts of effort into raising, "growing," feeding, and so "building" a child. Food taken into and made part of a child's body works like incorporated blood to create and maintain kin ties.

Adult spouses share food, too; by this, they "come like family." Because they are lovers the connection between food and blood is not strongly drawn. To overtly link food-sharing with blood kinship in this context would imply incest. The food-blood link drops out of the equation so that food-sharing serves as a direct, concrete, and indexical symbol of relatedness.

The "white" blood lovers share in nonreproductive sex only mixes temporarily. But in reproductive sex, blood mingles permanently in their offspring, creating an indirect blood relationship in hindsight. Siblings are related by virtue of having incorporated blood from the same source or sources; other kin links, such as those between cousins, are similarly traced to a consanguineal origin.

A big family provides, ideally at least, a big network of un-self-conscious, altruistic support. People are physically driven to lend it simply because they originate from or share "one blood" and are thus, as belief would have it, of "one accord." Kin terms express and add an enduring, unconditional quality to relationships and so cloak instrumental dealings that would otherwise seem self-centered, competitive, antisocial, and thus distasteful given the ideology of "one love."

Jamaican kinship terms and the rights and obligations that inhere follow the familiar pattern of daughters and sons, brothers and sisters, aunts and uncles, parents, grandparents, and so on. There exists one additional category of kin, the "babyfather" and "babymother." To call someone so simply means that s/he is the blood-parent of one or more of a person's children and, usually, that the relationship of lover has passed. But rights and obligations toward the children persist. The "babyfather" should provide financial support; the "babymother," caretaking services.

KEEPING "FRIENDS" AND "TALKING"

To be on a kinship-term basis with someone implies that, if "money runnings" get tight and "no food no diddeh" (food is not there), the relationship still holds. Friendships between "strangers," however, are transient and always understood as motivated by selfish desires: friends, being nonkin, are always "looking [for] something."

A "friend," pure and simple, means someone with whom one has sex. Only when the adjective "social" is inserted before "friend" does one refer to a nonkin, nonintimate colleague. Social interactions are traditionally confined to the area of one's yard and the width of one's circle of kin: with the excep-

tion of "brothers" and "sisters" seen in church, Jamaicans prefer to keep very few public contacts outside of the family. But
sexual relationships with kin should not occur (although they
do). Therefore, for sex, one must keep "friends." People tend to
assume that any nonrelative of the opposite sex with whom a
person "talks" must be an intimate, and that anyone not called
by a kin term but called "friend" must be a lover; there is no
such thing as "just friends."

Many Jamaicans say that they do not keep "social
friends" nor do they "talk" to many people. To "talk" with a
person means more than to talk—it implies that the two are
involved in a healthy social relationship. Two who "don't talk"
"have something": an argument. Should one try to greet the
other, his or her attempt is met with the insulting entreaty,
"Don't call my name!" (meaning "Do not give people cause to
think that you and I have any kind of relationship").

"DIRTY, BLACK NAYGURS": THE EVIL OTHER

Nonkin will surely try to "trick" you and "dance you
around," an adult man rewiring a house a few months after
Hurricane Gilbert informed me. His helper, a neighbor,
related to him through his common-law wife and volunteer-
ing his unsolicited labor, agreed: "You see me? Me is a man
who don't like people. They is too terrible." Villagers warn
each other not to "walk too much" and to keep to themselves.
Many, ignoring the necessarily social nature of my work,
warned me to stay out of others' yards. "Keeping company"
would only "give problem" because others are "wicked." They
not only "fasten inna you business" and "carry tales" concerning you all about, but they also "take set upon you" and your
belongings, and "suck you out" with their desires.[1]

People refer to their fellow villagers as a group of "dirty,
black naygur [niggers]," and claim, "So they stay." They por-
tray their own neighbors as selfish, vulgar people. For example, when hurricane relief was trucked into the village (over
two months after Gilbert struck), people refused to form a

line or heed the list of names the workers carried. They squabbled and swore and bored their ways in through the crowd that surrounded the tail of the truck, never fearing the rifle-waving soldier astride it. This lack of "civilized" behavior was seen, even by those who participated in the melee, as proof that "blacks can't cooperate".

Resentments, wary maneuvers to guard resources, and efforts to undermine others' economic positions are common between nonkin. Ideological smoke screens notwithstanding, these things also pervade interactions between blood kin (albeit to a lesser extent because one's interest in the well-being of one's true kin can be vested). The fiction of egalitarian kinship may cover but cannot quell self-centered thoughts and deeds (see Jayawardena 1963). Every greeting, every "Beg you something from the bag now man," every false utterance of "auntie" or "brother" loudly reminds that things are not what they seem. Loyalties are often feigned, trust is fragile, and all that one owns may be demanded and all that one is may be destroyed, even by relatives.

R. T. Smith points out that conjugal bonds among impoverished rural Jamaicans are generally "dissociated" as opposed to "segregated" or "joint" (1988, 142). While with "segregated" or "joint" conjugal relations (Bott 1971), each partner, separately or as part of a team, does what is necessary for a common good, lower-class Jamaican couples do not "think of [their] activities constituting a unitary whole; the stress is on exchange between two distinct entities" (R. T. Smith 1988, 142). Conjugal bonds, substantiated through food-sharing and embodied consanguineally in offspring, have a tangibly instrumental basis.

I return to this when discussing gender relations. The point here is that, although they may call each other "husband" and "wife," one's mother and father often deal with each other as "only necessary objects for the achievement of their respective ends" (R. T. Smith 1988, 137). Complementarity and intrinsic satisfaction or "one love" are overshadowed, often on a daily basis, by the pragmatic considerations each parent has.

There is an underside, then, to the touching pretense affected by euphemizing networking and interdependence with pleasant kinship terms. Using the idiom of kinship implies that all exchanges are based on trust, are uncompetitive, and lack selfish motivations and that relationships have long-term stability. But everyone knows that with fictive, affinal, and even some blood kin these ideological assumptions do not always hold.

GIVING AND SOLIDARITY

When I asked one grandmother how she could "share out" supplies she would need in another month, she laughed, "God will surely provide." She must give, she explains, or a time will come when she "must hungry." If she "lives good," according to socially accepted norms, those she shares with will return her favors. This seems a strategy for survival in a land where stable incomes are rare. Exchanges create alliances. Interdependent relationships bind two parties as one egalitarian "us" in opposition to a big "them." But giving goes deeper than that: people give because they want to—giving feels good, and people who do not give feel bad as well as guilty, she and her son told me.

People expect each other to willingly part with anything that is "begged," or asked for. "If they have it, they will give," explained a young girl; if they can, they willingly do. One must take care, however, never to ask another for something s/he has not got. Not being able to give causes sure embarrassment: refusal implies antisocial intent and a lack of the will to participate in a relationship. Granting requests and displaying solidarity is the norm and people say they "gladly give a stranger the tripe from they belly." This "slogan" (saying) draws on the understanding that difference and social distance is overcome by gifts of—and the subsequent incorporation of—bodily substance, leaving those involved sharing "one blood."

RECEIVING AND OBLIGATIONS

Jamaicans complain that as soon as you have given something to someone, that person will "never tire fe see you." When you have few (or unwilling) kin around, having a "regular" or daily visitor can be beneficial. Gift recipients voluntarily cut back bushes for their benefactors, fix broken fences, or help with the wash. "Black people" give things away to gain devoted companions, explained a (black) "young miss" of twenty-one years. They buy allegiance and keep followers around in case they "feel lazy to sweep the yard" or "a big work come up." People give when they know they will receive, in return, the kinds of benefits that true kin would, traditionally and ideally, provide.

Asking for something involves obligating oneself to a benefactor, and people are sometimes loath to beg favors because of the unequal relationship debt implies. Although giving and receiving promote solidarity, exchange also provides an occasion for establishing social distance. The first meaning attached to giving and receiving is solidarity; refusing a gift implies a refusal to articulate oneself into a network and to obligate oneself.

Sometimes, people infer an antisocial attitude (and often rightly so) from a gift refusal. A would-be giver can question, "Why you don't take nothing from me?" as did a man trying to buy a woman a drink at the local bar. If angry, a rejected giver may insultingly accuse, "You go on like you somebody—you go on like you better than we!" The rejector is accused of acting "stooch," or too proudly. Would-be givers may publicly assert that rejectors, acting "lucky" (a negative term for someone who needs nothing and no one and thus will not enter into the social network), would forget blood ties, antisocially refusing the obligations that normally obtain between kin.

Aware of the burdens accepting gifts involve, people hassled to receive yell: "I don't want nothing from you!" If "vex," they try to humiliate would-be-benefactors: "You can't give me nothing." Nonacceptance of an offer allows one to maintain one's independence and one's right to self-direction. A woman who declines a drink offered by a courting male has no obligation to please him, as "strangers" are "nobody" to each other. One woman, happily confiding news of a recent scandal to my landlady, paused to claim that because she had never taken a thing from anyone involved in the affair and so owed no loyalties, no one could question the truth of her story.

SELF VERSUS SOCIETY: FISSION, FUSION, AND "CIVILIZED" FLOW

Jamaican culture links the ideas of cooperation and civilization with the whiteness of skin. Concomitant associations are made between Africa, "tribalism," and uncivilized anarchy. The legacy of colonialism and slavery that includes the color and class system is evident in prejudices held. The masses are said to be fickle people who, because of their African heritage, side with their providers, whoever these may be. Associations shift as better deals are offered.

People know that the ties that bind fictive kin are themselves fictions. People also know that even true kin are interested in achieving social rank—rising from the base of the color and class pyramid—even though this contradicts the prescribed egalitarianism of kinship. The tension between solidarity and inequality leads to the constant swelling and shrinking of "in groups." There is a continuing, situational redefinition of boundaries between "strangers" and kin.

The egalitarian ideology notwithstanding, Jamaicans see most all relations as primarily instrumental and fear others' ambitions. With the general exception of mothers and children, they never feel sure just who will "grudge" them and who will "suck rice grain" with them when they cannot afford to offer better. Talk of self-interest can even refer to a mother and child dyad. Egoism here meets much more shocked disapproval than it does in the context of other relations where, however castigated, it is resignedly expected.

Innumerable loving, unconditional relations involving the continued exchange of resources and aid do exist among

Jamaicans. Nonetheless, and despite the national motto of unity, "Out of many, one people," Jamaicans see each other as self-centered, divisive, "craven," and "wicked." Ideally, self-interest and broken obligations "can't go so" between kin. "Nothing no go so" in "civilized" countries like England, they say.

Taylor (1988) argues that social pathologies and individual pathologies are homologous: ideologies and etiologies are linked. For Jamaicans, social problems involve disruptions in the flow of resources and aid, while sickness ultimately stems from disrupted internal flow. Matter must circulate freely in both the collective, social body and the individual, physical body if the health of each system is to be maintained and debilitating social and physical decay are to be avoided.

So, if they could, Jamaicans would safeguard networks by ridding their villages of irresponsible and egoistic individuals. They would purge their nation of "bad elements" by sending all "bongo Africans" back to "Congo-land." They would sweep them out like debris as they did Edward Seaga's labour administration after his party's defeat in the 1989 election: unprompted and spontaneously, people all over the island took their brooms to the streets, indicating their pleasure at the election's "washout" of the governing body. A "washout" of the citizen body would be just as welcome by the majority of Jamaicans who wish to "live good" or "live clean," without social problems that can block individual or collective success.

Chapter 5

Becoming "Big" in a "Bad-Mind" Land

Jamaicans are generally hard-working people but they criticize themselves for being lazy. Davies and Witter's lament that "too much [Jamaican] creativity expresses itself in techniques for avoiding work and study, or is dissipated in various forms of antisocial behavior (1989, 100)" is typically Jamaican. Other islanders forthrightly blame national problems on the "free mentality": a feeling that everything should come free and easy. The sharing idealized in kinship backfires by weakening the independent productivity of those who hold a "free mentality," creating a group of individuals that have little to share themselves and only drain their kin networks.

Excessive demands for sharing made by those who will not work, or by those who cannot make ends meet, dissipate or level wealth and so block people from achieving social "uplift." In addition, cultural ideals for altruistic generosity mean that those who try to become "big" are judged antisocial and greedy. Others' envy and disdain is easily aroused by those who might rise above the rest, and this can lead to negative repercussions.

THE "FREE MENTALITY"

A complaint commonly made concerns the perception that "Jamaica people love to sit down." The idea is that they believe whatever their parents have is rightfully theirs, and so see no need to work. This "free mentality" (as well as the understandable assumption that life is easier elsewhere) is seen in the common expectation that any relative who has made it to "foreign" must have a good job and so must send money. People checking for mail at the postal agency look for envelopes fat with dollars and pounds, tossing "pure letters" away with disdain. People may not hear from relatives "gone a foreign" for years. Those who have not yet found economic "uplift" cannot write home "caused from shame." Even those who have done well may not write: free of Jamaica, they dismiss distressing obligations and deny family ties.

Government agents are expected to provide for their constituencies, just as relatives—ideally—provide for each other. Many Jamaicans have not completed census forms or registered to vote because they feel "politics business" gives them nothing. Many who have not benefited directly in the form of cash, food, jobs, or farmwork visas from their local M.P.s (Members of Parliament, known for favoring party members and for alleged grand acts of embezzlement) refused to vote in the recent election. Hurricane aid was regarded (when little bits of it did reach the people) as if it were payment for a debt. People assumed that their prime minister (then Seaga) would and should "build back" their houses and felt he owed it to them as their leader to make provisions after "Kill-bert mash up Jamaica."

BRIBERY AND THIEVERY

"Blacks love easy money," Jamaicans tell each other, complaining that they take bribes too easily and are too quick to steal. When picking up barrels of goods legally shipped from "foreign" at the docks, for example, people expect to have to bribe customs authorities and wharf workers. People building houses who want piped water say they must set aside bribe money if they want that water before a year's time. After the hurricane, work crews demanded payoffs from people who wanted power restored, and they got them despite media campaigns against giving in to coercion.

Many men "resort to criminal activity," says Brodber, because no jobs are available to offset "the pressure to establish one's maleness through the abilities to disperse cash and the kind it can buy" (1989, 69–70). Most Jamaicans write criminality off to "wickedness" and laziness: for example, it is easier to steal a cash crop than to grow it. The distribution system, which depends on "higglers" (middle merchants) allows for this: roadside vendors commonly sell other people's crops. Some farmers, expecting robbery, are said to poison their food so that thieves can be traced. Knowledge of this persuades some shoppers to buy only from higglers they already know "long time."

One person told of a farmer who tainted his yam crop, went to market, found the yam thief, and told all customers they would be poisoned. Feeling violated, they moved against the "wicked" thief. The storyteller, who could not say how the farmer identified the yams or the thief, stressed the point that buyers would have been poisoned, making the thief's crime all the worse. The farmer's use of poison was expected, just as people thoroughly expect that many of the goods they buy are stolen.

Sometimes, boys and young men are encouraged to steal by their mothers or caretakers, who pressure them to contribute to the household. Caretakers "must know" that their landless, jobless charges "thief" what they bring in. Some foods, like yams and other tubers, are bumpy when grown in the wild and everyone knows this. Cooks who accept smooth yams from unemployed household members without question were cast as accomplices by a man who explained "the runnings" to me, as out on the street before us a machete-armed farmer threatened to "chop" a boy he accused of stealing his yams.

One man taking a trap down to the river walked with it wrapped in a large banana leaf, so no one would see it and try to steal it, he explained. Several young adults informed me they stole water from their neighbors' tanks during dry spells. "It happen all the while," they laughed. People lament that "these dirty naygurs" even steal clothes right off the line (in 1988 one pop song commemorated the "line stripper"). A missing chicken is sooner written off to thieves than to mongeese or dogs. Children are the culprits in almost all tales of familial theft. The heinous nature of stealing from one's own, especially one's parents who have given so much of themselves already, is always noted.

But "blacks don't love work," Jamaicans say, alleging that they steal like no other race. (That many are landless and the little work available is menial and ill-paid never figures in complaints made in this context.) People explain even supernatural things by pointing to the "free mentality." For example, "Chiney" and "coolie" ghosts are unshakable because they "love" work. Once "set" or ordered to make trouble (something a covetous neighbor might do), they persevere until done, while a black duppy mutters "cho" in disgust after receiving an order and sneaks off for a nap beneath a shade tree.

LONG-TERM PLANNING

Although many Jamaicans strive to ensure their future security, they commonly characterize each other as lacking in the ability or will to think ahead. Given the conditions with which people struggle, there is reason for the common invocation of the caveat, "If life spare and all is well," and truth to the saying, "Anything could happen." One ten-year-old boy acted with this in mind when he put on a brand new shirt, which was to have been "put down" for a celebration still several months away. When his grandmother asked, he said that by the day of the party he might be dead. Grandma laughed, declaring how like his father this boy had become.

One villager, noting that most successful businesses in

Jamaica are not owned by blacks, observed that blacks locate death close to home: space permitting, tombs are built on family land, sometimes very near to dwellings. Because blacks know with certainty that "every man must dead," he said, black shopkeepers buy goods in small quantities. Perhaps, he thought, "Chineymen" buy large quantities at discounted prices, planning a year in advance, because they do not "consider about" death as do blacks. He also said that many blacks (and he included himself), spend what money they get quickly and often foolishly, without concern for tomorrow.

POVERTY, SHAME, AND ATTEMPTS TO "LOOK GOOD"

Impoverished people are constantly bombarded with media images of wealth and prestige, and interactions with the rich (whether as maids, gardeners, beggars, or neighbors) are commonplace. People are aware and often ashamed of their poverty. Poverty brings disrepute, and people try to hide it. They know that others are watching, so they try to project images that protect their self-esteem (see Foner 1973). I remember one mother scolding her daughter for eating a dinner of steamed rice by the roadside instead of behind the house: any passerby might look into the dish and see that all she had provided for her child was "so-so" rice—poor folks' food. Outdoor kitchens are usually behind the house, where no one can see what is cooking.

Some go to such lengths to impress that their neighbors find it appalling. One woman had a run of luck and married a man who "carried" her to England, where she spent six months. She kept up a broad English accent on her return and would not associate with the single women she had once "moved with." She often complained that her body had not yet adjusted itself again to cold showers (and this in a village where river baths were the norm) and lamented the tendency she now had to "take up cold." People resented her pretentiousness, especially since (as rumor had it) the man had divorced her and sent her back.

In addition to demeanor, bodily appearance can be manipulated to indicate prosperity. The "foot bottom" and toenails should not be thick and tough, as they are when a person has no shoes. The head is important, too: one woman scraped her pennies together to purchase hair oil because she had gone without for four days and did not want people to begin to "chat her" as someone who "don't have it" ("it" meaning money). Jheri (treated, loose) curls and "creamed" (straightened) hair also bespeak wealth.

Skin hue, called "complexion," is important. Lighter is better: dark skins and hard outdoor labor (indicating low status) blend together in Jamaican thought. Facial features that imply a link with white society and therefore to the upper class are coveted. Men and women know which brands of hats, shoes, and clothing mean heavy spending. People take care not to wear the same clothes outside of their yards too often, lest others think they only own one "suit."

Men who can find the money often opt for a gold-capped front tooth. Women boast assets with big hips, as their measurements show how well they eat and the amount of stout their men can provide. People noticed when one woman began to "mauger down" and lose her once-broad bottom; they knew (and they broadcast) that her affair with a rich old man had ended.

THE EASY LIFE

Money easily spent implies money easily secured, and best of all is big money with little work. But this does not mean hard work engenders no respect. Despite the negative perception most Jamaicans have of their fellows, each village is full of hard-working men and women who take pride in jobs well done. Many testify that others work hard, affirming their good character and good standing in the village. The gatekeeper at one club insulted a group of "idlers" who were hassling him and trying to gain free entry to a video show by demanding, "Ease off! Move and g'way! I work for I money!" he exclaimed, adding indignantly "Respect due!"

Reputation also hinges on how easily money "runs." Hoarding bespeaks an antisocial nature. Describing a man as one that "sure can leggo money" is complimentary. To freely "spree" or "sport" others by buying drinks demonstrates sociability and financial potency. Brodber (1989, 67) notes that, unlike blacks, Asians indentured in Jamaica "with no pool of friends around to impress with one's earning capacity and without the immediate sight of needy dependents" were better able than blacks to save and so have met business success. Those with many kin nearby have a hard time amassing resources because of the emphasis on generosity. Other survival strategies are necessary.

Anansi, a folk-tale spider and a culture hero handed down from "first time" slaves, is well known for getting things free through hilarious tricks that "disadvantage" those who would control him. A trickster-hero, he does and says things real people, especially those ruled by others, cannot (see Kerr 1963). Often, he wins at the games he plays. But Anansi sometimes loses: his plots backfire, and he becomes an example of "man turn fool-fool" by his own antisocial greed.

The easy life, self-indulgence, instant gratification, big spending, and the notion that everyone can and should be a generous billionaire is promoted through television, music, and film—much of it imported from rich northern nations such as the United States. Coming into money without work and outsmarting one's fellows—especially one's social superiors—is, in Jamaica as in many societies, enjoyed.

THE GAME OF "BEGGING"

A person who "begs" or asks for something gets something easily, instantly, without work, particularly if s/he does not feel (or denies) the obligation incurred by accepting a gift. People commonly complain that "Jamaica people too beg." A young girl explained, "If you don't ask, you don't get." At the same time, there are those who refuse to "beg" and are uneasy with presenting themselves as dependent. They fear that, sooner or later, the giver will "tell them about it," embarrassing them by exposing their poverty and announcing their obligation.

An older woman, denigrated as "beggy-beggy," said she always asks for what she needs and, "thank you Jesus," always receives. In a rare moment of self-revelation, she boasted that she is a "born hustler." Others call her a "John Crow," after the Jamaican vulture, a huge, ugly, and black creature that eats dead meat: the woman has a reputation as someone who will "beg anything" and is "always hungry." A John Crow has such greed for food that "nothing sick him." This imagery is fitting because human sickness generally occurs as the body tries to purge itself of vile, offending things of the sort that vultures willingly take in. A John Crow's body must either be very rotten inside, or guarded from sickness by sorcery. Both conditions indicate moral corruption.

"John Crow" people "eat out" money parasitically and seek free lunch. Being scavengers, they love funerals because they can get a bellyful of "graveyard food." They populate wedding receptions and church festivals simply to "taste cake" and get fed. Although food is taken in, no social obligations bind the vulture. Like the vulture, people labeled "too beg" maximize benefits but feel no debts. This type of behavior separates the "dirty, black naygur" or "bongo African" from the "civilized" Jamaican.

Obligated or not, beggars can be a nuisance. One woman confided that she hated banking because "beggy" people from the district who happened to be in town and see her would find her later, "looking money," figuring she had it. It is good to give, but if you are not careful, one young man who people mistakenly thought had won a truckload of money in a lawsuit warned, people will "suck you out." These same people have money in their pockets but would never even buy you a beer, he said.

People looking for money and goods often congregate on the streets near bars on weekends because people who get paid on Friday like to "sport" at these locations. Claudell, a young woman of twenty-three, liked to leave her year-old baby at the one-room house in which she lived with her mother, her sister, her sister's common-law husband, and four cousins; she would "walk out" to the bar and work all night long to get grocery money. She operated by getting people, usually unrelated men but sometimes also kin who had money and felt like showing "kindness," to buy her drinks and refreshment.

When people gave her cash, Claudell bought the least expensive thing and pocketed the change, for groceries. If someone insisted on making the purchase personally, she would order an expensive treat. She laughed behind their backs, boasting that she drank "pure Suppligen," a protein-rich and costly canned drink made by Nestlé. If her host was intent on conversing with her as she drank, she would oblige. But frequently, those buying drinks cared more for their images as "money men" than for her company. She would then add her prize to her stash bag to carry home.

This type of operation is common, although the lengths to which Claudell went would not be tolerated for long in the small district where she lived. Already, she had a reputation as someone "too terrible." She was known for being "mean," "licky-licky," a neglectful mother, and for "eating out" her boyfriend's pay (he eventually left her). Her family was infamous for its "bangarang" quarrels and for covetousness. Her father had, it was said, poisoned another man out of jealousy. Claudell, like her relatives, all known as "pure Satans," came to serve as a village symbol for all that Jamaicans consider antisocial and bad.

BEING "MEAN"

People are embarrassed when others put them in a position where they must deny a request, so sometimes they hide things lest others "take set" on these and "beg too much." In defense of such "meanness," people speak of the "free mentality." They claim things lent will come back broken if at all and that others never return favors. Jamaica, they explain, is full of "rats." Pests, rats "eat out" the insides of things like coconuts or bread, leaving only hollowed husks or crusts. Living off someone's money self-centeredly, ignoring obligations, is to "eat it out." People are wicked and "if God no pressure us so, man eat man."

"Kindness" involves altruistic, kinlike sharing. "Kind" people give what is asked for and offer things beside. A "mean" person, like a "stranger," never shares and refuses requests. Everyone hates a person who is "near," or "exact," such as someone who never cooks extra dinner—someone stingy with food and so with his or her sociability. People concerned with their reputations are "free" with what money they have, buying drinks and putting on a show of "kindness" so that others cannot call them "mean."

Bodies and cooking styles give "mean" people away. Those who are "near" have a "cubbitch hole" or dent of covetousness at the "neck-back"; in other words, they are thin. Their bodies "dry down" and "come skin and bone." "Mean" people use very little salt when cooking. Their food is unenticing; most Jamaicans feel that "fresh" (unsalted) food is inedible.

Vy and her brother, both in their early twenties, were sent to live with a "mean" old woman fifteen years ago when their impoverished mother could not "keep" (support) or "care" them. The lady's thin body and flat cooking betrayed her "nearness." Stingy people "draw down mauger" because, on top of not feeding others, they starve themselves, Vy explained.

When the woman did share food, it was "fresh" and otherwise ill-prepared. She doled out small portions not big enough to "fill belly" but only to "nasty up teeth." The woman boiled soup from the same piece of dried fish every day for a week, removing the piece each evening to use the following day. The soup carried nothing of substance and lost any taste by the third day. It served as a sign of excessive thrift and a lack of a will to nurture, as did the woman's thin, dry, husklike body; a body with vital juices inside would have held a social and giving person. That the woman had a large lovely home fits with the image Jamaicans have of "mean" people: they have money but never spend.

"SELFISHNESS"

Just as no one likes others calling them "mean" or insulting them by claiming "You can't give me nothing," "I don't want nothing from you," or "You is nothing to me," no one wants to be known as "selfish." I was scolded for acting "selfish" when I neglected to tell a church sister about my birthday. In doing so, I had denied her the privilege of telling me "happy birthday" and organizing a birth-night prayer meeting. In other words, I did not allow her to give me anything. A "selfish" person cuts others off, denying them the chance to engender obligations, and so denying them the chance to call in debts.

Mr. Tilkins lived in London, where he worked at a succession of low-paying, made-for-foreign-labor jobs. His brother and his brother's wife had managed to "go foreign" too, and Mr. Tilkins lived in a flat adjacent to them. His sister-in-law worked outside of the home but found time every day to cook for him, believing that without a wife he could not manage. She left dinner for him before she went off to work and, after an interval of about four hours (they worked in different places and on different shifts), he would arrive home—to a cold meal.

Mr. Tilkins, who (like most Jamaicans) loved his food hot, told this story one evening while his wife and a neighbor sat sewing. He neither heated the food by himself nor did he make his disappointment with his sister-in-law's service known. Mr. Tilkins simply moved to another part of town. His behavior, his wife exclaimed, epitomized "selfishness." A "selfish" person lives alone and never asks others for favors. The women berated him loudly and energetically for not "expressing himself" and for acting so "selfish." "You can't live apart from others," they proclaimed.

"GRUDGEFULNESS"

While "mean" people are actively antisocial, "selfish" people are inadvertently, or passively so. "Grudgeful" people are those who feel that others who have succeeded, for example, by landing a job, do not deserve their success. While some people are simply "red eye," or covetous, "grudgeful" people directly aim to "keep you from lifting up."

Ideas about people kept from "coming up" (and the techniques by which this can be managed) preoccupy Jamaicans. It can be done by coercive illegal means. Two men on a "country bus" heading to Kingston discussed this, agreeing that no sane Jamaican would want to work hard and build up a business because a "bigger boss" would simply shut it down. When a small businessperson begins to "come up" s/he gets forced out by a big businessperson who wants no competition.

"Uplift" is good in comparison to remaining in a "low station," but not wholly so. As people say, "One man's rise is another man's fall." Foster (1971) connects this kind of thinking with a real scarcity of resources, calling it the "Image of Limited Good." Also, "uplifted" people use their power to create dependents rather than to help others rise. Two poor farmers, discussing goings on in local political circles, said that politicians never like to see their aides "come up." Instead of taking pride in having trained a young one well, politicians fear that those who work under them will try to usurp their power. Once higher up, people quickly forget old debts. Loyalty is an unenduring, perishable product when engendered by vertical relationships. It works like capital for those on whom underlings depend (see Bourdieu 1982).

Even in small businesses and for people who have few established dependency relationships, the importance of shutting others out is clear. One woman said that when she tried to "do a thing" by selling oranges in the village, others envied her success and tried to do the same. This flooded the market and ruined her business. Had she been a "bigger boss" she would have eliminated competition through sorcery or more direct action.

Sometimes, "bigger bosses" even resort to murder to control a business area. Men trying to make money by meeting Jamaica's mounting transportation needs have met death instead. My neighbor's son drove a van and died by a gunshot fired by a more powerful driver's henchman. Accidents sometimes happen because of bus route competition; engines and brake cables are interfered with. There are other kinds of sabotage: one bread delivery van driver and commissioned salesman found seaweed in his gas tank. He "picked sense out of nonsense" and concluded that another driver who wanted his customers' business had done it. His boss, of course, assumed that he did it himself simply to shortchange the bakery of business.

People blaming things like this on "grudge" often have some doubts about themselves and their right to success. "Grudgefulness" happens when one person thinks another is not "good enough." So a person who feels "grudged" knows at some level that his or her character has flaws onto which others may "rivet." People's shortcomings gain publicity when others discuss the reasons behind a "grudge" held against them.

"Jamaica people can't stand success," my older "brother" said. A well-known folk song celebrates the death of a man called Sammy who "plant piece of corn down a gully" in an effort to "uplift" himself. The field "bear til it kill poor Sammy." The chorus repeats the cry, "Sammy dead, Sammy dead, Sammy dead oh!" As his story unfolds, listeners learn that "wasn't work" itself nor thievery that killed "poor Sammy" but the ire that the unshared fecundity of his "corn piece" aroused in his neighbors. His neighbors were "vex" about losing status as Sammy's own rose, and they "grudged" him: "a grudgeful and a bad mind make them kill him." Being "mean," he did not merit such good fortune, and so his neighbors arranged his death.

"Bad mind" people actively try to "spoil" those they "grudge." The surest way to "mash down" a person is to attack his or her health—to make the body rot and decay like a spoiling fruit. "Sore foot," for example, which involves festering foot ulcers that will not heal, might be "set" on a person who obtains a visa for work in "foreign" so that travel plans are disrupted.

Bad advice can also "crash" plans. Raychelle, twenty-two, was fortuitously chosen by an old and wealthy man to be his bride. Everyone she "moved with" congratulated her—everyone except for the older woman who had been employed by the husband-to-be to "care" some of his young children. The "grudgeful" woman advised Raychelle to remain "free and single" instead of going through with her plan to marry. This advice was certainly not sound, the bride-to-be told me.

Considering the amount of social "uplift" the proposed wedding would bring and also the fact that the older woman's upstanding daughter was in need of a good husband, Raychelle announced: "Grudge, she grudge me." Raychelle had a tainted past, and she knew it. A woman once pelted her with stones in public, saying she had carried on with her boyfriend. Also, Raychelle's mother went off with Raychelle's "babyfather." These things, Raychelle thought, could have led the older woman to decide she was "not good enough" (and that the daughter was more deserving of a good marriage). When the older woman, touring the couple's new house with a small group of the bride's relatives, went off alone into another room, Raychelle believed that her suspicions were confirmed. The "grudgeful" woman, alone in that back room, might have been working "iniquity"—witchcraft—with which to "mash down" Raychelle and her marriage plans.

"MASHING DOWN" OTHERS WHO FEAR GHOSTS AND SORCERY

Cohen writes that Jamaicans in the farming community of Rocky Roads have "deep-seated hostilities which rarely are expressed directly. They fear one another, and each is convinced that there are secret conspiracies which aim to destroy him" (1955, 382). The tendency to blame failures on others also has been analyzed in the often cited work of Kerr

(1963). It is revealed very clearly in my own data.

One poor farmer had "worked up" his herd of cattle to eight head. Suddenly, they all "took sick," and five died. Wondering about their foul, black feces and "the way things look funny," the farmer decided that someone who "grudged" him had gone to "work" on him through the cattle. Another man, a merchant, had a sudden run of bad luck. Nothing sold, he could not stop drinking, and he fell ill. He dreamed he saw a certain (dead) person "playing" in his market stall. On his wife's advice, he washed his body and everything in his stall with a mixture of salt water and lime juice, to "cut" and "suck out" the evil "destruction" his enemy had "put 'pon" him.

Jamaicans fear supernatural "tricks," but few claimed that they might go so far as to turn down a promotion or refrain from building a house (both rare and wished-for things) in order to avoid them. Few said they would venture to a "professor" or "Obeah" worker—a sorcerer—for a "guard" (such as an amulet or ring) to avoid the threat of "grudgefulness." As "wicked" and "bad mind" as Jamaicans might be, they also describe themselves as easily frightened.

Jamaicans often berate the "fool-fool way" others "go on," "directly ignorant," "superstitious," and scared of their own shadows ("shadow" carries a double meaning, also referring to duppies). Terror does strike easily when one cannot simply flip a light switch to illuminate the cause of an unknown sound. But fright is cultivated. People terrorize each other "fe joke." They also do it when they want to steal or when they wish to exert control over another. Parents, for example, tell tales to keep children from tarrying on the street as night comes down.

Stories about frightening others sometimes come up during interludes between "true" ghost tales, or in stories about early childhood. People—mostly men—tell tales of pranks they played and imagined ghosts, caused by wind-rattled "bush" or "funny" shadows. One man happily described how, in his younger days, he would walk about at night dressed in banana "trash" (leaves), scaring other people. "Light posts weren't as popular first-time," a woman said, claiming that duping others has lost popularity because street and yard lights (among the monied) now expose would-be pranksters. But tricksters still walk about late, or jump from the bush at the side of a track to terrify, sometimes dragging chains, sometimes holding captured "blinkies" or giant fireflies in front of their eyes, sometimes entering yards surreptitiously and knocking on the wallboards or calling out names.

One woman, Deena, asked a man to spy on her boyfriend as she suspected that he had an "outside" girlfriend. The boyfriend encountered the spy on a dark lane and ran home to her in fright, thinking a duppy was after him. Deena kept her secret and let his story "stay." People take advantage of others' fears, calling up beliefs about sorcery by wearing a type of jewelry that suggests that they command some "high power science" (black magic). One man wears a key-shaped charm and a number thirteen medallion to convince those who would harm him of his links with "evil."

Many are "too coward" to really engage in "evilous negromancy." "Man fall on his own sword" so the best and safest way to fulfill an ambition is through hard work and "natural means." To involve oneself in supernatural workings is a dangerous thing—"No, Bubba! Me no business with that." Some do "deal in unclean business" but many of these brave folk do so only in a most roundabout way. For example, I was warned never to give anyone my shoes, or they would try to give me "sore foot" so I could not travel again. In that way, they would attack others who they thought had benefited by relationships with me.

ACHIEVING "UPLIFT"

Austin (1984), Brodber (1989), Comitas (1973), and Foner (1973) have shown that lower-class Jamaicans are blocked from upward mobility by structural and institutional barriers. Brodber and Comitas discuss the ill effects of occupational multiplicity, while Austin and Fonor concentrate on the shortcomings of the educational system. Blaming one's failure to "uplift" on fellow community members leaves the barriers intact, making substantial mobility impossible. But even the littlest bit of "uplift" is a drastic and highly desired improvement for many.

Often, and against large odds, people try to improve themselves through hard work and perseverance. Some resort to "unnatural" means. Magic for increased prosperity usually involves "bending" someone's "mind." This is done through special substances that must be incorporated into a target individual's body. As long as the dosage is controlled, sickness should not ensue.

One woman, Cat, sold pudding at the school-ground and is reputed to have used "magic" in her cooking to compel children to buy. She saved her daughter's bath water, dirty with sweat and bodily exuviae, for the mix. Once a person "taste piece," thereby ingesting and absorbing those bodily substances, s/he would feel compelled to come back again and again to buy more. I doubt Cat saw an increase, as she is no longer in this business.

Another vendor procured a magic powder and sprinkled it in her shop to increase sales. The powder, which people claim gives her dry goods a "funny" taste and makes the air around her shop smell peculiar, compels people—even those just passing by who breathe the air near the shop—to buy. Some thought that her sales have risen, but many said they stay away from her shop now to avoid being drawn in (some boasted, "She can't catch me!") and because they fear the toxic effects of the powder.

Through the powder, the "wicked" and "greedy" shop-keeper was "forcing" people's decisions. "Bending minds" is strictly wrong for Jamaicans, who value independent decision-making. Besides, things not arrived at through hard work and regular or "natural" means later crumble. This gladdens the hearts of those who have not managed to "make a way" and should deter those who would "mash down" others from attempting such wickedness.

BOASTING AND "TRACING"

"Boasy" (boastful) behavior in a person who does "come up" is not condoned. As long as a person is "kind" and not "boasy," something symbolic of a position "on top," like owning a house, does not cause problems. Being a householder or housewife is desirable and admirable. It is part of full adulthood, so "that no say" (it does not cause strife). But the kind of boasting that happens when people get into a quarrel and "tell" each other what they have brings trouble. Having another person announce their strengths and your weaknesses (for instance, that you neither own or run a house and are, therefore, not a "somebody") is cause for anger.

"Jamaica people" like to make each other look bad, they say. When others know of your social and moral foibles, they love to "tell you about it." "Tracing" refers to a public bout between disputants, when each traces the shortcomings of the other or traces out a personal version of the argument, maligning the other party. For example, a woman vexed might validate her anger toward another by telling her, "I cook my own pot"; in other words, "I am an adult and you are not, since you do not run a household; therefore, my anger is more valid." Her behavior is "boasy" and her target feels slighted at being shamed in public.

Although there exists no categorical name for a gifted tracer and "tracing" is not a condoned activity, those blessed with rhetorical skills provide amusement for the audience that gathers to listen. Though often concerned about their conspicuousness and wary of seeming too "talkify," those assembled may offer their views to each other and some will even advise the main players. They may laugh and poke fun at the target of abuse, especially when a scene has gone on long or one participant is obviously winning the row. Those "tracing" often use the audience to their advantage. For example, instead of directly addressing their opponents, arguers may turn their rhetoric onto audience members, describing the offense and asking, "Now tell me, do you think that right?"

Jayawardena (1963) has demonstrated the functional nature of institutionalized forms of conflict in the West Indian setting. Guianese "eye-pass" disputes, he has shown, contribute to the maintenance of egalitarian norms in plantation communities. Brought about when one person offends another by claiming superior status, "eye-pass" disputes involve a stylized idiom of abuse that marks the quarrel as one between equals (who look each other in the eye, and do so without envy), with an aim of reestablishing unity.

The functional nature of "tracing" is a bit more complex because the majority of Jamaican villages are not plantation communities. Unity in the face of the planters is not a goal, and status, power, and prestige differences within the community do and should exist (the plantation laborers Jayawardena discusses would not accept this). Differences involve rights and obligations that must be adhered to but should not be flaunted by those close in rank and should never be used to humiliate.

Like the "eye-pass," "tracing" assumes shared values. "Tracing" concerns problems *within* the system, not *about* it; "tracing" presupposes that opponents share the same social and moral values. Egalitarian norms figure in "tracing" as in "eye-pass" disputes; "boasy" behavior or an affront to another's dignity often brings "tracing" about. But status differences also carry weight and the nonfulfillment of obligations or the denial of another's rights can trigger a "tracing" too.

Whether egalitarianism or status and role-related rights and obligations are appealed to, "tracing" functions to reenforce norms and resolve tensions. It brings a quarrel to public judgment so it can be resolved. Beside its directly structural functions, "tracing" helps reconfirm cultural expectations. Victory frequently hinges on verbal agility and legalistic "reasoning" skills rather than pure rightness, but standards and expectations for behavior always come clear in bouts of "tracing." In arguing a point, a participant often compares ideas about what "should" be with what has actually taken place. S/he puts forth ideas about proper thoughts and deeds. Even if between status equals, "tracing" resolutions leave one party an inferior for having acted "out of order."

In truth, no one can live up to all expectations. People are cautious about with whom they share which secrets because during quarrels opponents can "trace" these (sometimes enhancing them; sometimes inventing more: "biggest lie win war") for everyone in listening range to hear. One woman with a rather sordid past told me she never has "words" for anyone on the street; she wants to avoid arguments. She fears what others might "throw" back at her and bring to the public's attention. Another woman, illiterate, confided that she would not ask "just any and anyone" to write for her because they would "turn around and tell about it" in a public quarrel.

GOSSIP

Some people always "want some news to carry." People believe others "bring carry" news to those involved for personal gain. This might take the form of a few yams given in return for information concerning an adulterous lover. Often, information is solicited; many admit to keeping "spies." People know that anything they say may be used against them. A simple question can be taken as an effort at gossip reconnaissance. If the person inquired of feels troubled enough, s/he responds "You ask too much question," "Come out of me life," or "You a private detective?" Even close companions cannot be trusted: enemies can use them without their knowledge or can bribe them for information with which to carry out evil deeds.

Jamaicans consider it vulgar to "fasten into" others' "business," and speak with disgust about people who "lap frock tail and labrish"; they disdain those women known for tucking their skirts up diaper-style as they sit down for long sessions of gossip in which they "chat" others. Although men "labrish" too, women are more often called out for it. Perhaps because men generally talk little about their personal feelings they do not realize that women, for a variety of cultural and psychosocial reasons, do. Women talking are not necessarily "chatting" others: often, they talk about themselves. Men's guilty projection ("they know what they would do [or say]") and vain worries about the exposure of potentially embarrassing exploits help account for male allegations about females engaging in character assassination.

Many insist that only "compulsion" brings them out of their yards. Some do not even go to the shop if they can help it because then "any and anybody can know your business." At the shop, others note what you buy as well as that you buy at all and draw conclusions. Opaque plastic bags—"scandal bags"—are necessary for privacy. They hide what one carries and so conceal information that might otherwise be used in a scandalous fashion. Keeping to oneself is sanctioned as long as avoiding "problem" (and not an unfriendly attitude) motivates such behavior; staying in one's yard suggests a respectable disinterest in gossiping.

THE POWER OF TALK

The danger of allowing an enemy to "trace" or "carry" talk of one's (mis)deeds or to call one's name is based on more than fear for one's reputation, fear of implied social ties, and fears of pollution. Words themselves have power. The act of "chanting" something again and again can cause it to come true. Prophets and soothsayers are called "chanters."

To "wash mouth 'pon" someone is to "chat" them in a bad way. People named are profaned through polluting contact: aggressors' mouths and so their bodily filth sympathetically touch their victims as they utter their victims' names. Belief in this powerful aspect of speech underlies the seriousness of commanding a person, "Don't call my name in your mouth," or "Don't dirty my name with your stinking breath." A name is excreted through the aggressor's lips as if phlegm, bile, a bite of rotten fruit, or as one villager put it, as if washed out worms or intestinal parasites. People often spit after "calling" names, as if removing bad tastes from their tongues. Sometimes, spitting substitutes for "chanting." One man offered that women spit more than men for lack of words—he believed that women have smaller vocabularies than men and little command of English.

When someone "washes" their mouth with a name they usually "bad mouth" (say negative things). Speakers gifted with "goat mouth" are especially successful at creating "bad minded" effects through speech. Goats ruin everything their mouths touch ("Goat nyam [bitten] potato can't plant") and so too do "goat mouth" people. Villagers try to keep their names out of the local gossip mill and protect them from those with "goat mouth" as well as from those who would simply "bad mouth" and so contaminate them. The success of efforts to "uplift" or to avoid a downfall hinges on cautious comportment. The next chapter explores this further.

Chapter 6

"Unclean Deeds" and Careful Eaters

A status system involving positions ranked on a social ladder—as well as greed and jealousy—rivals the overt egalitarian ideology of "one blood" and "one love," and every Jamaican knows it. Others' motives are always in question, making social interaction a potentially dangerous endeavor. Anything can arouse rumors or suspicion, as people carry with them a fear of being poisoned or otherwise punished for their successes. Talk of poison and of having one's "mind bent" to the will of another expresses the tension generated by the expectation of sharing and the demands kin can make. It can also be used to validate responses to problematic relationships.

SENSITIVITY TO INSULTS

Anytime one crosses another's path, accidentally steps on a foot, or inadvertently nudges or bumps somebody, a loud apology that goes quite beyond what Americans would see as common courtesy is made. "When a man step on my toe and don't say sorry," Mass Beck told his niece after she did the same to her sister and had not apologized, "I consider it a kick. He just kicked me." To ensure that an accident does not get interpreted as an aggressive act, a "beg pardon" and profuse "sorry, sorry, sorry" is in order. Even leaving a room requires an "excuse [me]" to show that no slight was intended.

Profuse apologizers are attempting to protect themselves from suspicion. Without an apology, people may feel that they have been slighted on purpose, that purpose being the pure jealous "hatrage" (hate and rage) that might produce a physical kick or a metaphysical one, such as the planting of powder to "sore" one's foot. Sensitivity to insult goes beyond a self-conscious fear of being ascribed a socially low position; an unexcused and abrupt exit might indicate foul play, such as the surreptitious wafting of poison dust. One must be careful not to attract suspicion or to offend for offenses (intended or not) may provoke retribution.

POISONING

Jamaicans have long feared poison. Many West African cultures had traditions of poisoning, generally for divination. Patterson (1969, 265) reports that the poisoning of masters by slaves (especially those who knew "Obeah," or sorcery, and so were "extremely expert" with poisons) was "not uncommon." Emerick describes the "prevalent fear of being poisoned" existing "among all classes" in an essay written almost one hundred years after abolition and emancipation (1915, 333). More than life is at stake: beside its ability to "sick" or kill by altering the natural balance of the body, poison can compel action if it alters the body in just the right way.[1]

Because people do poison one another (howsoever infrequently), Jamaicans exert the utmost caution about food and beverages. Many pray over their food. One man, hoping to turn bad into good, offered this grace daily: "Thank you, Father, for this daily bread He has provided for us.... Join with us and consecrate it into a medicine and a tonic for this body of yours and mine. Amen." By this, he protected those at his table from choking or being poisoned and ensured that the food would both nourish and taste "nice."

Temporal precautions are also taken. With any food or drink, one must note color, taste, and smell. Over and over, people warned me to watch from whom I took food, explaining by way of example that they never ate "from just any and anybody."

"UNCLEAN" COOKING

Cleanliness provides the simplest reason for dietary caution: some cooks do not keep their cooking utensils, their foodstuffs, or themselves clean. Jamaican kitchens, which run the gamut from simple, open-air wood fires to coal stoves or kerosene burners housed in zinc and wood sheds, to indoor arrangements with gas stoves, tiled floors, and plumbing, are kept quite clean. Hands are always washed, food kept covered, and scoured pots wiped clean again before being taken up for cooking, in case dust or anything has touched them.

Because "you can't never sure," lots of people avoid street vendors and restaurants (which usually close at six in the evening, since eating late is not a custom). In addition to the possible threat of ingesting something "unclean," people report that the "meat kind" used often comes from animals humans should not eat. These include pests (such as insects and rodents that compete with humans for food), reptiles, and animals kept as working pets (such as cats, dogs, and donkeys).

Carrion is not to be eaten, even indirectly. Many prefer farm-bred, "factory" fowl because the common type, scavengers, eat "dirt," that is, bugs (which carry disease and themselves eat "dirt"), carrion, feces, and other rotting matter. Land crabs are even worse: besides resembling insects (they scuttle like Anansi the spider), they eat corpses in tombs. Carrion-eating creatures must be avoided by people not wishing to ingest fellow humans or the contagious "filth" of decomposition.

Tales involving duplicity and meat substitution at butcher counters and restaurants are very common. A popular (and funny) song concerning this came out in early 1989, just after the highly publicized arrest of a roadside soup vendor for selling goat soup (a traditional dish) actually made with cats. One woman explained that the cook had slighted his girlfriend, and it was she who, in "tracing" him, exposed his evil deed. But a young man claiming to know "what really happen" revealed that the vendor had been trying some Obeah "science" that called for boiling a black cat, got caught, and explained it away as a soup scandal because practicing Oheah is both illegal and shameful.

"UNCLEAN" FOOD AND POISON

Food paranoia is common, runs deep, and is more than a matter of simple hygiene. Saying a person's "hands are dirtied," their cooking "unclean," or their food is full of "dirt" carries much more meaning than a non-Jamaican might think. People who deal in Obeah "dirty" themselves. Jamaicans truly fear that those wishing to harm them will do so through their food. A meal is something taken into the body, and poison can be ingested along with it by an unsuspecting eater.

People who do eat in restaurants and from street vendors claim that no vendor or restaurant worker would purposefully harm them as they could never "have something" between each other. Because they and the workers are "strangers" and never socialize, the workers would not "bad mind" them. This justification negates, of course, any claim that one's in-group is in complete harmony. And the possibility that a worker could be bribed by an outsider to poison a customer's food or the chance that an "evilous" worker might "take set" on someone and do him or her wrong does exist, so care must be taken.

No one accepts a drink that has been opened out of sight. Many actually pry bottle caps off with their teeth, saving themselves from "worries" about whether or not the buyer, bartender, or vendor has slipped something in. No one eats or drinks from a plate or cup left standing while s/he looks about other business; no one comes back to finish something left out in a public place. Even if no enemy "interferes" to "try a thing" or "trick," flies and other disease-spreading insects might "pitch 'pon it." Some people never order the same things twice to foil plotters who might watch for patterns. Most eat a big meal before embarking on any lengthy trip so that they do not have to eat away from home.

More care must be taken when dealing with fellow villagers because of the likelihood of rivalry. People are loathe to let their children leave their yards unfed, because children (not yet fully "sensible") are apt to accept food. Often, however, no refreshment is offered to guests unless it would be awkward not to, as when a visitor has traveled far or stays a long time. Of course, in such a case, chances are that trust is well established. At times, such as when an influential or otherwise potentially useful person stops by, refreshment is offered to impress and to initiate a relationship. Fellow villagers hear if the guest accepts food and they make assumptions about alliances.

Some people, adamant about taking food only in their own yards, will sit "empty" in others' yards for hours. No matter how much gas the empty "belly" generates and despite the unpleasant sensation of hunger "twisting" the "tripe," they never consider eating. But it is quite rude to refuse food when offered. Refusal signifies suspicion and distrust, which are bound to cause offense. Sensitive hosts realize this and may allow their guests easy escape by phrasing offers as negative assumptions, like "You don't want fe me [any of my] dinner?"

Greedy hosts can take advantage by not offering food to people with whom it has never yet been shared or by making negative declarations about the possibility of a guest's wanting to eat. Now and again, they are surprised by willing visitors, either pleasantly or not depending on the intents with which they made their offers. Knowledge about food-sharing beliefs can also be used in play. People can banter with close relations who, when visiting, get hungry and ask for food, teasing that the visitors never used to trust their cooking.

Understandings about sharing food are used when people "trace off" others. An elderly woman baked several sweet potato puddings as gifts for certain people. Her grown son Joe never eats away so always feels "hunger bite" upon returning to the yard. Arriving home very late one evening, he took a big cut of pudding from the pan meant for Mr. Winslow. When, the next day, the woman saw what had happened, "vex she vex." Joe grew defensive and insulted his angry mother, asking what made her think Mr. Winslow would ever take food from her, implying that his mother and Mr. Winslow had no relationship except one of mistrust.

This same son's mother still has a good relationship with his ex-girlfriend Marie, whom Joe feels acts like a greedy John Crow. Joe conceived children with Marie but has no money to give them or her, hates her as she does him, and has another girlfriend anyhow. To his chagrin, Joe's mother often gives Marie money. He cannot stand these insults to his pride and is ever alert for food that Marie may have left at the house, believing she might poison him. Joe always asks his mother who made any prepared food she offers him, in case she has unknowingly become a cat's-paw for Marie or some other enemy.

Joe's caution is typical. All Jamaicans are very aware of the ramifications gifts carry and are particularly wary of gifts of food. Taking the utmost care about what goes into one's body is common and thought of as wise. Accepting a plate of rice and peas can have dire physical consequences as well as social ones. People know this and act accordingly.

Any sign of irritation in the "belly" or "structure" is a cause for suspicion. One young man woke with stomach cramps and immediately wondered who might have poisoned him. He "considered over it" between trips to the chamber pot. After a lot of thought, he recalled the oil nut seed (*Ricinus communis*) that he had placed on his gum for a toothache the preceding day. Realizing that the seed must have slipped down his "food tube," "operating" his "belly," he was relieved to conclude that he had not been poisoned after all.

As a white foreigner and one from a place considered "civilized," I was assumed to be unaware of the terrible possibility of ingesting poisoned, "unclean" things. My landlady and my friends made sure I never felt hungry: they kept me well fed. They also questioned me constantly about what and from whom I had eaten and warned me of particularly suspect foods and people.

WHO TO WATCH FOR

There are several people in each village known for their "wicked" ways. Where I stayed, "beggy-beggy" people and members of "that Poco church" aroused suspicion. The Poco church is actually a poor Revival church, one reputedly dealing with Satan (thus the Poco label: short for "Pocomania," itself a distortion of "Pukkumina," mainly an African religion that most Jamaicans, in their concern for "Chrisitian" principles, have come to believe involves demon worship). The church "Mother" (note the kinship idiom), a certified, licensed pastor, had had two children by the age of sixteen and allegedly engaged in prostitution before turning to Revival, a religion in which only angels still in God's heaven and the Holy Trinity are supposed to be worshiped.[2] Her conversion notwithstanding, she could not shake her previous reputation as a "harlot," and those who followed her suffered for this.

Nonconformist attitudes and lax, "careless" lifestyles or "slackness" typify the "wicked," who must be avoided. People known as "just too terrible" are always involved in quarrels and frequent the street, or they have amassed wealth but do not act as the well-off should. Mistress Lee, for example, does not part easily with anything and keeps to herself inimically. She wears pants, drinks gin, and smokes. The last three behaviors might be accepted (as they are in certain cases), but the first two are not, and that fact renders everything else Mistress Lee does suspect. People find fault with her: they see her as "wicked" and "selfish." If her cat comes by looking for water, they assume that in her "meanness" Mistress Lee has not given it any.

PART TWO

"Sin," or desire (see Cohen 1955, 390 regarding this gloss), and the propensity for evil may "show in the face," making a sinner ugly, causing ulcers or bumps, but "you can't directly know" who will attempt "a thing." Sometimes, when a person cannot look another in the eye because of guilt, ill-intent is revealed. Still, even a close companion can do someone in, whether through bribery, a "grudge," or an outside agent's covert commandeering, as when someone with "bad mind" asks a person's relative to give him or her a piece of secretly poisoned cake.

The best way to avoid becoming a target (or a dupe) is to avoid unnecessary contact with others. Sociability can bring destruction not only because people view an overly social person with suspicion and may therefore decide to "set" a "trick" on him or her, but also because things sometimes best kept secret can get exposed to public scrutiny more easily when a person "keeps company." During interactions evil people can secure material things or information needed for intended "dealings."

One can avoid those known as "wicked," but "any and anybody" might bring about another's downfall. People are born "directly wicked and envious." A Revival preacher explained how and why we inherit "wickedness." Impertinent angels (Lucifer and his colleagues), expelled from heaven for "slackness," drifted to Earth. They "interfered" sexually with humans, "mingling" their evil blood with ours and so forcing "wickedness" into the gene or blood pool. Criminality and other character traits pass to children (one reason blood transfusions are feared). Accordingly, since some "lines" have more "wickedness" in them: some families are more "terrible" than others.

WASHING WICKEDNESS OUT

"Wickedness" inheres in the human species, and children are likened to "little Satans" until they learn self-control. Socializing only with upstanding citizens helps: the influence of others on one's ability to check evil desires can be great.

People judge others by the "quality" of those with whom they "move." Securing respect depends on avoiding disreputable people. Respectable people are known as hard, honest workers and do not occupy the lowest "stations" because they have managed, through "natural" means, to "uplift." People of low "stations" are often accorded low moral standings.

The Christian church is one of Jamaica's strongest institutions. Its numerous branches hold many teachings in common, and all students take religious education classes. Few citizens are uninfluenced by the church. One teaching holds that personal evil can be washed out with Jesus's or "the lamb's" blood. A very popular hymn tells us, "There is power, power, wonderworking power in the precious blood of the lamb.".

"Sin" is something "dark—it blackens the heart." The link between blackness and evil has been mentioned as, for example, in the phrase "dirty black naygur," the boiled black cat, and the term "black magic." Only those interested in "negromancy" and demons use black candles, as whiteness is associated with purity, godliness, and cleanliness. One hymn asks, "What can wash me white as snow? Nothing but the blood of Jesus."

Long ago, some of the "first time" Jamaicans made sacrificial offerings of goat kids (goats being referred to like sheep as "mutton" and "lambs") during "Kumina," a ceremony involving the dead, with ritual drumming, dancing, and rum. Now, they just feast on them. Hurston, one of the first anthropologists to work in Jamaica, recorded how the blood, called the "power," was caught in a glass for the main participants to drink from and purify themselves (1938, 73).

Over and over, preachers tell their congregations to "live pure and clean" and "keep pure and clean" to receive God's blessing. A "good" life is lived "clean and sober." Quoting the Bible, they point out that good wine should not be poured into dirty vessels. Many parallels are drawn between the vessel and the body and the wine and the blood. As wine fills a vessel, God's blessings can "fill" the human body, including the "mind" and "heart." But the body, like the vessel, must be clean to receive God in his purity.

Pastors draw other analogies directly from popular health

beliefs. Blood functions to maintain good health by cleansing the body of impurities as it washes through, and wine—especially "tonic" wine—fortifies the blood, itself sometimes called "wine." The belief that "wonder-working power" rests "in the blood of the Lamb" makes clear the logic of the metaphors pastors love to use. The body must stay clean for a person's good health and for his or her religious grace. As human blood washes out toxins, Jesus's blood washes away "sin." As "tonic" wine fortifies the body, the blessings God offers strengthen spiritual resolve. And as a dirty vessel would soil clean "wine" and God's grace if poured in, so too would a body dirty with "sin" contaminate that which might enter.

People who "red eye" or feel envy toward a "clean and sober" neighbor's "booked passage" to heaven try to "spoil" her or him. They sully the reputation and bodily cleanliness of the person who has his or her "visa," "passport," and other "papers" for heaven in order. The body is desecrated and "spoils" or "rottens out" when penetrated by poison.

"COMPELLANCE"

Jamaicans have demands made on them constantly and "downpressers" fill their world. They cannot exhibit "meanness" in response to the obligations that exist between kin, even though they admit that altruism is often a pretense. They often resent others' demands but do not forget the "kindnesses" others owe them. They know that establishing oneself as a householder by "natural means" and upholding one's independence are indicators of social adulthood, but saving money or building equity for the future is often frowned upon as hoarding, which undermines the supposed egalitarian relations with kin.

Many openly contend that most relationships are instrumental associations. They often project their own competitive wishes onto others, and see them as lazy "John Crow" parasites who "beg too much." Many take glee in getting away with "a thing," fooling bosses and authorities as Anansi always did.

Surrounded by needy, judgmental relations and by tricksters who fool you into parting with all you have, struggling against the poor job market and institutional barriers to success, it makes little sense to try to hold onto things.[3]

"Chants" of "one blood, one desire" notwithstanding, Jamaicans fear and loathe the ever-present specter of manipulations and demands, whether explicit, discreet, or disguised. A person is easily manipulated when something that compels is put directly into his or her body. Powders and the like, available at special shops, procurable through Obeah workers, and often easily made from ingredients found in nature, can enter the body through any opening. Some work purely by magical means; others—poisons—alter the physical body as well as or instead of working magically. Poison can be inhaled or absorbed through pores but is most easily incorporated when disguised in refreshments and ingested.

"Compellance" poisons usually work on the "mind" part of the body, changing it. Using magic to manipulate is serious, but it is more discreet than to kill or "directly sick" someone, two other Obeah options. If the "compellance" works as it should, it attracts no attention or suspicion. For example, a person "looking" money from another might cook her a meal and drop "something" into it. The additive affects the consumer, causing her to return time and again, bearing money, which she would not have done "naturally," of her own accord. Her decision to share funds is understood as "forced" because her host used a magical poison to "bend" her "mind." If all goes well, only her host knows. But administering "compellance" poison is a delicate art. A targeted person's physical "cleanliness" and health are easily "spoiled." The dose, particularly if administered repeatedly, can irritate the "belly," causing sickness symptoms which can spark a victim's curiosity about "what really a go on."

TIES THAT BIND

Poisoned refreshments enter the targeted person's body,

mingle with its physical substance, and bind the person to the food-giver in a way that makes the person's actions seem uncompelled and altruistic—much as the fulfillment of kinship obligations should, ideally, be. As noted, kinship is based on shared physical substance. Mothers feed fetuses and children with blood, which the offspring incorporate into their bodies. Once incorporated (or traced by two people back through time to an intersection in one common genitor), blood binds kin together into interdependent, "natural" networks in which instrumentality and coercion, ideally, do not figure.

The cultural model by which "compellance" poison does its work follows the procreative model of consubstantiality that underlies kinship. It generates, through a poison's incorporation into the body, kinship-like, un-self-conscious bonds of obligation. But just as true kinship bonds can in actuality be resented, so too can the ties that poison binds.

People resent being compelled to do anything. But when kinship obligates, unless they can fault the behavior of those demanding their compliance as in itself not kinlike, people must come through in good humor and should not complain. Often enough, obligations to kin are quite willingly met. However, often they are not. The idiom of poison provides an important foil for the idiom of kinship just as egoism and altruism form the cultural dialectic underlying social network behavior. Accordingly, some kinship resentments are expressed in poison beliefs. When poison (and not kinship) motivates actions, people gain the right to rebel against obligations and obligators.

One man tells of a woman who baked him a cake. She added "a little something" to secure his love for her. He liked cake and ate this gift up, only to find himself later plagued by nausea and cramps. Luckily, he vomited and otherwise rid his body of the offending ingredient. Needless to say, he rid himself of the woman too, who he assumed had tried to "trick" him into a tighter relationship. He does not "too love" cake anymore.

Another man laughs as he boasts about foiling such an endeavor. A lover he often visited and who would have liked to see him more asked if he ate pudding; yes, he said, he did ("pudding" can also mean vagina). The next time she saw him, she gave him a large cut of a pudding she had just baked. He took it home, intending to eat it. Accidentally, the piece slipped to the floor and "Puss" bounded up for a share. But the cat, after sniffing it, turned up its nose. Realizing (or assuming) that "witchcraft business a go on," the man disposed of the suspect sweet and never called on this "friend" again. By talking of poison, he validated this decision.

"FORCING NATURE"

Poison, like any toxin, "spoils" in the body and "sicks" it. Poison endangers the person intent on "binding" as well as the person bound: found out, s/he faces embarrassment and ostracism. This can happen when a poisoner errs in the application or dosage of whatever substance is chosen to work a "trick." Targets then get sick from poison meant to "bend" the "mind" because the "belly" is a sensitive place. "Funny" bouts of "bad belly" alert sufferers to "unnatural" situations. And any "forced" relationships are doomed to failure after a time. Not established by mutual consent or "naturally" mingled mutual substance, these relationships must break down because the desire to hold them together does not "naturally" inhere (as in kinship).

A person "forced" to give money to another may dislike the relationship but stay in it. S/he feels "contrary," "impossible," and generally irritated with the contradictory emotions the relationship evokes. "Tied, like a donkey" (donkeys are kept as work animals), s/he resents the rope. Still, the person "tied" cannot leave, and feels "a way" even without the knowledge that s/he's been "tricked." One day, s/he may feel compelled to grab a machete and hack off the hand or the head of the master. The person "tied" feels out-of-control, especially if s/he has no concrete sense of having been unnaturally "tied." But since "unfair games must always play twice," the master's suffering "must come."

"TYING" AS A RATIONALIZATION

Many stories are told of couples who bicker and fight but stay together because one has "tied" the other and bound the relationship. Chronic and seemingly unfounded quarrels are often taken as proof that an "unfair game" occurred. So are relationships in which people stay although no children have been produced or one partner is not receiving the benefits s/he is supposedly due. Otherwise, the endurance of these untraditional, nonideal relationships would make little sense.

"Tying" claims can provide answers for questions like "A what make him go on so?" and "Why don't she leave him? Him and she no family, after all." People use their knowledge of "compellance" to malign others and to denigrate their own relationships, to excuse or validate otherwise unbecoming behavior, and to rally support from fellow villagers by setting them against an offending person. They can defend themselves against accusations of acting unwisely in keeping a lover of low "station" or for staying with an abusive one. While women who stay with men who beat them may claim to have been "tied," the men may likewise claim that their bad behavior comes from their resentment of having been forcibly and deceitfully "tied" into an "unnatural" relationship. Who in a quarrelsome couple will win the most social support depends in part upon who makes the most compelling claim of having been bound by an "unclean deed."

EGOISM AND ALTRUISM

Jamaican social interaction relies on a model in which all sharing behavior is un-self-consciously and altruistically motivated because of "natural" substance linkages. Mingled or shared blood ties promote the survival of kin groups, naturally bringing about cooperation. Where no blood is shared— where people have no consubstantial identities with each other—cooperation is based on instrumental egoistic desires.

The tension between maintaining egalitarian social relations and getting ahead is high. It is linked to extensive and supposedly altruistic obligations and to the belief, itself largely engendered by the emphasis on altruism and disapproval of self-centered behavior, that others will bear down on those trying to "uplift." Denied, egoism must burst out stronger elsewhere and, indeed, it does so in the undercurrent of cynicism concerning the "real" (instrumental) basis of relationships. Expectations for assistance cloaked in the idiom of kinship, as well as malicious actions meant to undermine the success of others, both help to create and at the same time give expression to this atmosphere of resented relations and competition.

Jamaican social interaction occurs along a continuum that places egoism (competition, wariness, and no shared blood) and altruism (cooperation, trust, and shared blood) at opposite poles. Fictitious kinship bridges the assumed gap between supposedly competitive "strangers" and loving "family." While this sort of continuum is found the world over, Jamaicans have linked this bipolar model of social interaction into a specific cultural system in which resentment of obligations and unfulfilled desires to "uplift" get voiced through health concerns that include a dominating fear of being poisoned.

In the following chapters, ideas about dependence and independence are discussed further. Childrearing and gender relations are examined because ideas about kinship both effect and are made tangible through action taken in these realms. I shall later show how and why the ideas about dependence and independence revealed and enacted in childrearing and gender relations lead men, more so than women, to fear food-borne poison, and I shall then explain the different kinds of fears women have.

Children at Play

PART
THREE

Reproducing Society

Chapter 7

Sociable Procreation

The tension between egoism and a commitment to society—to kin group and community—is seen in attitudes about having children. The people among whom I lived disparage those who do not want to have children as "useless" and "selfish." Having children symbolizes a sociable commitment to community and kin, while childlessness (whether through infertility, celibacy, abortion, or contraception) signals one's antisocial tendencies.

THE VALUE OF CHILDREN

Children are valued additions to almost any household. They provide company, comfort, and an extra pair of hands for work. "No one eats for nothing," Mummy says, giving her four-year-old a broom. Some caretakers still subscribe to "slavery fool-fool bongo business [and] treat pickney like hog," one woman awaiting a bus told another. Children nonetheless must help with household chores.

A neighbor of mine who has only a few grown "boy-childs" still living with her can hardly wait for her daughter's child to "come up" in age enough to be helpful with those tasks the men cannot "manage" (because of the sexual division of labor).

Then, my neighbor will send for the child. She and my landlady cannot understand their church sister's refusal to take in
children. Sister Evangeline, about sixty-five, worked a job,
kept a house, and raised her "lot" of children in England before
repatriating and settling down on her family's land in the village. Her refusal to consider having another child around is
"selfish," "stupid," unthinkable, and unfathomable—most
Jamaicans would "[be] happy and glad" to incorporate a
helper. There "must" be times, my neighbor and landlady tell
each other, when Evangeline "well wants" someone to run an
errand, boil some tea, "keep company," or "[do] any little
thing—after all!"

In addition to gaining household help and a sort of health
insurance (a child can send for help should a person "drop
down"), those who "grow" children hope to have financial security for their senior years. One woman calls her children her
"pension." Women with children "doesn't must" depend upon
or sell out to men, she says (despite the fact that most women
with babies must look to men for money). Her words ring true
for those whose children are grown and have done well; she
herself has four children and should her husband leave her,
will still do alright.

PROCREATION
AND SOCIAL REPRODUCTION

Having children affirms one's link into a consubstantial
social network and is required for full adult status. In mingling one's blood with another's, a person returns the gift of
life blood his or her parents gave, confirming and tightening
his or her bonds to society. In caring for dependent others,
one demonstrates his or her commitment to the kinship
ideals of interdependence and obligation.

Fecundity represents reciprocation: blood for blood. The
practical and immediate nature of this reciprocity was illustrated above; my neighbor's daughter, who my neighbor gave
life to, gave a life to her mother in return, in the form of her

young child. Procreation and birth confirm male and female virility and fecundity, demonstrating that one has life inside to give and that one's vital essence or life blood will persist. Like the mule, a person who does not reproduce only serves to work. His or her blood disappears from the social circles that individuals, joining together, create and recreate.

NONFECUNDITY AND MULE SYMBOLISM

Like women, mules are known for their carrying capabilities; women carry wood, water, and so on, and mules serve as pack animals. "Drop pan" number meanings (discussed in the context of growth and decay, in Chapter 2) reveal a popular association between old women and donkeys (no. 37 denotes both). Hurston reported a common saying asserting that God made two kinds of donkeys, but one cannot talk (1938, 76). Nonfecund women are "mules": unlike fertile women and donkeys (the more common beast of burden), mules do not breed.

Mules are associated with prostitutes and whores, as the assignment of all three to "drop pan" no. 21 demonstrates. In addition to defying female role expectations and therefore posing an antisocial challenge (whether intended or not), nonmonogamous and nonfecund women fill the sexual but not the procreative needs of men (nor do they fulfill their own culturally constructed childbearing needs). Although as sexual and subsistence workers nonfecund women, like prostitutes and mules, are useful, those who do not provide society with children "have no use" in the end. This implies that the ultimate purpose of the individual (and of sex, which ideally ends in "discharge," the release of sperm and eggs) is to recreate society.

Mules (I discuss prostitutes in Chapter 9) do not reproduce and so cannot establish any enduring form of society. They do not establish relationships confirmed by offspring. They are stubborn and uncooperative. Mules represent particularly antisocial and "selfish" beings uninterested in growing up to establish new bonds and unable to return the gift of life by fulfilling the obligation of procreation. Nonfecund women can never achieve social adulthood because they, like mules, do not overtly signal childhood's end by having babies and establishing bonds—blood bonds—with the larger society outside the immediate family circle (infertile men can, of course, claim to have fathered children not really their own).

BESTIALITY AND ANTISOCIAL BEHAVIOR

Infertile, hard-working mules symbolically capture the core of cultural beliefs that surround nonreproducing individuals. Discourse on antisocial behavior often draws on animal symbolism, as structuralist analyses would predict. One night, during a round of bingo played illegally and quite rambunctiously in the dingy backroom of a village shop, a young woman named Alta got caught cheating. A ruckus ensued. Alta's father raised her after her mother ran away and a woman "traced" this, making the insulting inquiry, "Where fe you daddy get you, back of cow?"

Alta's insulter insinuated many things with that thrifty symbolic statement. First, the insult likened Alta's mother to an animal or social outsider; second, it implied that her father was a twisted, antisocial man who preferred to copulate with cows. The insulter told Alta, in effect, that she was not truly human; her blood mix contained nothing from the human female. Her antisocial tendencies, evidenced by her cheating, were a product of her breeding: an inheritance from her sexually aberrant father and her socially alienated mother. Her cheating at bingo confirmed, in her insulter's eyes, that Alta did not really belong to and should not be included in the social group.

Those who do not have children and complete the social contract—the obligation to return some blood, incurred through birth—are, like animals and those conceived "back of cow" or fathered by donkeys, not articulated into the social network. Having children expresses the readiness to fulfill obligations to society and one's relatives. It demonstrates a willingness to reproduce the social environment into which one was born. Children represent, concretely, the fresh social bonds established between "babymothers" and "babyfathers." People who do not maintain and create these sorts of links tacitly release themselves from their social group's hold as they subversively (albeit sometimes unintentionally, as in cases of natural infertility) reject it.

Like mules, people who "mingle" with animals are "selfish." Those rumored to have "interfered" with dogs, goats, or cattle, usually have "plenty money," no "kindness," and spend most of their time alone. Tales of bestiality are often told, and scandalous stories appear almost every week in tabloids such as Jamaica's *Weekend Enquirer*. As antisocial as it is, Jamaicans say, sex with domestic animals happens frequently. No one likes to eat meat from a female animal because it can be "nasty" with semen; they patronize only those butchers they trust to sell "clean" flesh.

Tabloid accounts in the spring of 1989 left some Jamaicans thinking that entertainer Michael Jackson's face was caving in like a rotting pumpkin. His "vanity," "meanness," and general "sin" "spoiled" his body and caused his health problems, my friends said. Jackson was known as a "greedy" man who spent vast amounts of money on himself in trivial, "useless" pursuits instead of sharing with others. Although rich, he had not married (a costly endeavor), had never kept any special "friends," and so had no children to support. He was considered self-centered.

Jackson had fired his "yard boy," my friends continued, "caused from jealousy." The worker had been spending too much time with Jackson's monkey. Granny now piped up, explaining that Jackson had been sexually active with his pet and did not want to share the pleasure with his "yard boy" (or bodyguard). When I asked how she knew this, as it was not printed in the particular article we were discussing, she and the others looked at me incredulously and asked for what other possible reason would Jackson have fired the boy? Jealousy is always sexual, they said. I teased them, accusing them of "bad mind." They defended themselves, pointing to a

Weekend Enquirer story (1989c) about a man so jealous over his donkey that he "cut poor Ginny's punani to shreds" one day when she would not have him ("Ginny" is any female donkey; "punani" means vagina). They repeated tales (all known to me because other villagers had recounted them too) about local animal lovers, asserting that bestiality might be vile but is not unusual.

My friends defended Jamaicans, claiming that this sort of thing happens all over the world, all of the time, and that "evilous" whites do it too. Glory, a neighbor and Granny's sister-in-law, came up to the yard with some chicken for Granny and, hearing the topic of conversation, sat down and offered confirmation. During her years as a guestworker in England, Glory often saw one particularly solitary woman with a dog. In the village, yard pets are kept for pragmatic reasons and people rarely call them anything endearing. The English woman not only named her pet but also took it everywhere she went. One day, Glory spied her in the grocery with the dog standing up against her, resting his front paws on her body. She had to quiet it, Glory reported, and begged the dog to come down while reminding it that such was not proper in public. Even in England, warned Glory, interpreting this scene as proof that the woman and dog were sexual partners, "sin" goes on.

One commonly told tale concerned a famous, wealthy white woman living just to the west who supposedly used her dog for sex. Another tale referred to a rich Indian man who had gone off with goats frequently enough to father some half-human kids. I learned from many sources about a specific poor black man who had been caught with a dog in Kingston. His neighbors "ran" him from "town"; they could have killed him for such a vile deed.

The various protagonists, all real people, shared neither racial qualities, socioeconomic background, or taste in animal "friends." What connected them? One young woman explained succinctly why a person, in this case a man, might engage in bestial relations: "Goat don't wear panty." In other words, "minglings" with animals do not involve debts.

A male lover should bring gifts, like panties and other

such presents, to his women "friends." Women expect this: sex is immediately and financially costly for men. When a person wishes to insult a man by pointing out he has no money, s/he may accuse him of cavorting with animals because no woman would have him "poor so." But accusations of bestiality are serious enough to keep them uncommon. Heterosexual human contact involves debt of another kind when children are conceived or enduring relationships formed. To deal with the long-term costs of such relationships, people create further bonds with people who might help. But taking on too many obligations is perilous.

Those accused of bestiality reject the costs of sociability for the benefits of solitude. The young woman quoted above noted that animals cannot talk back or gossip; they can "beg you" nothing and never "chat" you. In Jamaican eyes, Michael Jackson remains "selfishly" uninvolved socially. Because of "sin" and "meanness," they say, he sent the island no hurricane aid. Like him, the white woman to the west and the Indian mentioned above are known for "unkindness." All three "have it" (money) but "don't nice." The English woman, even though not known to be "mean," was obviously "selfish." The black man was poor, but he had a reputation for rejecting village women in favor of "foreign" tourists. He had a history of "meanness," and was well known for treating his girl-friends "rough" and refusing them the money and food that men are socially obligated to provide for women "friends." Like the others, he preferred animals.

SELF-ESTEEM, JOBS, AND SOCIAL ADULTHOOD

Sociable humans "mingle" with other human beings. Children are the passport to social adulthood; without them, self-esteem and the respect of others are hard to attain. Only a good career can save the situation. Even so, women who delay or exchange childbirth for careers are stigmatized as "selfish" in its fullest Jamaican sense.

Very few Jamaicans need to make a choice between children and career. Career opportunities are few, and positions with prestige are mostly closed to the impoverished. The employment situation for men is bad; for women, it is worse (see Massiah 1986 and 1988; Senior 1991). In the village where I lived, 63 percent of the males and 73 percent of the females between the ages of fourteen and thirty-four were unemployed in 1982. Figures were even higher for the parish capitol, where 76 percent of the men and 79 percent of the women below the age of thirty-five were unemployed (STATIN 1982). The few salaried jobs that do exist for unskilled workers are menial and ill-paid and can hardly provide a foundation for self-esteem. The jobs reserved for women are more suitable for mules than for human beings. Many of the women who do find jobs eventually quit and try to become self-employed (Barrow 1988, 167).

Aunt Lynn is one who gave up "working out." She swore off the harsh task of plucking chickens and the demeaning chore of washing other people's dirty clothes in favor of other survival strategies (she now roasts peanuts to sell by the pub on weekends and sells cigarettes from her house). Like the majority of women, Aunt Lynn wants and needs to work, but most jobs are unstable and involve taking orders and neglecting one's yard and family in return for meager and often delayed pay. Having children (and using many methods to gain a livelihood instead of keeping a paid position or attempting to build a career) is the simplest way to increase self-esteem and establish adulthood.

Having a child does not in itself bring womanhood, as the Jamaican Family Planning slogan "Before you are a mother, be a woman" indicates, but womanhood requires children. When two women on a bus began to quarrel over an accidental shove, the fact that one had not borne children was used against her. "You front never burn [hurt] you; you never have no pickney," shouted the aggrieved woman. "You is no woman—you a man!" To quarrel with this "man" would be a waste of time, because as opponents the two were no match. To argue with the "man" would be, in this context, like arguing with a "girl-child."

FAMILY PLANNING AFTER THE FACT

Jamaicans would never agree with the blanket statement that children are a burden. Only those with conflicting interests see them this way. Schoolgirls with high hopes for their futures may practice birth control (school rules bar pregnant girls from classes). But most women are unemployed and have no career demands or workplace limitations standing in the way of childrearing responsibilities.

Women seldom use "the planning" until after having a few children, thereby gaining social adulthood and a houseful of helpers. Jamaican women use birth control to limit family size rather than to delay or space childbearing (Powell et al. 1978, 56–57). This does not mean that women who do not use birth control specifically want to conceive; only one of every ten users who stops does so because she wants more children (Powell et al. 1978, 36). Concern over reliability and one's health and reputation underlie women's lack of interest in "the planning." Men are often concerned with genocide and the promiscuity of women taking contraceptives. The penchant for living each day fully "should in case death [come]" and a love of gambling also works against the use of birth control.

CONCEPTION AND THE THRILL OF RISK-TAKING

Gambling is a highly visible and greatly enjoyed aspect of Jamaican life. People take risks in other areas of life as well. The folk-hero Anansi is celebrated for his risky tricks, and people love getting away with even small things. Risk-taking has physical and emotional effects, and in altering one's biochemical balance (as when adrenaline pumps), it can truly induce good feelings.

Gambling goes on at nearly every celebration, dance hall, pub, and on any street corner in bigger towns. People gamble on dice games like Crown and Anchor. When business is slow, concessionaires allow little boys (who "thief" change from their mothers or get money by returning empty pop bottles) to take their chances. Bingo is popular, and many organizations, such as schools, raise money through occasional all-day bingo fairs. Bigger money can be won with dominoes, cards, and at the track. English races can be bet on at special shops. "Drop pan," the lottery-style game in which people "buy" or put money down on a number, is also popular.

Risk-taking in sexual behavior may enhance the pleasure of sexual activity. Ignoring the likelihood of pregnancy and doing "the work" "skin to skin" increases the chance of conception, adding to the excitement of copulation: danger can thrill. This is even more true when sexual activity is clandestine or when rebellion is involved, as it often is for the young.

BIRTH CONTROL CLINICS

The importance of keeping a "fit" body far outweighs the benefit of birth control. One head clinician guessed that two out of five women who participate in "the planning" suffer side effects, but noted that everyone worries about sickness, because birth control "mash down" the body. Birth control blocks the procreative flow of sexual substances between individuals, and in doing so it blocks the flow of substances within individuals in ways that cause sickness. People's health concerns, as well as dispensing problems and practical barriers to compliance, reduce the efficacy of "planning."

Family planning clinics are held, usually twice monthly, at the local health centers, which are everywhere in Jamaica. There were two within seven miles of the village where I lived—one within walking distance and the other easily reached by bus. Birth control is discussed with new mothers at the clinics they are required to (but do not necessarily) attend when their infants reach six weeks of age. Practitioners currently favor "Perle" (pills) and "injection" (Depo Provera, an injectable hormonal ovulation suppressor not used until 1992 in the United States because of its link with cancer).

"Planning" services generally cost ten or twenty cents (about two or four U.S. cents) a visit, depending on which clinic is attended. Supplies are usually free. But few take advantage of "planning" services. Only 19 percent of four-teen- to twenty-four year-olds who have used contraceptives got these from a clinic; the majority used store-bought supplies (Powell and Jackson 1988, 39). Although young adults are more apt to opt for methods other than intrauterine devices (IUDs) or "injection," both of which require clinic visits, this statistic is still telling.

The National Family Planning Board keeps a good record of the number of visitors clinics receive each year and the number of "new acceptors." They note that for every six women seen, one man visits (National Family Planning Board 1988, 2). But information about how many people actually use contraceptives is not readily available through the board which, for understandable political reasons, would have Jamaicans and the world believe that everybody practices "planning." In reality, half of all women between the ages of fourteen and forty-four have never used birth control, and only slightly more than half of those who ever did use it were doing so when surveyed (Powell et al. 1978, 50). Use is often quite haphazard and irregular. Only one-third of the users Brody surveyed reported using any method for as long as four months (1981, 94).

Many of the clinicians I interviewed prefer "injection" because of the "low I.Q.s" and tendency to forget things which they allege plague the women they see. Most clinicians think their patients are superstitious and few acknowledge that women's views, experiences, and expectations encourage docility in the clinic and influence (mis)understandings about family planning methods. Clinicians say that many clients lie about why they came: some want "planning" so they can give themselves abortions. Heavy doses of hormones cause hemor-rhaging; eating a month's worth of birth control pills at one time can induce a miscarriage (and can make a woman very ill indeed).

Women are affected by clinicians' attitudes. The tendency

women have to present themselves as involved in permanent, monogamous relationships reflects this. So does the diaphragm's unpopularity. According to a senior public health nurse, diaphragms have been available for over ten years, but not one clinician mentioned this method to me. Some had not even heard of it. All doubted that anyone would use such a method, "cause from shame" as well as the reluctance women claim to have to touch their genitals.

STERILIZATION AND IUDS

Sterilization and intra-uterine devices (which basically deter implantation by irritating the womb) are available and used, but both methods are labor-intensive and require sterile conditions for implementation. They cannot be dispensed by clinicians at health centers, and so clinicians do not promote them except in special cases. That is what officials say. Women, however, report that sterilization papers are often thrust, with pens, at drugged mothers in hospitals just before or after delivery.

Sterilization through tubal ligation, called the "tie off," is understood as a process wherein the "tube" gets knotted so no sperm can enter. The IUD, or "coil," is thought to work by blocking and preventing sperm from climbing all the way up to reach the egg. Tired, they fall down and out. Women often complain of pain and odor, and sometimes of bleeding or hemorrhage. Some "run yellow water," as if "rotten" inside, they say. Clinicians report seeing many infections and many unexpected pregnancies, too. Usually, abortions are offered to women who conceive when supposedly "tied off" or when fitted with an IUD. Women using other methods, even those on the roster of a family planning program, cannot be sure of being offered a safe and free abortion when their method fails. Because abortion is illegal (in part due to restrictions imposed by the United States in exchange for family planning aid), appeals are taken on a case-by-case basis.

CONDOMS

Condoms are abundant. But only 8 percent of those who visited family planning clinics in my parish elected to use them (STATIN 1988a, 151). Condoms have a reputation as being unreliable and dangerous. They burst or slip off, often lodging inside women, resulting in conception and illness. This happens, people say, because they come in one size only (too tight for some and too big for others), are poor in quality, and also because many men enjoy "cruelty." Sometimes men "force" them off during "discharge." Men also may "pinch" holes in them.

Supposedly, only doctors can remove condoms once they get stuck inside women. Everyone knows someone to whom this has happened. One woman I was told about did not know that the condom had burst, leaving the tiniest bit of latex behind. The rubber stopped her urinating and also caught up waste that began to rot. The infection, coupled with her inability to pass urine, caused a painful, swelling "bad belly," which eventually killed her.

Clinicians told me that many of the condoms dispensed in clinics are sent from the United States. I saw condoms with past expiration dates, and one clinician confided that a fellow worker, using condoms from the clinic, experienced so much bursting that he and she decided to check the boxes in storage. They found them all defective. Hot weather, stifling storerooms (heat damages latex), and shipping delays probably account for the defects.

Condom packets have no instructions, and none of the clinics I attended had explanatory pamphlets, although clinicians said that printed information for all methods was sometimes available. In 1989, the senior public health nurse at parish headquarters could find only a few outdated brochures (from Planned Parenthood of America) to show me: a one-page spreadsheet of options and U.S. reliability figures from 1973 and a small pamphlet from 1977 on vasectomies (which are hardly ever considered by Jamaicans). The head of an urban clinic did better; in addition to a pamphlet on "injection," she rustled up a thin comic book written in patois called "Put Off Joe." This told of the physical hardships child-bearing causes women and the money troubles babies cause men; both are prominent cultural themes. Although it urged men to use condoms, the comic book did not explain how to use them.

Instructions for condom use are verbally given and, in the demonstrations I witnessed, very vague. For example, proper removal, cleanup, and disposal techniques—important for this method's success—were not addressed. Nor was the fact that condoms stored in back pockets or other hot areas lose strength. People receive no warning against lubricating the dry rubber with petroleum jelly, which is found in almost every household because of its indispensable value as a hair and scalp moisturizer. Petroleum jelly ruins latex. It also lodges in the vagina, harboring germs and causing infection.

Those who use condoms usually learn how, whether properly or not, through trial and error or from experienced others. Individuals do not usually get condoms from clinics by themselves but rely instead on one cohort member to procure a supply. Alternately, and for the sake of privacy, people can buy them at most any general shop. Like all forms of birth control available in Jamaica, they are relatively inexpensive, costing about seventy-five cents (fifteen U.S. cents) apiece, but often even this is hard for a poor Jamaican to find.

Condoms are now receiving more attention with AIDS education. In the spring of 1989, eye-catching white stickers printed in black and red with "Only you can stop AIDS; use a condom" were distributed throughout the island. The *A, D,* and *S* of "AIDS" are red while the *I* is black and penis-shaped.

BIRTH CONTROL PILLS

Despite clinicians' claims about the popularity of "injection"—perhaps reflecting their own preference—women say pills are more popular. So do national statistics. Of all "new acceptors" in 1988, 44 percent chose pills, and only 23 percent

asked for "injection" (STATIN 1988, 154). In my parish, 53 percent preferred pills (151). Birth control pills, like condoms, can
be bought over-the-counter (but a month's supply costs $10–16
Jamaican or $2–3 U.S.). Pharmacists often claim that they can
ascertain proper dosage by talking with clients, but most do
not actually take the time to do so because of their many customers. They rarely take blood pressure and other readings
that might contraindicate particular selections. A woman or
"young miss" would shy away from such special treatment
anyhow. Most decide themselves which pill to take and learn
how to use them, rightly or wrongly, by watching others.

Poor self-administration of birth control pills and faulty
understandings about how to use them frequently lead to
health problems. Many women are hospitalized for hemor-
rhaging induced by improper dosages. Many experience
untimely breakthrough bleeding; some experience amenorrhea. Emotional side effects and headaches, weight gain, skin
eruptions, bad odors, and changes in blood pressure and
libido can occur with great strength when dosages are not
professionally prescribed. Often, through misunderstandings
or a lack of instruction, women get pregnant. Sometimes,
they take pills only after having sex because they imagine
the pills work by effecting uterine "washouts." This assumption makes cultural sense, considering the way in which
many Jamaicans understand their bodies to work.

DEPO PROVERA SHOTS

Clinicians favor "injection" as it demands nothing more of
a woman than four clinic visits each year. It also brings menstruation to a halt, and women who rely on their menstrual
flows to "washout" their reproductive organs find this quite
disturbing. Many worry that others, particularly partners
who oppose "the planning," will know by the amenorrhea that
they are taking birth control. "Injection" also causes changes
in bodily odors, making women feel fetid and causing "jumpy"
behavior. One woman explained "what really happen": chemi-

cally induced body odors cause small "Gingy" flies to swarm around injected women as they do around rotting fruit. The flies bite at their ankles, making them "dance."

Many women say that it takes too much time to get injected. Clinic attendance may require a whole day of waiting. Sometimes the clinics run out of drugs. Moreover, while a woman sits waiting, people who know her come and go. They see her as she makes her way to and from the "planning" clinic. Like potential health problems, public exposure deters many from taking "injection."

WHAT BIRTH CONTROL CONNOTES

Birth control compromises the cultural ideal of social reproduction. It blocks the establishment of enduring social ties by blocking the procreative mingling of sexual substances. It blocks the flow of resources and aid that a procreative flow between partners would have involved, so blocking the sustaining growth of reciprocity systems. In a homologous fashion, birth control blocks the flow of substances within women and leads to physical debilitation.

Birth control carries suggestions about sexual behavior that women who value their social standings would rather avoid. People assume that women using "planning" sell sexual favors indiscriminately, are adulterers, and "too love sex." Many men do not like to see their lovers use contraception because, in addition to concern over health dangers, they believe that "planning" leads to "outside sex." Male control over female sexuality is limited by "the planning," and men are its most vocal opponents.

Abortions are frequent because people are reluctant to use contraception (and because they misuse it). Pregnancy termination is seen as murder, much in the way that women using "the planning" are seen by some as "walking cemeteries," and so abortions (illegal anyhow) are kept secret. Because most would never admit to having aborted, abortion statistics other than those culled from hospital records are not found.

The taking of life is an antisocial act. The wasting of blood, which should be recycled back into society in the form of human beings who will reproduce the social system, is a sinful, instrumental, and "selfish" assertion of egoistic power, especially as it denies men control over their route to reproduction and pollutes and wastes their blood and essence. In its way abortion, like "planning," renders men as "useless" as "mules."

Controlling one's reproductivity implies a hatred of children as well as "selfishness" and a lack of social commitment. Disliking children in a society where they are so highly valued is aberrant and even subversive. Yet, as the next chapter shows, childrearing techniques and the traditions surrounding birth reflect much more than the professed unconditional love of children, which encourages bountiful procreation.

Chapter 8

To "Grow" and "Care" Children

Childrearing practices affect character development and perpetuate certain patterns of interpersonal relations and certain kinds of concerns.[1] The ideas rural Jamaicans hold about kinship, human nature, status, initiative, aggression, food, cleanliness, gender, and sexuality are learned during childhood. These ideas, along with traditional health notions and the cultural emphasis on sociable, procreative relations involving shared blood and mutual aid, inform the culturally constructed syndromes explored later.

Because of the understandings rural Jamaicans hold about human nature and the inborn tendency people have to act badly, raising children demands a stern eye and hand. Physical punishment and strong admonitions are far more often dealt out than praise for deeds well done. Caretakers often use aggressive measures to help children "come up proper"; nonetheless, love and affection do gain expression.

BIRTH PAIN

When a woman takes "nine long months" and suffers with pain which "hot, it hot, it hot," she does not take lightly to

145

expectations dashed by "out of order" or otherwise "ungrate-ful" children. Mothers emphasize how the "burn" of child-birth hurts, not the trouble children cause, when explaining why they want no more. They never mention childbirth costs as a deterrent (hospital fees are $50 Jamaican, or about $9 U.S.). Physical pain is highlighted. Children are admonished to appreciate the burning pain their parturition caused their mothers. Physical pain is understood and experienced as more important than emotional pain, which is not a highly developed part of childbirth culture. Talk of birth pain is used to express the emotional pain experienced by mothers when offspring fail them, and to engender guilt in children.

Villagers "chat" young girls for becoming pregnant, claim-ing that once they feel the "hot" pain of labor "cut," they will regret it: "Let that baby tear out her what's-it-not [vagina]; then she will see." One sixteen-year-old, just after giving birth, was told by her grandaunt that the "hard part" was over; raising children is easier than giving birth. Although mothers must "take an interest" in their children lest the pain they endured go to waste, childrearing is thought of as needing no special techniques. Caretakers say that their charges learn to do things like walk, control their bowels, and eat real food "when they ready."

FAMILIAL IDENTITY

Pregnancies bring no congratulations. This is because people avoid appearing as if they "fasten into any and any-body's business" and because "birth is a thing that happen every day." When babies come, they stay with their mothers. This may be impossible when the mother is without "suppor-tance" from a man, jobless, working in "town," irresponsible, or unwilling. Babies then get sent to live elsewhere, after weaning. Usually, maternal grandmothers but sometimes aunts, older siblings with the same mother, or other matrilin-eal relations take them in (and use their labor). Sometimes, paternal grandmothers provide homes. Children rarely live with their fathers alone.

Usually, many people live together: children "grow" with constant company, and even though they may not always interact directly, they feel lonely, "boring," and often "frighten" when no one else "da about." In the yard next to mine lived a grandmother, one daughter not currently involved with a man and her child, another daughter and her common-law husband, and four grandchildren (belonging to a daughter now working in a distant town). Another daughter and her infant lived there for a time while her common-law boyfriend was off working in another parish because, although her rent was paid and she had near neighbors, she felt "boring" and lonely living by herself in the room that her man had set her up in. "The need to be with people" (Phillips 1973, 95) instilled through living conditions, childrearing techniques, and traditions about loners continues in adulthood.

Children are named after their fathers. A woman's children's last names provide an oral history of her procreative sexual exploits. Names also bind fathers to children, publicly announcing that relationships exist and reminding men of their obligations. When a man accepts responsibility for a child, he "owns" it. The answers to the questions "Who fe punkin'?" and "Who own the baby?"—meaning "Who fathered it?" and "Who will pay for its upkeep?"—are suggested by the baby's surname.

Not all fathers fulfill the expectations for child support that naming exposes, but social pressure to do so is there. It is there unless public knowledge has it that the name given is a "suit jacket cut to fit." To "cut" a "jacket" means to tailor things so that someone other than the true "babyfather" is named and so indebted to mother and child.

Many men support their children if they can. They do not want to waste the "nine months of hard labor" which they put in, sexually and otherwise, to help their "babymothers" "grow" their offspring; if supported and raised well, even a "jacket" child can enrich a man. But not all responsible men have access to resources, and many cannot contribute. Some leave to avoid the shame.

Many men exhibit hypermasculine behavior instead. Cultural beliefs that men's sexual instincts are overpowering provide justifications for their exploitative promiscuity. These behaviors, in turn, attest to manhood when earning power is low (see R. T. Smith 1988, 147).[2] If she does not have access to resources herself or through family, a lone "baby-mother" must "look a next man" for help.

One little boy, whose father did not "own" him and who slept with his aunts in his mother's natal yard but spent his days with her in the yard of her new common-law husband, was teased by a woman who asked him repeatedly who he was. She questioned his identity by offering three different last names: his father's, his common-law stepfather's, and his maternal grandfather's name.

The teaser "grudged" the boy's mother's good fortune at finding a mate whose pockets lay "heavy" with money. She felt that the man, her uncle, should have given her and her family the money which went to support the boy. By teasing the child she slandered his mother who, besides having lost her argument with his real father (the boy had been given his surname but to no avail), shuffled the boy from home to home. This is something a "respectable" mother who does not "make her own bad luck" by "taking up with a man who breed and leave her" does not do. There are, of course, contradictions between the expectations invoked here and the cultural belief that men are irresponsible and "leave" children more often than not.

Whatever their last names, most children—"cared" by their birth mothers, usually "grown" by them as infants—feel strong ties to their birth mothers. Owing to household instabilities, says Clarke, a child learns early that "it is to his mother he must look for any security or permanence in human relationships" (1957, 107). The mother-child tie is reinforced by the belief that children want to be with their mothers and vice versa. A baby, sleeping on a bed with many people, will crawl over them all when seeking Mother, one woman said. Baby knows Mother, just as his or her body knows (and so does not react negatively to) his or her father's "white" blood, contained in the mother's milk.

The boy who was teased loved his aunts but knew full well who his true mother was, and he loved her more, as Jamaican ethnophysiology would dictate. Also he had been "shown" and had heard that this is proper. His mother, he was told, and not his aunts had "hot" and bled so he might be born. She, not they, had fed him in her "baby bag" and "belly" and at her breast with food she ate for him and with her blood (his father, like many fathers, contributed only the starter "germ"). His identity and his strongest bonds of inter-dependent obligation were tied up with her and he, like most "boy pickney," relied not on his biological father for a role model but on men related matrilineally.

GENDER IDENTITY

Most women "father" in addition to mothering their children because economic and traditional constraints keep "babyfathers" from fulfilling the provider role and from participating greatly in the upbringing of their offspring. As mentioned earlier, men remain "marginal to the solidary relationships of the household" when partners' distinct and sex-linked attributes are highlighted instead of their relational complementarity (R. T. Smith 1988, 138). Even when unity is stressed, men and women maintain segregated role responsibilities. Bott found a positive correlation between this pattern and extensive extra-familial networks (1971); R. T. Smith (1988, 138) confirms this pattern for Jamaica.

Chodorow (1978) shows that when women are children's primary caretakers and have appreciably fuller relationships with them than do men, boys must work harder than girls to secure sex-appropriate gender identities. To this end, they try to become all that they figure women are not, casting the feminine as negative and undesirable. Girls, for their part, have a harder time individuating and establishing themselves as beings separate from their female caretakers because they spend so much time with them, but because they can imitate these women, their gender identities are less problematic.

Jamaican girls have immediate role models to teach them cooking and washing skills. But boys, more often than not, have no easily accessible male models to follow within their yards. Caretakers' male relatives and lovers are often unapproachable when home. Because of this, boy children must actively seek maleness. They venture out to locate and learn about men (traditionally found on farm "ground," fishing, or engaging in recreational activities such as rum-drinking and dominoes). Boys must disassociate themselves from their caretakers. This is hard: boys identify with their female caretakers just as girls do, not only because of proximity and the circumstances of infancy but also because acting mothers assume principle parts in their children's lives.

The culturally encouraged ties between children and nurturers are bound by everyday interactions, such as sleeping together. Men have a hard time breaking free from childhood. Boys know that men—even schooled ones—can rarely fulfill the very impractical standards set for them and worry about meeting expectations. They are ambivalent about prolonged dependencies (both emotional and economic) and fear and resent the strong ties to and reliance on women that socioeconomic constraints (such as high unemployment rates) and traditional behavior patterns perpetuate. (Women's reliance on men is viewed differently because of the economic and ideological underpinnings of gender interdependence).

Male sexuality is not confined to the yard. Men usually seek lovers "outside," as they did when boys. Food, clothing, and shelter needs are met within home yards by mothers and later by girlfriends or wives; recreational needs are not. Permanent girlfriends, supported by the men who keep them, must cook, wash, and keep house as if they were their men's mothers. After seeing her housekeeping spoiled one harassed woman expressed a common sentiment, complaining that with both her son and lover in her house, she "must care two pickney."

Women in relationships, like mothers, expect their men to bring dirty wash only to them and to take food only from their pots. In this way, women guard against food-related sorcery, aiming to keep control of the men. No one can have two mothers (or masters) and, although he may have many lovers, no man can have two wives (whether common-law or legal).

The difficulties of growing up and taking on the male role are a great concern to men. Men fear the feminine aspects of themselves much more than women fear the masculine sides of themselves. Men's gender identities are so much more conditional and tenuous. Their genitals—so different in both form and function from the female's—take on great symbolic potency for expressions of manliness.

KEEPING CHILDREN UNDER PRESSURE

Children of either sex are supposedly born wicked, and caretakers must "bind" themselves to the task of "breaking" their charges well. As children "come up" and while still "tender," caretakers must get "firm." They must "bend" children young by exerting pressure for, if left to age without training, children will be bad. Cohen reports that the object of Jamaican socialization is to eliminate the aggressive tendencies children are born with (1953, 40). Ideologically, this is true. But in reality, only aggression toward caretakers and elders gets eliminated. Aggressive activity forms an important part of childhood play and adults and older siblings often instigate it for fun. This teaches children not only to contain aggression when inappropriate but also to stand up for themselves. They also learn the right targets for aggression. Aggression is socialized, not eliminated, and often this is done by aggressive means.

"Never let the pickney rule," advised Aunty Etell, a housekeeper paid by a well-off man to live with and "care" his three young girls while he stayed in a distant village with his new "babymother." Never let a child in on a secret because then s/he has the upper hand. When sending them to carry messages to "big" people, be vague: tell them to ask for "the something," which the person sent to should know about. Caretakers do not explain their "business," and children do not ask "What for?" Like wild horses to be trained, children should be "penned in" and (except for errand-running, which they should do with haste) not shown "the world." Once over the fence, caretakers are hard put to re-pen and close the gate on them again, Etell says. A good caretaker "structures" her charges' lives and sees to it that they follow orders instead of initiating plans of action.

By calling her "Aunty," the children she "cares" fictitiously draw Etell into their circle of kin. Although they should treat her with respect, they "love cause problem." These children, shown "the street" early on, are "too lie," "too rude," and "love romp too much." Their father tried to "manage" but had it hard because, in addition to his reluctance to use "pressure," they have sucked "the pilted milk"; that is, their mother was evil so they are especially evil, "grown" as they were with her blood. The fact that they hate sharing their food attests to their "craven" tendency.

Greed ultimately brings pregnancy, Aunty claims, and she "shows" me that children who "can't content" with what their parents can give them "look boys" for money. A greedy or "craven" girl's "salt thing [vagina] can't never dry," so she "love boys too much, and get problem." Boys (like male dogs) do "give trouble" but do not bring it home (like female dogs or "sluts," which people are reluctant to keep). Girls, liable for pregnancy while boys are not, carry "problem" back to their yards in publicly visible "bellies."

What all this says about procreation and gender relations is discussed in Parts Four and Five, but the messages of Aunty's teachings on childrearing procedures are clear. Human nature is inherently evil. Children must be raised with stringency if they are to bring home pride instead of shame, the bad feeling caused by public scrutiny. Caretakers constantly remind their charges in acid tones that they are still "pickney." Children who act "rude," who initiate action themselves, and who "go on like they big" are bound for beatings.

CHILDREN WHO ACT "BIG"

Mummy's two girls love to talk back to her, probably because she has a sense of fun and does not "go on" too strictly, but also perhaps because they are, as she claims, extra bad. One day, these active four-year-old "gal-pickney" decided that they would bathe or "hold a fresh," put on "good frock," and go "walk street" or venture up to the crossroads where the pub and shop are situated. When Mummy, rather irritated that day, told them they would take a nap instead, the smaller one, "arms akimbo like she big," announced she had no need to sleep in the day, for "me a big man." Her uppity claim brought hidden laughter, but her "rude" assertions got her and her sister spanked.

Another instance of "rude" and "out of order" action left one little girl fearing for her female anatomy. While her mother was away this "young miss," "romping" on the road in front of her yard, stole a boy's hat. Grandmother heard the commotion, came to the roadside, and ordered the girl to give it back. The girl got sassy and "wouldn't hear." Mother came home later and, learning of her daughter's misbehavior, was irate. When her boyfriend, the girl's acting father, came back to the yard, he was informed of the day's event by the mother and grandmother both. Poppa (the boyfriend), already upset because his dinner was not ready, swore to the girl that if he could he would pry, or "get off," her "titties." This brought laughter to the mother and to her sister, who had been waiting to see the "young miss" get "flogged" or beaten. They offered a screwdriver, but Poppa angrily declared that he needed a sledgehammer, to hammer the "titties" back down. I have also heard adults threaten to chop budding breasts off with a machete as punishment when girls "go on" like women.

When girls begin to grow breasts, Poppa later explained to me, they get "too big"; they think themselves women and get out of hand. Sometimes, they "break down Mumma's door" in their rush to be "big" and "in the world." When children "forget they's pickney," "rudeness," or self-initiated and disrespectful behavior, results. Caretakers resort to aggressive physical punishment in an effort to make children "hear."

Children, like clients or indebted followers, are obligated to "mind." They should do what caretakers make them do, not what they want to. Ideally, they do so in a "willing" fashion. Sometimes, caretakers lie to their charges to get them to act. One mother consistently told her young son she would "soon come" when she sent him along with her sister to her sister's yard, where he slept. She had no intention to go, but the two-year-old boy would not leave without this promise.

As children grow, they learn that they must obey. Though children are expected to see to chores and can play quietly among themselves, other kinds of action must wait for instruction. This is especially true for actions involving the world outside the yard. While children are curious and some of their actions are let to pass unnoticed, the rules of blind obedience and noninitiative always get invoked when their decisions peeve their caretakers: when they get underfoot, decide to bathe before doing chores, try to rush the caretaker to some action, or most importantly, question his or her decisions in any way.

The ban on taking the initiative can be evaded by asking to be made to do a thing. For example, to look at a photo one's mother holds, one begs her rhetorically: "Make me see." When ready to leave on a planned outing and tired of waiting for others, one suggests "Come, make we go." Expressions like these effectively hand power to or "make it stay" in the hands of those who have a right to it, leaving their decision-making power figuratively intact. Commands phrased this way also metaphorically relieve would-be commanders from responsibility for their own dictates.

Children should do the bidding of anyone older than them with good will and should act toward them with respect. "Rudeness" or too much independence invites physical violence. Although frequently only threatened, beatings do occur—often with no explanation. Villagers say children "know full well" the reasons for which they get hit. Yet many adults recall getting beaten indiscriminately every day, "for anything." When she was a girl, one woman's grandaunt beat her for making "handicap dumplings" as well as for making them correctly. No matter what, "she just beat me," the woman lamented, even as she agreed that elders and other superiors have the right to act aggressively. Adults, recounting their beatings, claim themselves better for having been raised strictly. The woman, for example, points to her perfect dumplings with pride. She and others like her feel that not enough caretakers "go on strict" today. Kerr found the same nostalgia voiced by parents two generations back (1963, 42).

Children misbehave in private and in public. Bad behavior in the yard, especially if raucous or dealt with noisily, can bring neighbors to "wash mouth 'pon" a family, caretaker, or child. Bad behavior in public surely will. People explaining why they behave in socially acceptable ways often say that they do not wish to "bring disgrace" to those in their yards. A policeman, explaining why he could never involve himself in corruption, cited the disgrace getting caught would bring to his people as an even greater deterrent than the shame it would bring to him. A woman waiting for the bus regretted that today's youth "forget they have a mother or any relation in fe them yard" whose reputations their bad behavior will affect.

In the yard or out, children know how their caretakers "stay" and can usually sense when word will turn to deed; they try to run away when beatings are too near, giving caretakers time to "cool down." Otherwise, and before things reach a peak, children heed caretakers' advice and do their biddings. A skilled caretaker, Jamaicans know, turns an inherently "wicked" child into a docile being whose aggressive instincts are acceptably contained.

CHILDHOOD ACTIVITIES

Children are kept in their yards as much as possible, but school (if caretakers can afford to send them) and errands sometimes draw them out. Children welcome errands. They can "romp" a bit with little companions down the road, visit with friendly relatives and neighbors, beg hard candy "sweeties" from a congenial shopkeeper, and look for fruit or other edibles in the bush. They must take care, however, not to stay away too long or get caught doing mischief.

Time in the yard is spent doing homework, chores, and playing. When caretakers can take an interest in homework, they see to its neatness, not its content. Children are also occupied with chores. Water must always be fetched, firewood gathered, and dishes washed. Playtime comes only when caretakers backs are turned or all possible chores have been dealt with. Children are very resourceful and make toys of cast-off junk. Sometimes, if a small ball is available, children gather stones and play "jacks."

Most young boys collect old wood, old tire rubber, old rope, and other odds and ends to create toys like slingshots and "bikes" (scooters) with elaborate pulley-operated steering systems, brakes, tires, and tin-can headlamps. One group of boys pooled resources to build a car. They crashed it often and so always arrived "up street" in a late (re)model. Eventually, the oldest boy in the group took the boards to build a "divan" bed, reducing the car to scrap rope and rubber, and asserting his independence, through the symbol of having his own bed.

Girls, more confined and more put upon to help about the yard and "care" the younger ones, cannot play in the same fashion as boys. They do create toys but spend less time building and fixing things. By twelve or so, girls are too busy doing wash and other chores to "romp" often. Interests run toward men and free time is spent combing and plaiting each other's hair. As young girls, they learn to sit still while others groom them and decide how they might look; by their teens they have grown used to fashion mandates. As they "come up," girls grow increasingly reluctant to leave their yards in dirty clothing or without having bathed.

KEEPING "FRESH" AND CLEAN

Keeping the body from getting "nasty" can be a challenge. Jamaica is hot and everybody sweats. Toilet tissue, for the sake of economy, is not used after urination. Women and girls must find out-of-sight spots in which to "heist they frock" and squat, taking care not to wet themselves. They can feel and smell quite "renk" by day's end. This is especially true when women have moist or runny vaginas. Those nursing or "caring" infants have more than their own salty fluids to contend with: babies, with only cloth "nappies," constantly "pee-pee up" caretakers. In this environment, the frequent need to "hold a fresh," or bathe, makes sense.

Unclean bodies carry their own sweat and sometimes also the urine and spittle of infants or others' sexual fluids. This is very unhealthy. Bathing removes the effluvia of others as it removes one's own substances, rendering a bather salt-free and "fresh" (unsalted food is also called "fresh").

Often, the insult, "You stink like!" means that the scent and so the fluids and sweat of sex have lingered on one's body. So when others insult them for stinking, people may claim "Is only me alone sleep." This can imply chastity and good standing in the church. More often, it simply implies that a person cannot stink, not having had sex recently (ruder individuals say this explicitly). Not having engaged in intercourse, a person cannot be "nasty" (like semen-laced animal flesh, also called "nasty") for no one has "nastied" them up.

Although not sexually active, children "nasty" themselves with their own bodily substances (as well as with other forms of dirt) and so bathe or are bathed at least once daily. Plenty of vigor and soap suds are used. If money allows, skin is oiled for smoothness and to make it shine (and as a protective layer) after a thorough cleansing.

Hair is washed two or three times a month, as needed, but is combed at least once a day. Tomboyish girls who keep short hair and those whose hair stays short because it is dry and brittle and breaks off are insultingly called "dry-head pickney"; they lack vital and feminine moistness and may turn out infertile. If available, hair oil or petroleum jelly is applied. Little "dreadlocks" or "nats" (knots), which make hair look bumpy or "nappy," are given no time to form, for children cannot look "uncared." They cry if teased that they are "nasty," "stink like," or look like little "dreadlock Rastas," Rastafarians being considered unwashed and abnormal.

Even at a "tender" age, children know the social stigma attached to foulness and to marginality.

ANIMAL TORTURE

Children continually poke about in their yards, looking for interesting insects and things to play with. Like their parents, they fear lizards and frogs, but most love to torture other small creatures. A few girls found a rat drowning in their water drum. They removed it to a small basin with tall sides and added about two inches of water. Every now and then, when otherwise bored, they would check it, poking it to see if it had died yet and teasing it when they saw it had not. They planned to play this way "til it dead," then give it to the dogs.

A rat is a pest and "it no nothing" to kill one. Likewise, bludgeoning a lizard to death, picking the wings off of a "night wasp," smashing a "forty legs" centipede, or pouring salt on a frog to make it dissolve are considered fun. When it comes to domestic animals like dogs and pigs, this does not hold. A woman of forty explained the difference between fun and "cruelty": "cruelty" to domestic animals kills them. Though this limits the things one might do, much fun can still be had. People laugh as they tell of such antics as tying newspaper bootees around cats' paws and watching them dance, and getting chickens to stick their heads in rigged coconut shells from which they cannot pull out.

Children's play time is often spent imaginatively imitating adult activities. Even torturing animals can be imitative: shortly after Peaches demanded I "make" her take my broom to kill a lizard that had scuttled onto the veranda, her mother took up a broom against her. Everyone later said she knew she had this coming. Her actions toward the lizard probably reflected her knowledge of the impending beating and demonstrated the tendency children have to imitate elders and to channel aggression toward acceptable targets.

LEARNING THROUGH IMITATION

Many imaginative games of mimicry are violent. In "house," the child who acts as caretaker punishes misbehaving "pickney." There is a special version of "school" called "Teacher, Teacher," in which one child (as "teacher") simply beats the rest (Wendoja, personal communication). Children imitate more than violence, of course, and learn more than how to bully one another. They learn farming, washing, cooking, and other chores by watching. One young boy, for example, took it upon himself to grow pumpkin in a vacant patch of the yard as he had seen his grandmother do. He donated most of those he harvested, known as "his own," to his sister, who cooked for him. Had there been a farmer in the family, this boy might have "studied" and learned how to plant and grow yams or potatoes.

One woman who takes in wash describes the children who mimic her actions down by the river, trying to wash the clothes they wore there. She laughs that they are annoyed when she notices a piece left dirty and takes it away to wash properly. This is typical: if one person cannot "manage," another takes over the task, often brusquely. Only rarely do people have the time and patience to sit and teach. Even then, direct lessons are hard to give—there is no model for this except the rote learning system of the schools.

One "young miss" named Tracy explains that she learned to cook simply by "studying" her older sister and sometimes doing small tasks for her. One day, "when me feel say me ready" at the age of eleven, she decided that she would cook for the group. That suited her sister and, since the meal came out to everyone's satisfaction (and the sister has other things to tend to), Tracy now cooks every evening.

When adults are out of earshot, children step to another level of mimicry. They may attempt to "dance punani" (very sexually suggestive winding) or "lick domino" (clap them down violently in playing them) as they have seen grown-ups do at pubs and dance halls. They "cuss bad word" and tease each other with sexual innuendoes. They also "romp" much harder than they do when adults are watching, although even then things can get quite lively.

THE AGGRESSION OF PLAY

A young girl of twelve was charged with caring for her aunt's one-year-old son. Other adults were in the yard. The girl handled the baby very roughly, swinging him from side to side, slapping him in the face, bouncing him like he truly was a sack of potatoes, and yelling "whoop, whoop" in his ears. She ran back and forth on the cement-covered part of the yard, holding the screaming baby on her head. She was having fun, and no one tried to stop her; in fact, a related aunt came over to the child and put a chick down his shirt, just to see him squirm. Although extreme, this scene was not atypical.

Children often run after one another with knives or fire from the kitchen and are even urged by adults to throw stones at an aggressor and "lick him down." Caretakers teach children to protect themselves from others and sometimes throw stones at the children themselves to get them to retaliate (caretakers stone children out of anger too). This type of teasing use of threats is common. A group of girls, frying up some bananas, threatened each other with hot oil. They burnt each other (until tears came) with newly fried banana: one girl offered another a tasty-looking morsel before it had cooled and then, pressing firmly, seared this hot gift into the recipient's upturned hand. All was in fun at first but things soon got out of hand. One of the girls, growing "vex," threatened to "jam" another's "ting," or vagina, with the broom handle. The "game" soon ended.

Unless an adult is in a bad mood, rough romping is fine until tears or arguments take over. All children might get punished for an incident but at other times only some are scolded or beaten while others get soothed. Children being beaten by caretakers can sometimes squirm free but may never hit back. Once "flogged," children are usually banished from sight and return silently only after the aggressor has had time to "cool out."

FOOD AND PLAY

Violence and aggression commonly figure in Jamaican life, and although they hate beatings and the shame they bring, children can grow inured and can be heard to say "hot will cool," "cut must well," and "swell will draw down." One form of punishment that always impresses is the denial of food. As a Jamaican schoolyard mnemonic for the notes of the treble scale goes, "Every good boy deserves food." In contrast, in the United States it is "Every good boy does fine."

Cohen links early childhood food deprivation with hoarding resources later. In adulthood, many a Jamaican has a "belief that he never has enough money, that he is poor, and that everyone else is undermining his opportunity for earning a satisfactory livelihood" (1955, 389). Ideas about food are directly related to the resentment of others' demands on one's resources, a desire to amass, and a concomitant feeling of guilt over one's own "meanness."

Because gathering and preparing food takes a lot of effort (which bolsters its cultural salience), because solidarity is signaled by eating from the same pot, because sharing food symbolizes relatedness, and because of the rareness of and bad feelings associated with being alone, a child's exclusion from meals is harsh indeed and second only to total exile from the yard. Sometimes, children simply disappear upon seeing their plates empty. They return quietly a week or so later, when tempers have "cooled." Children usually run to grandparents, aunts, uncles, and the like. Often, they simply announce their intent to stay at their chosen sanctuaries when night comes down. Relatives usually oblige, asking few or no questions and sending no word to a child's primary caretaker.

Meals are not often actually withheld, but the threat of losing one's food share is impressed on a growing child. S/he comes to fear not only punishment through real denial but also that "Tingo Lingo," a folktale ghoul, will steal his or her food. Versions of this tale differ, but in extreme cases, Tingo Lingo eats the children too (or carries them off). Caretakers tease their charges with this and other fantastic warnings concerning appetite. In play, caretakers may threaten or pretend to have poisoned the drinks or the pot of seasoned rice. They may also do this in anger. Youngsters learn that food can bring harm. They also learn to use this belief on others. After trying to keep her brother in order, one girl of eleven loudly told him she would poison his lunch; she won her way (if at least momentarily). Children learn early that while food can "build" it can also endanger life: "What don't kill [makes you] fat; what don't fat, kill."

Caretakers tease children by offering and rescinding edibles until the children start to cry. Then they are given the promised morsel. The girls "romping" with fried bananas imitated this type of baiting. Sometimes, caretakers demand food from children: "Beg you a dumpling now." Children sadly acquiesce, not daring to refuse and risk punishment.

Caretakers push children hard to strengthen their resolve to hold back tears, to teach sharing, and to discourage "meanness." After a time, children become distraught; food is returned just before they cry. The association between food and comfort made during nursing is thus extended. A sense of proprietorship over food is instilled, too, as is the feeling of violation that food stealing provokes when, unpredictably, a borrowed morsel goes down a caretaker's gullet.

Weaned early, often by having the breast withheld at six months or less, infants eat cornmeal or other porridges made with sweetened condensed milk. They drink water mixed with sugar or a little powdered milk. Those who can afford it feed their children processed baby food and tinned preparations. They do this partly to show that they have money and thus the backing of a man. They also do it because the media and milk companies bombard them with images of babies in affluent countries being fed processed baby food and because the clinics sometimes give them samples strategically donated by milk companies such as Nestlé. Thus they come to believe that such food is beneficial and worth buying.

Fat babies are considered healthy, and every effort is made to plump babies up. But food is not always readily available. Even when "plenty" or "nuff," a diet of porridge and sugared water cannot provide the nutrients of breast milk. Sanitation is often poor and babies "draw down" from diarrhea.

Some mothers, especially young ones whose motherhood provides the sole source for their self-esteem, make a production out of preparing food for and feeding their infants and seem to be feeding them all day long. Others try to adhere to a schedule so as to "break" their babies well. Some say that infants crying off schedule are not really hungry but just "craven." Everyone knows that "Jamaica pickney too lie" about hunger and "eat too soon" (too often). Hungry children learn that "begging" food from their caretakers brings reprimands, not relief. One man prefers, however, that his children do ask for what they want. Even if he says no, he believes that if they do not learn to ask they will simply steal what they want.

Adults usually eat only breakfast and dinner (sometimes saving a bit of dinner for a supper). Adults teach themselves to tolerate hunger and consider eating "soon" a problem much graver than eating "plenty," which many do (and with much gusto). Snacking promotes laxness in meal timing, and when a person does not eat "on time," s/he risks a belly full of gas. Inconsistency and nibbling also promotes general discomfort, as the types of things that can get eaten on demand are not proper, cooked victuals. And the more often one eats the more chances others have to administer poison.

Eating often is impractical as well as dangerous: many people have no easy or pest-tight way to store food or enough fuel for extra cooking fires. Cooking is time-consuming (taking an average of two hours) and labor-intensive. One old knife, one mangled spoon, one big "dutch" (or round and lidded) "family pot" worn smooth from scouring, and one low coal-burning stove in an open-air shed form what many people call a "kitchen." The belief that, for reasons of health, people should eat only a few times each day provides women with a justification by which they excuse themselves from the chore cooking really is, maintain a type of dominance over others, and retain a degree of control over their own labor. Asking others to wait with a promise, "Soon come," then executing a chain of chores like sweeping, ironing, and bathing before calling "Come, make we go now man" is a similarly manipulative expression of dominance and control.

Grown men often announce, "me no business with pickney food" when offered a cut of cake or a handful of biscuits because dinner is not yet ready. These are considered poor substitutes for cooked food, but children are allowed to love these things and revel in the instant gratification they provide. One girl told of a school outing to Dunn's River Falls (a tourist sight). The van carrying her classmates stopped along the road (on request) many times. By the time they reached the falls most children had spent their entrance fees on roadside treats; many were sick. The trip was ruined.

Children like to gather berries and make expeditions to catch shrimp-like "tumpy" or hunt for land crabs. With their homemade slingshots they shoot more than each other—they down small birds and roast them in wood fires. As her son gets set to fry up some small fish he has just caught (he purchased the oil with returned soda bottle deposits), Adina declares that "all Jamaica pickney love fe cook they own pot." When others are present they will share but children also hoard, sneakily and guiltily, knowing that should an elder discern their "meanness" they will be beaten.

Children get little direct positive feedback. Now and again, caretakers treat their charges to a "cream cone" or a pack of "cheese chips," but usually this has nothing to do with achievement. Elders are more apt to find fault than acknowledge accomplishment. Demands for neater schoolwork, better pressed dresses, cleaner floors, and so forth seemingly never end. The only time a child receives praise is in tandem with another's scolding. A caretaker might tell a neighbor that s/he has "no complaint" with a given child, but the absence of unhappiness is not the same as being pleased.

SEX AND PLAY

Although often aggressive, offering little in the way of positive reinforcement or concrete rewards, and always nagging
their charges to reach for "higher heights," caretakers are
nonetheless affectionate. Hands are held, children hugged,
laps sat in, and bodies stroked. Children are frequently asked
for kisses and are kissed all over and on the lips. Close proximity, touching, and affection often borders on the sexual.

Female caretakers offer sexually styled affections to little
boys, especially their own. Although generally expected,
accepted, and not seen as a problem, limits do exist. One
mother who carried her two-year-old with her up to the pub
cuddled him in a fashion that provoked another to note that
because he was not her husband, she should not have kissed
and held him so. But the complainer "grudged" the mother,
who had recently acquired an employed boyfriend.

Similarly provocative demonstrations often took place at
the pub, but laughter rather than disdain was the normal
response. "Slack" caretakers commonly brought their charges
with them "up street" and encouraged them to mimic the sexually suggestive winding and "rub-a-dub" (partner-rubbing)
dance styles for everyone's entertainment. One mother took
her toddler over to another woman and pressed his crotch
against her hip, telling him to dance with the woman.

People frequently tease little boys about their genitals.
Caretakers ask what they are called and why they are there.
A girl of twelve told her littlest brother she would cut his
penis off if only he could show her where to do it. A mother
playing with her baby son repeatedly pretended to bite his
penis. Another teased a younger boy about having a "puppy
taily" (a term that might come from the nursery rhyme that
asks "what are little boys made of?"). The same boy's mother
teased him another day for hiding his penis after he noticed
it had slipped "out the door" of his briefs. Later in the month,
when they played "doctor" on her bed, she threatened to
inject his penis with a make-believe hypodermic needle. He

was visibly upset. Once, an insect bit one of his playmates on the penis, causing it to swell. He suffered merciless taunts about its size (large penises are undesired, for reasons discussed in Chapter 11).

Little boys are also teased if they want to nurse. "Big men don't suck titty," Samantha said to her boy when he cuddled against her bosom. She asked him to grow up, to act like a man. Then, as he silently resolved to give up "pickney" habits, a canny smile crossed her face, and she forced his head to her chest, demanding that he suck. He protested loudly and squirmed his way out of her grasp as she laughed. Later, as they lay together peacefully, she affectionately sang him love songs, tugged his penis, and sucked his fingers, which they both enjoyed.

"Gal-pickney" also receive lots of affection. They are cuddled and held and kissed like boys, but their genitals are generally ignored except for when "vulgar" caretakers threaten them with talk of punitive mop-handle ramming and the like. As girls grow, they become aware of the need for hiding their "privates," also called "pum-pum," after a type of yam which swells, or "cho-cho," after a rather wrinkly skinned, pear-shaped squash. Girls wear skirts or dresses and take pains to tuck these modestly between their legs in order not to expose themselves, which makes any type of "romping" quite a feat.

SEX TRAINING

Girls are warned from early on that men and boys must be avoided because they want nothing but sex. They learn that men seek young, tight "needle-eye pum-pum" and that rape is frequent. They know that men "give" women children. Four pre-teen girls kept by an older man for sexual favors were held in prison (as was he) for two weeks: villagers told me they "had no business with that man." Having been warned about men, they were expected to have had more "sense." "Wicked, they wicked," for they "wouldn't hear," and so they had to suffer.

Girls know that men like intercourse, will pressure girls for it, and that it can bring physical pain. Nothing is said about pleasure. Menstruation, too, is not discussed. When menarche occurs—the current average age for this in Jamaica is 13.1 years (Powell and Jackson 1988, xiv)—girls are merely told to "expect this thing" and that pregnancy is a near and present danger. How pregnancy happens and why menstruation exists is left unsaid. But boys are now completely off-limits. Caretakers get stricter and "gal-pickney" are kept in the yard more than before menarche.

Children do grow up in a sexual world despite caretakers' efforts to deny them entrance. They know genitals exist. Their own are often threatened or denigrated. Living without privacy, children see others' "privates," and they also observe animals. No drawing of a male animal is complete without genitalia, nor are female animals complete until rows of teats are added.

Children see cocks mount hens and know about human sexual intercourse. People commonly have intercourse near the beach or in the bush, where banana leaves are cut to make beds in "green grass motel." Often, they have sex less discreetly than they believe, sometimes even seeing to their "family life" in shared bedrooms if they think the others are asleep. People try to be quiet while having sex, but children hear and see things and often try having sex themselves. They play "dolly pot" (a bawdy version of "house"; the name reflects the cultural salience of couples and households sharing food from one pot), experimenting secretly until puberty catches up with them. Until then, caretakers turn a blind eye to childhood sexual play because it cannot lead to pregnancy.

R. T. Smith notes that a girl's first sexual experience is likely to be thought of as "traumatic" (1988, 138). My findings confirm this. One woman commented that "many young girls need stitches" afterward. People estimate that a large number of virgins are introduced to sexual intercourse through rape. One man set this at 20 percent; women (and fathers concerned for daughters) generally put the figure higher. Half of those interviewed at a local clinic mentioned force being used on them. One young man asserted that force "helps" girls who might otherwise never try intercourse: once they know sexual penetration, he said, they enjoy it.

Girls know rape may happen, and like those who care about them, fear encountering "man gangs" on the road. They wear clothing to bed partly so that night prowlers cannot "trouble" them and do not find them "easy fe rape." Some even wear shorts under the slips or nightdresses they sleep in. Two sisters, forced to seek refuge in a neighbor's house during the hurricane, feared that, even in a room with twenty-five others, the boys and men there might "fingle" or "interfere" with them if they tried to sleep. This did happen to a friend of theirs who also stayed in that room, although they do not know it because she did not tell them.

When physical force is not used, verbal coercion usually will be. Boys and men hassle girls and women who do not respond by accusing them of acting "heggs up" or too full of pride and by pretending to be insulted that they do not trust them. "Troubling" happens in the family, too: the people interviewed at the clinic mentioned that incest among stepfathers and stepdaughters is a common problem. During my stay in the village, at least one "young miss" was impregnated against her will by her mother's lover.

Negative aspects notwithstanding, some girls seek out intercourse. They are interested in this "thing," so commonly spoken of and so often seen in the media. Some girls are encouraged by their caretakers to "look men." Their caretakers cannot afford school fees and see "outside help" as a solution. Girls get lunch money, bus fare, tuition, and clothing in trade for sexual favors. Unfortunately, as one man pointed out, when girls become comfortably kept, they often forget their original goals and then drop out of school. But then they age and their "features" change; soon their supporters leave them for younger "beef" (a term related to the insult "back of cow").

Childhood learning about sexuality, gender, food, cleanliness, status, aggression, initiative, human nature, and kinship affect adult behavior and the perception of experiences.

Gender relations, adult sexuality, and the different types of precautions each gender must take in both intergender and intragender dealings are explored in Part Four.

Lovers in front of a snack cart

PART
FOUR

Gender Relations

Chapter 9

Finding "Work": Sexual Solicitation

Adult gender relations are affected by childrearing practices, traditions concerning the value of children, ideas about the reproduction of society, and beliefs about male and female "nature." Understandings about transactions involving gifts or money also come into play, as does the tension between moral and instrumental relations. Attitudes toward prostitution and other denigrated practices reveal beliefs about gender relations, just as ideas about infertility, bestiality, and family planning reveal the importance of reciprocity and sociable reproduction.

BODY TERMS AND SEXUAL ADVANCES

The vagina has many nicknames. These generally refer to edibles, as in "panty pudding," "fishy," "ranking meat," and the aforementioned vegetables, "pum-pum" and "cho-cho." People point out that the vagina is figuratively but not literally something men want to taste. Like pudding, it "sweets" them—it "make they feel nice." One type of pudding is, not coincidentally, called "blue drawers." The pudding mixture, secreted inside pieces of banana leaf as a vagina in panties or "drawers," takes on a blue-green tinge when boiled.

One older man explains that the vagina has many more "pet names" than the penis because it is much more "dangerous—that thing could stop a truck!" Another man tells me that the vagina warrants more nicknames because of its strength: "before it breaks, it stretch ten miles." Most simply say that nicknames for vaginas abound because unlearned people do not know or are ashamed of using the proper term. They also point out that men want sex and must ask for it— men approach women, not the other way around. Names for the penis are not needed because women do not directly "beg" access like men do.

Jamaicans rarely "talk it plain" and commonly ask for an item or favor as "the thing" or "the something." This helps one maintain privacy in a community where others are always "fast inna you business." It also helps keep children who act as go-betweens uninformed about adult matters. With ambiguity, people conceal intent, guard knowledge, and make tactical yet nonconfrontational maneuvers. Moreover, Jamaicans enjoy making listeners laugh and forcing them to puzzle out meanings.

Keeping others guessing places them in danger of making mistakes while removing speakers from such perils. While others make themselves vulnerable by overtly verbalizing or acting on suggested but not explicitly stated things, speakers retain control and power. A speaker can reject an interpretation, stating, "You don't get me," or "You nah see it, true?" Sometimes the speaker notes, "You nah catch my meaning," and surrenders: "Arrite. I go talk it straight."

Men do not always "talk straight" regarding sex "because shyness": women might reject them. Out of need, one man explained, men developed a rich vocabulary describing sex and the vagina—a vocabulary full of words and phrases with many meanings. Women accepting male offers acknowledge one meaning. Those who would not comply take another.

Since men always want sex, women need not fear misinterpretation. Yet, if a woman interprets a statement as a sexual overture and shows scorn or otherwise irritates her suitor/aggressor, he can "throw" immorality accusations back on her. He can tell her he meant no such thing—that her own "bad mind" and propensity for prostitution caused her to think in terms of sexual solicitation.

Sex is "out of order" for those related through others because it undermines preexisting ties and exchange arrangements. Incest is despised (it does happen, but efforts are made to hide it lest "scandal and contention," outwardly centered on economic rights and obligations, erupt). Ideally, a woman interacts on a purely social level with her sister's son or father to avoid rivalries over resources (and so affection). Similarly, a man and his wife's church sister are platonic, "social friends" and sexual intimacy is inappropriate. Nonetheless, as one woman remarked, "even your very husband you can't trust."

Men simply cannot help pursuing women when the opportunity arises, even when their chances are slim. Men advance on women in bars and dance halls and also in shops and on the street. They even joke about sex with women who are supposed to be exempt. They "trouble" women everywhere; "A so men stay. A so God made they."

A girl asking a policeman directions receives a polite solicitation. A shopkeeper taking money grasps a woman's palm and rubs his finger up and down its middle, smiling sweetly, asking if she has a husband. Bus riders are instructed to "move on up in the pussage," after which the conductor mockingly offers "I mean the passage" ("pussy" means vagina and so can "passage"). Bus conductors often take "liberty" with female passengers, slapping their bottoms and speaking of "rudeness" (sexual matters). Many male passengers rub up against women on tightly packed busses, using crowded conditions as an excuse for "fingling" female bodies. Women expect such abuse.

"REPUTATION" AND "RESPECT"

Older or married men keep their invitations inconspicuous, offering them quietly and to one woman at a time. Men with high social statuses have more to lose than to gain through overt flirtation because calling attention to receiving "outside" satisfaction is considered poor form for those in high "stations." The implied disregard for their wives and for their own "position" would detract from the "respect" these men have earned. Men of "low station" need not worry over retaining "respect" because they command little. They can, however, maintain manly "reputations" for numerous and productive sexual exploits and for having the money to "keep" many women.

Wilson (1973) differentiates between "respect" and "reputation," showing how West Indians act according to a dual, dialectical prestige system. "Respect" involves stratified relationships and draws on understandings about the different level of "respect due" to each social "station." "Reputations" are established in a context of equals. Establishing a "reputation" as a man or a woman involves living out gender ideals and demonstrating one's membership in a group of peers. The sense of solidarity that "reputation" mobilizes resembles the loyalty that appeals to kinship can provoke.

"Respect" depends on living out class-based expectations. If it is to be maintained, social difference rather than unity with others must be stressed. For example, smoking *ganja* with a group establishes one's "reputation" and demonstrates fraternity. But those who want "respect," such as bosses, must abstain as *ganja* smoking collapses status distinctions, limiting one's power over others (Dreher 1982).

THE VALUE OF INEQUALITY

Wilson (1973) gives each half of his dual system equal importance, but in Jamaica attaining and maintaining a high social status can bring a person more than a good "reputation" ever would. This explains why overt emphasis on "reputation" decreases as age, ambition, and class levels rise, but it complicates Wilson's distinction. For example, having the money to keep several women depends on one's class and thereby mobilizes ideas concerning "respect," even while funding the sexual exploits on which "reputation" relies.

"Respect" carries more social value than "reputation" not only in terms of the loyalties and obligations that it can be used to call in but also in terms of the resources those who can be called upon have to offer. Just one high-status ally can give more than several low-status allies can. And no matter how "respectably" they behave, low-status people can never command "respect" as members of the higher "stations" can. They lack the political, social, and economic "backative" necessary to sustain claims to it.

Bourdieu (1982) calls the social value of attributes such as "reputation" and "respect" "symbolic capital." People appeal to others by invoking the ideas about rights and obligations which "reputation" and "respect" connote. By using these concepts as "symbolic capital" to mobilize others, call in debts, push credit limits, and otherwise utilize loyalties, people can accomplish certain ambitions. For example, "symbolic capital" can be used to win a political office. The more "symbolic capital" one commands, the more debts one can call in, and the more votes one can control. "Respect" carries much more value than "reputation" because the inequality "respect" involves means that those with "respect due" have more owed to them than they owe others.

"Respect" is especially important for women. Womanhood brings less prestige than manhood. A reputable woman therefore has less "symbolic capital" than a reputable man. She would, however, command more if she had "respect."

EXCESS "REPUTATION" AND "RESPECT"

Different aspects of Wilson's "respect-reputation" dialectic gain prominence depending on a participant's intentions and his or her social position. One appeals to "reputation" or "respect" depending on whether one wishes to invoke ideas about equality or about stratification. The "respectable," high-status man need not prove his value through "reputation" because he has already established his unequivocal maleness by achieving social position. He could never have found "uplift" without the "symbolic capital" his "reputation" brought. He does need to maintain his "reputation" to some degree and can invoke it when he needs to demonstrate his solidarity with other villagers. Nonetheless, his position "on top" gets most emphasis because "respect" buys more than "reputation."

At the lowest social "station," getting "love" (sex) cheaply, to "breed and leave," or otherwise have a "joke" on women increases a man's "reputation" by demonstrating his virility. As mentioned, the exaggeration of "manly flaws" is necessary for self-esteem when economic power (and the "symbolic capital" that accompanies it) is out of reach. An "idler" may build a "reputation" within his peer group by sexually molesting a teenage girl, but a rich man never could. Similarly, a low-status woman can increase her "reputation" by holding her own in a "bangarang" (quarrel), but women who command "respect" cannot engage in such "common" business. Those of higher status are expected to behave in a more "civilized" fashion.

When viewed from a high "station," the exploitation of women is "vulgar." Moreover, a man of low "station" could never really support large numbers of lovers properly—he would not have the funds. "Loving" boosts "reputation" but must be accompanied by "conscious" responsibility toward those "loved" and by other types of social awareness if "respect" is to be achieved. "Big men" do engage in and boast about sexual exploits, but they usually do so quietly to avoid undermining the "respect" they command and to protect their wives' positions. One "big man" explained that although restraint is expected of higher-class men, they are still men so can never wholly control their "natural" hunger for "pum-pum."

Women wronged by men seeking to boost their "reputations" through brute virility can take revenge. They can spread tales of their aggressors' socially irresponsible actions (such as not "owning" children they sired) and can tell other villagers that these men are "soft" and "have no use" (whether financially or sexually) or that they "eat under the two-legged table." This refers to oral sex, which people say is disgusting and, for reasons discussed in Chapter 12, dangerous.

One very "big" man confided that he liked to keep his exploits "in the family" to avoid "chat." He provided his nieces with radios and such while they provided him with sexual favors and promised secrecy. He believed that they would not want to hurt his wife and counted on the fact that their relationship with him (and his wife) meant that their own behavior, too, would be condemned should it have gained publicity.

LIFE WITHOUT SEX

Life without sexual energy or tension between men and women is unthinkable. People openly talk of sex and expect that men and young couples will want it. Many believe in quarantining AIDS patients because the "natural" need for sex (and the human tendency to seek vengeance) will drive them to continue with intercourse. "Eunuchs," people with no sexual appetites, do exist. But having a "nature" that demands expression signals a far more healthy state. Denying oneself sexual gratification or failing to "discharge" brings "madness" to women and causes back problems in men because the "sinews" are affected and toxins build up. These "facts" get told to those practicing celibacy and especially to women refusing male advances.

RESPONDING TO MALE PRESSURE

"Reputation" expectations, cultural traditions concerning intergender relations, and the psychological motivations and propensities these encourage lead men to make sexual advances when they can. A farmer walking to his "ground" or relaxing with a beer at the shop before heading home will try to get a woman to "talk." Even "big men" will do so when they feel inconspicuous.

Those who most often "trouble" women are the "idlers." These unemployed men congregate on roadsides and at pubs and shops to talk, "chat" others, and "look 'pon people." They usually ignore Christians and "big women" but always hassle less-established women and schoolgirls.

Any response on a woman's part encourages a man in his belief that she may give him sexual pleasure. Women need not talk to pursuers just because pursuers talk to them. Still, to avoid drawing attention to their predicaments and to fend off the accusation, "You go on like you is somebody," women—adolescent schoolgirls in particular—respond with uncomfortable giggles and telling glances at girlfriends. Many women prefer to "run joke" when approached for sex, leaving themselves unbound, offending no one, and keeping real messages of acceptance unsent. When a man called to Lisa for "pussy" she pretended to toss him the cat.

Some "rudies" (conspicuously sexually active women) and schoolgirls tease predators back. For instance, one "young miss" waiting for the bus one morning in front of the shop on "the main" sat just so a certain "idler" could see beneath her skirt. A schoolgirl "begged" a different "idler" for a pencil with which she said she would do her homework, knowing the obligations debt incurs and understanding that men buy and give things to women to seal relationships. When a woman initiates exchanges or cooks for a man he can be sure of eventual gratification because otherwise she would not try to make the connection. I earned a neighbor's wrath by naïvely offering her common-law husband tea my first month in Jamaica.

Men can reject women by refusing food gifts. This often happens during quarrels. For example, when one man's marriage plan "got crash" by dissenting relatives, he signaled defeat by sending his lover's dinner offering back to her yard uneaten.

Males making sexual advances enjoy, like all Jamaicans, good teasing sessions. In childhood they learn the fun of pushing others to their limits of mental and physical endurance. Men make physical approaches when possible, touching a forearm or reaching for a breast. They laugh when women so vexed lash out with loud accusations: "Heggs up! Feisty and liberty!"

One woman stridently berated an aggressor who had moved too close for her comfort, "Don't dirty my earshole with your stinking breath!" Sometimes, women respond to pressure by questioning their suitors' masculinity, announcing that they are not lesbians (as if the men pressing them are women), or declaring no interest in "soft" and "useless" (financially insolvent, sexually unskilled, etc.) men. They may "trace them off," "tell about" their past mistakes and embarrass them, or call out, "You can't give me nothing," so others can hear. "Go along and suck titty," some command, implying that their solicitors are not yet independent, act like children, or have incestuous relationships with their mothers.

Public rejection is generally verbal, but rare cases do occur when men—usually not those in their prime—suffer physically for unsought advances. A woman told of a young girl from the next village who had to pass an adult male's gate on her way home from school. Each day he stood there, penis erect, calling her name. One day, she carried a length of wood. When he bid her come near, she gave him a big "lick" (a hit) seriously injuring his penis (usually, it is men who "lick" women with "the wood," or penis). All too often women cannot strike back, but hurting a man's penis is horrific because it affects his ability to express manliness through sex, explained my friend.

Some other girls were constantly molested by their "sprucey" granduncle, who had a room adjacent to the one in which they shared a bed. He often crept in as they slept to stand by their bedside, sometimes touching them. One night, the girls lay in wait, and when the old man arrived, they grabbed his penis and shoved a hairpin right in, the storyteller claimed. She felt sorry for the old man as, in his embarrassment, he did nothing for his condition and his penis got infected. She allowed that the man was at fault, and regretted that so many men "go on so" while girls must let them, but felt that the girls should have told their mother about him instead of taking such violent action, maiming his manhood.

SEX FOR SALE

Men "ask sex" and women do not because, as an old man said, "What women have fe sell men want fe buy." When they need to, women can exchange sex with men for gifts or money. People assumed that because I could pay my rent and buy food that I would not accept any invitations from men. They warned of the village men: "None of them can give you a penny." Yet my protectors mystified the use of sex as a commodity by emphasizing the idea that accepting things from men indebts women. They advised me, "Don't let none of them able to say to you that they carried you down a seaside [for sex]. They can't say that, and you can look them in the eye." Only a woman with no debts to or dependences on a man can "hold her head up" in dealings with him: no deference is needed.

One woman, seated on a typically Jamaican low wooden stool and hiding its rectangular seat, shiny and smooth from use, beneath her bulk, was jokingly admonished by her daughter to readjust her skirt. It had fallen from the typical, diaperlike style in which she had tucked it between her legs, exposing her crotch as she peeled bananas to boil. The daughter laughed that she did not "look pum-pum yam" to buy, playfully combining the slang term for vagina and the idea that sex can be bought.

THE LIMITS OF COMMERCIAL SEX

Only prostitutes accept money when sexual services are given and only they have no debt to their partners, who are truly customers. Money transactions fully instrumentalize sexual relations. Men hire prostitutes for sex and sex only, relieving themselves of responsibility for any progeny. One woman, Moms, told of a girl who took ten shillings from her boss for sex and got pregnant: he "owned" or admitted to having sex but would not "own" the baby he "left." He had paid for her services so considered things "done."

Women who charge for sex cannot enjoy it, Moms said, since men feel they can do anything to hired bodies. Monetary transactions for sex promote the objectification of women and the abuse of their bodies, as "owning" something involves "commanding" and "controlling" it. Owners "run things" and "rule." This idiom comes straight from the economic realm of personal property. "Owners" retain the right to handle their property as they wish, even if this means to "mash it up."

Most anything can be "owned." For instance, one woman not directly involved in a public fracas was said to have "bought out the argument" from those involved when she gave her opinions in a loud and clear fashion. A man who admitted to stealing a goat thereby "owned" the deed. One who married a woman with a son felt he now "owned" her child. As in slavery days, "owning" people entails taking responsibility for their provision. Feeding, schooling, and clothing a child in turn supports a claim over him or her. Men who do not want this responsibility refuse to "own" their progeny.

A woman discussing prostitution with her daughter illustrated the concept of ownership as it applies to sex with a story. A girl asked for $20 Jamaican (about $5 U.S.) in exchange for sex. Her customer took her to an area of overgrown bush, "pushed" her body into various "harmful positions," and abused her until she offered to hand back the money if only he would stop. He told her to keep it for her doctor fees. He knew she would need medical attention but insisted on doing what he pleased, having paid for the use of her body.

PROSTITUTION AND INVERTED NORMS

Women's economic and therefore their social power hinges on their sexual "use" when they lack capital or work skills. A heated exchange between two women on a bus illustrates this. Lashing out angrily after her foot was stepped on, an older fat

woman maligned a younger, slim one as "young and green"—
as immature, with no sexual "sweet water" to "fat" her nor any
sexual experience. She claimed that the girl had "no use to
any man" and so no "backative" to render forceful the "hot
words" she did "throw." The fat woman then boasted of her
own sexual prowess and so of her economic and social power.

Many women have occasionally sold sexual favors to men
for "dollars," and women involved in long-term sexual relations for profit even have a term for their benefactors:
"boops." A man who solicits bears no ill repute. One who
becomes a patron or a "boops" is awarded a legitimate social
status through the application of this nonpejorative label.
But women deeply, admittedly, and profitably engaged in
prostitution are called "vulgar" and are despised for "specu-
lating with their bodies."

Prostitutes refuse to mystify the instrumental dimension
of sex. They do not develop expressive, intrinsically fulfilling,
kinlike relations with customers and do not limit themselves
to one man's money. They invert or overturn cultural traditions and are held in disdain as antisocial. Those few able to
come out ahead of rent, food, and childcare costs "go on like
they nice," parading about in "criss" new clothes, but people
scorn them, and men treat their bodies poorly and leave them
worn. Eventually, their bodies "tired" from "the work," perhaps with teeth missing, scars from fights, breasts which no
longer "stand up" firm, and often suffering the long-term
effects of sexually transmitted diseases, prostitutes must
seek other means of "supportance."

PROSTITUTES AND SOCIAL BONDS

Because they do not seek to infuse their heterosexual
liaisons with kinship qualities, prostitutes do not create
bonds of obligation with men. While their sisters establish a
moral dimension in their unions, women in "that harlot business" have no "claims" on any man's money in later life, having "tied" no one to them with kinshiplike altruistic bonds.

The "drop pan" number association between "prostitute," "whore, and "mule" discussed in chapter 7 indicates that popular belief links nonmonagamous women, like infertile women who work but cannot reproduce, with mules. Ethnophysiological beliefs about intercourse hold that "what one man put in, the next lick [knock] out," so prostitutes would have problems conceiving. Also, by having many partners a woman decreases her chance of "fitting" with any one man and thus of getting pregnant. So people believe that prostitutes, like mules and infertile women, leave no progeny. If they become pregnant, they are apt to abort or "dash away baby." They are, supposedly, more likely to use birth control and to contract venereal infections, which can lead to sterility. But Ross-Frankson found that five out of seven prostitutes do have children (1987).

Unless they have working children or have been able to secure something for themselves by saving their pennies and investing, perhaps in a little shop, old prostitutes must "scuffle." Many end up sitting about at bars and "begging" drinks and peanuts from laborers celebrating payday, or taking up with men whom they scorned in their younger years.

TRADITIONAL SEXUAL LIAISONS

One woman bluntly denied that she would ever consider having sexual relations without financial gain. Another announced, "no man no go 'pon my belly unless I got something from his pocket." But the sex both referred to is not of the solicited sort. It conforms to the traditional model in which sexual relations are initiated by men, ongoing, and only indirectly paid for. Money is properly and respectably exchanged, with a time lag. It serves not to compensate but to attract—to "keep the women them coming back." It becomes part of the expression of kinshiplike altruism that traditionally overlays sexual relations.

A relationship's status can be inferred from the fashion and timing of payments made (Bourdieu 1982, 5). Cash is best because women can buy what they need with it but gifts of panties, food, and services such as yard work can do. Women receiving from men with stronger ties to other women must avoid "careless" gift-parading to keep resources flowing their way. One woman was berated for holding high the bottle of stout another woman's husband had given her. People said she did it as a way of "making claims" on her benefactor, publicly announcing that he was hers and she his. The money he had was, by rights, his wife's and "vex she vex" about having his infidelity and improper spending habits advertised. The stout-hoisting woman's "boasy" behavior made him end that adulterous liaison.

Ideally, each woman has her own man, and each man supports his women. Yet, as people say, "Hungry sleep with dog": sexual favors buy women subsistence. But to admit this exposes the egoistic side of sexual liaisons. Mystifying the instrumental aspects of sex by adding expressive dimensions to sexual relations (on top of indicating that they were initiated by men and involve long-term commitments) protects women from being considered prostitutes.

Women should be monogamous. Since women supposedly do not need as much sex as men, only the base need for money could spur them to casual copulation. Those who keep many boyfriends at the same time or participate in one-night affairs display their instrumental desires too flagrantly. A double standard exists. Male promiscuity is overlooked because it confirms "reputation" (and so fraternal equality) and patriarchal power over women. In addition, men are not the ones receiving money.

Nonmonogamous women all too overtly expose the tension between the cultural ideal of moral relationships and the instrumental side of sexual liaisons. They are called "whores." Although not as bad as the label "prostitute," "whore" nonetheless indicates that the cultural standards set for ideal-typic sexual relations (which should be enduring, male-initiated, and only indirectly paid for) are not well kept. The next chapter explores intergender liaisons further, especially in their ideal form.

Chapter 10

Love and Marriage

Although delayed payments give sexual liaisons an expressive dimension and make exchanges seem altruistic, villagers told me that "Jamaica people don't believe in love." Romantic love is never mentioned as a driving force behind long-term relations. As R. T. Smith (1988) found, lower-class men and women see each other instrumentally; instead of talk about the complementarity of the sexes, differing male and female attributes and needs are stressed in discussions of pairing. In certain contexts, cynics admit the obvious: men "look sex" and women "look money." This assertion exposes the thinness of the boundary that separates prostitution from acceptable relations—the kind that this chapter explores.

LOVE

To "look love" is to search for sex. R. T. Smith explains that "sexual relations are conceived as 'giving' one to the other rather than as the joint activity of a couple. Intense affect is not necessary" (1988, 142). Still, real affection and genuine attachments do exist. The expected expressive dimensions of lasting liaisons resemble the asexual, stable "one blood, one love" bonding of kinship; mother-child consanguinity (and concomitant ideas about commitment) serves as the model for all enduring ties (see R. T. Smith 1988, 114–115).

Romantic love does occur but it is not expected.[1] Because of its intolerance of practical matters, it is not always welcome. Romance without finance cannot "fill belly." And one must "expect complication" with romantic love: jealousy causes trouble, and rejection can physically cause "madness." While our society struggles with couplings made for economic convenience, Jamaicans struggle with unions based only on romantic love. It is easy to ignore economic motives when a woman keeps only one partner and he can provide, but it is hard to justify women staying with men when "no money no diddeh." Lovers are not really kin and so can, as logic has it, easily be dismissed. Still, lasting unions based on romantic love are admired.

One woman loved her man deeply but, because he was a poor provider, was forced to "scuffle out"—to "look money" elsewhere. She eventually "took up with a next man," who had been making advances, using the "supportance" he gave her to support herself, her children, and her original man. But she soon moved in with the second man. She still loved the first but felt compelled to make the transition into an economically sound and culturally justifiable relationship.

LONG-TERM UNIONS AND LABOR EXCHANGES

Marriage, common-law or otherwise, is seen as an enduring work partnership in which services are exchanged according to the sexual division of labor. One woman joked to another, who asked her to fetch some peanuts, that she would soon marry and so was not "working out." She would not bring the peanuts because her labor was promised exclusively to her boyfriend, as it should be in any male-female union. When her girlfriend then "begged" money for the nuts, she laughed, "Is me a man?"

Men, not women, should provide money. One man disgraced himself when he publicly "traced" what he saw as the shortcomings of the wife he had moved out on. Alone, she had struggled to bring up their six children. He now chastised her for not paying back the $100 Jamaican (about $20 U.S.) he had lent her. But villagers listening to the "tracing" felt that, since the two had a marriage contract (legitimizing overt instrumentality) and since he was her "babyfather" (a position requiring altruism), he should have been providing much more, with no expectation for repayment.

Ideally, in long-term relationships, men do the "hard" physical labor, such as construction, farming, and yard work, while women cook and wash. Men expect to give orders to women, who are expected to defer. One man remarked that he pitied anyone who married his sister because she likes taking charge. He joked that "two men" would then live in her house.

OVERT MALE POWER VERSUS COVERT FEMALE POWER

Although women should not express power overtly, they can use covert means to manipulate. In a pre-election discussion in the waiting room of a clinic, many agreed that women could and should rule Jamaica. Some joked that women can "tie" their constituents (create kinshiplike bonds magically) to secure their support and ensure good behavior. But one woman used this as proof that women are "too smart" to be trusted in office: "No man never think to cook food in no bath water," she said, referring to magic done that way. A man added that rebellious men had only to rape such rulers to reclaim power.

Rape, an overt show of strength which takes control of, disempowers, and subjugates the vagina—that key symbol of womanhood—keeps men "on top." In addition to its use against those who wield too much power, rape is sometimes said to be the proper treatment for particularly "mean" women. Many people of both genders think rape heinous but contend that men must sometimes "steal a little love" from a woman unwilling to share or give it.

The election discussion illustrates the overtness with which male ascendence is expressed and maintained. Men give orders and solicit liaisons. They use aggressive force, figured here as rape, to impose their power (which is out-front, as is the penis). This follows the model for heterosexual relations that prescribes genital intercourse (to the exclusion of all other forms of sexuality) and sets men against and on top of women.

Throughout the Caribbean, women are thought of as "smart, devious, and clever" (Henry and Wilson 1975, 193); Jamaican women are no exception. They must control others with wit and covert manipulations. Their power must be kept under wraps, secreted away like the vagina, which is "dangerous" and "strong" but also penetrable. The vagina or "buddy mouth," like the "food mouth," is a portal through which insidious forces can enter the body. This leaves women vulnerable, as the issue of rape implies.

MALE VERSUS FEMALE LABOR VALUE

Male labor is, like male power (and male "nature"), obviously and openly expended. Male tasks involve working up heavier sweats than female tasks do, as they are usually carried out in direct sun and involve more intensely spent energy. Male tasks culminate in peaks of visible bodily stress while female tasks, usually done in the shade, do not. This is not to say that women do not work hard—they surely do. Women cook, clean, wash, raise children, and provide their men with sexual fulfillment (which, for many women, is not a pleasure). These things may not appear as difficult as male tasks because they involve sustained energy expenditure and less visible stress. But they "work" the body rigorously nonetheless.

Most Jamaicans believe that the traditional sexual division of labor is "natural." It necessitates interdependence.

Traditional dress—men in trousers, women in skirts (their genitals easily accessed)—symbolically captures the notion of difference. But because men must give women money and because their work involves visible physical stress, men who "work out" in the public wage-labor sector are better paid than women for similar expenditures of energy and time. Men are ascribed greater economic value than women.

When "roadwork" comes around just before Christmas every year as part of a government-sponsored island upkeep effort, men (those favored by the party representative empowered to delegate work) are assigned to chop back roadside bush while women sweep it up and burn it. Village men received about 130 percent of the daily wage women were paid because chopping creates more sweat and is considered harder (and less menial) than sweeping and burning.

Women often do things like "take up machete" to chop wood or farm, some wearing dresses all the while. Likewise, men sometimes wash or cook. People may tease women who farm and men who cook, telling them, "Look a friend!" But it is understood that those doing nontraditional work either simply like to or are not involved in heterosexual partnerships and so have no suitable "friends" with whom to trade their labor.

Ideas about gender and labor affect the efficiency with which people can complete tasks not traditionally thought of as theirs. Sometimes, they deny themselves knowledge of how to carry out jobs assigned to the opposite gender. Needing help justifies interaction. The division of labor motivates the sorts of intercourse necessary for the perpetuation of society. Individuals who can do everything themselves have no need for others. If all were "selfish" and without interdependencies, society would not exist.

INDEPENDENT WOMEN

Typical women are strong in "mind" and character. They know their value. Men have more prestige and occupy more real power positions, but women actually esteem themselves above men, whom they see as lazy and incapable. Women can prove their worth: "Wasn't it a woman," one female pastor asked rhetorically, "who first knew Jesus had risen?" It is true that many women are submissive; with eyes downcast they answer others only with "yes" or "me no know." But docility inheres in beliefs about behavior proper to low "station" (or rests in minimal wit), not gender.

When they can—when financially independent—women demand "right and proper" treatment. For example, a woman who tends bar part-time threw a pan of boiling water at her empty-pocketed boyfriend when he grabbed her and pressed too hard for sex. "Higglers," traditionally female middle merchants who sell in the markets and along the roadside, are known for their brashness. They frequently engage in noisy debates with those who have wronged them, sparing no expletives. One woman explained that higglers have to "carry on so" because they must endure "all kind of problem" and abuse, a very trying task considering Jamaicans' hyperawareness of slights. This makes higgling less "respectable" as an occupation than housewifery.

Higglers, more directly in control of their lives and often richer than housewives yet less "respected," occupy a social position in which self-expression is nonproblematic. Self-employed and financially independent, they owe no patrons their allegiances. Not high status yet not so low in "station" that they must act with deference, higglers can voice the opinions they "own." But women who want to maintain positions of "respect," including married rural women, "leave off" such "pickney business" as "tracing" and otherwise "carrying on."

MARRIAGE AND CLASS

A higgler, even when legally married, can never claim high status because her work takes her into the market where she has contact with the lower class, against whose disrespect she must protect herself. "Working out" also excludes her, as the ideal "big woman" is kept by her man and need not mix or argue with those of lower "station." With "respect due," she has no need to quarrel. Anyhow, doing so arouses disrespect.

Legal marriage "uplifts" a person in the social system. Ideas concerning hierarchy (such as the direction of obligations and rights) are aroused by knowledge of the social structural positions of others relative to oneself. They can be mobilized by the strategic invocation of the "respect" villagers accord one another.

Using the term *mistress* denies equality and demands "respect" from those of lower "stations," advising them that notions about stratification are being called into play. And yet, commanding "respect" demands that the expectations for the class in which one claims membership be fulfilled. Married women must comport themselves quietly and must not mix with lower-class people (except as patrons or employers or as kin, but even then, they must mix very little).

MARRIAGE AND MONEY

Although marriage involves two people whose actions affect each other's social standing, a wife's comportment also stands alone, a component of her own personal social standing (see R. T. Smith 1988, 134–48). Many women view marriage as a move toward independence, not as an institution that promotes their dependency. It is a step toward establishing "command" in a yard where one may declare, "Me run things."

Marriage is less than half as common in Jamaica as it is in the United States. In 1988, only 4.4 of every 1,000 people married; the average rate over the fifteen years between 1974 and 1988 was 4.3 per 1,000 (STATIN 1988a, 87). For comparison, the U.S. rate in 1987 was 9.9 per 1,000. Only 15 percent of Jamaicans registered in the 1982 census had married (STATIN 1988b, 23). Brody, who worked with mostly lower-class women ages sixteen to forty-seven, reported that although almost half of his subjects cohabited, only 14.7 percent were legally married (1981, 187). Of the unmarried women, 87.4 percent expected no legalization of current unions (194). A full 43.3 percent of all women were committed to "visiting relationships" in which partners lived apart but frequently came to call on each other (187).

Changing residences is costly. For a start, one needs a place to go to. Rentals are scarce, building materials expensive, and good land is neither cheap or plentiful. Also, many people who want to move cannot because their beds are owned by relatives or are shared. To announce that someone does not even have a mattress shames him or her. Young men often stay in their caretakers' yards because of poor "money runnings." Although some argue that mother-son dependency is the key factor keeping young men at home (e.g., Kerr 1963, 69–70; Clarke 1957, 164), Jamaicans know the primary reason: they cannot afford to leave.

Lucky women escape their caretakers' yards with the help of usually older men who have money as well as a place to "put" them. Women are always looking for situations likely to lead "somewhere." Girls learn early that men who have money to share are good. One grandmother teasingly questioned her little granddaughter, asking her if her father or grandfather gave her money. "Grampa," the child easily replied. "So who is the better man?" Grandma asked. "Grampa," again.

Men know "women always looking something" and can come to resent this, especially when they have nothing to give them. Because economic conditions prevent many men from holding honest jobs, young men in particular, who more likely to be unemployed than older men, often turn to petty crime to fill their pockets (see Brodber 1989).

"Now days, men prouda being thieves," one gentleman lamented. He explained that "women loves money" and "these days" do not care from where it comes. Thieves have ready cash for "sporting," and so thieves have many women. They take pride in this. But unless they have the foresight to invest, they rarely get legal wives and only perpetuate "the system" that led them to steal in the first place. By providing women with cash, they reinforce the instrumental side of gender relations.

Men who have gotten work "in foreign" and have been able to save can afford to marry, and because of pension and insurance benefit disbursement regulations, they usually want to. They often stay long overseas and send funds back for wives to spend as they see fit. Women may build houses and start small home-based business with capital their husbands remit.

I lived in a village of 800 people (STATIN 1982). Three weddings occurred in the course of one year, which reflects the average rate of 4.4 per 1,000. All three grooms were successful overseas laborers of mature age. Cohen found that most Jamaican men who legally marry do so at thirty-five and concluded that most seek wives only after their mothers die because they need to replace them (1953, 127). While this does apply to many men who seek common-law partners to cook and wash for them, by the time a man marries he has usually long since found someone to provide the sorts of services for which he once depended on his mother.

One of the weddings did occur because the groom's mother died. The groom said this led him to wonder what might happen to his common-law wife should he pass away. His U.S. employer would certainly not pay her benefits. He did not marry to replace his mother's services; he had been living with his new wife for over fifteen years. He married to provide his wife "security" and to buy "respect." Men say marriage is "the Christian thing to do" (R. T. Smith 1988, 117; Clarke 1957, 80) People "living that concubine life" cannot attend church. The criteria for "respect" come directly from church teachings; active membership is necessary for full "respectability" (Wilson 1973, 100).

A look at previous weddings and those in other villages confirmed that marriages to men who have held jobs overseas are most common. These men are sought after and can most easily win a woman's hand. It is harder for the average man, working in the island, to amass enough money for marriage. And most island laborers receive no pension benefits anyhow. Women cannot afford to limit their options by tying them-

selves up with men who do not "have it"; marriage is "rigid
and therefore not appropriate within uncertain economic situations" (Barrow 1988, 163).

NAMES AND TITLES

Changing one's name upon marriage carries connotations
about kinship and conjugal unity, but a woman changes
names more to indicate "uplift" and to claim the "respect due"
to a "mistress" than to prove her incorporation into any man's
life. One woman instructed some little girls sent to her on an
errand that after her wedding they must call her *"Mistress
MacDonald,"* emphasizing the honorific, not the surname.
Another woman, not invited to the wedding, groused, "She go
on like her didi make patty": like people can feed off of her
feces—as if she has no corruption. Everyone knew the bride
when she had nothing, not even a bed, this woman said,
faulting the bride for making sure that everyone saw when
she had the mattress her bridegroom bought delivered to the
house he had "put" her in. Now, the uninvited woman grum-
bled, they must call her "mistress" and show "respect."

A husband's particulars do have importance. Some men
carry more monetary and prestige value than others. The
above bride's "master" was by all means a top prize. But his
standing means more to other married women (and to men
who might otherwise approach his wife for sexual favors)
than to the people a woman leaves behind as she ascends the
social ladder. To them, any "mistress" commands respect.
Even this one did: villagers confided that everyone used to
treat her poorly but now they courted her "kindness."

DOUBLE STANDARDS AND
THE DUAL MARRIAGE SYSTEM

"Big men" are encouraged to quietly seek "outside" partners while women must be contented within marriage. The

common-law unions of the lower class are easily penetrated by high status men in search of sex. R. T. Smith (1987) describes this as a "dual marriage system" because common-law unions function in tandem with legally bound ones.

Smith disagrees with Rodman's (1966) notion of a "value stretch," wherein lower-class couples stretch their values concerning marriage because they cannot afford to marry in "proper" fashion. The existence of common-law unions, Smith explains, allows women to take money from high-status men and provides these men with women for "outside" liaisons. Lower-class women, especially younger ones who still have dreams and are not dark in color (men look for light-skinned wives), favor common-law unions since these leave them freer than legal ones to accept help from above and, if offered, marriage. Lower-class men like common-law partnerships because they can then couple without being bound.

Usually, until older and settled into a common-law relationship, lower-class women hope to secure a legal union with a man of higher "station" but have no interest in marrying one of their own class, even if living with him. They do not wish to simply mimic or be *like* the upper classes (which Rodman argues); they want to belong to or be *of* them. My data supports Smith's view, in which common-law and legal unions function in tandem. Common-law unions differ in aim from legal ones.

WEDDINGS

Marriage takes place in later life, if and when economic stability has been attained and a family built. Weddings, which are expected to be big celebrations, symbolize the status claims that inhere in legal marriage. The religious ceremonies are usually held in another district's church so that everyone can see the couple "drive out." The most important part of the church ceremony is the marriage license signing, which highlights marriage's legal and binding dimension. Anyone with a camera is commandeered to photograph each person—bride, groom, maid of honor, best man, and pastor—signing his or her section.

To go to church one must dress with impeccable grandeur so most attend only the reception, where people feast on goat-head soup, curried goat, rice and peas, boiled banana, cake, and wine. No one should leave without a full "belly." Men drink rum with water and cut limes. They are usually far outnumbered by women, who take more interest in weddings. People say that many women want to "fasten into" bridal "business," check out expenditures, and "mash up" celebrations. At one wedding, people swore a spiteful young woman purposely knocked the bride's bouquet from her hands. The bride, however, had no recollection of this happening.

The main part of the reception occurs before dinner when, after arriving, the bridal party assembles around a table in an open-air "booth" or thatch-roofed structure. The table is "decorated" and "dressed" grandly with ersatz linens, fake crystal and china place settings, and a variety of festive foods, such as whole oranges with squares of cheese and maraschino cherries impaled on toothpicks. Most formal gatherings, including birth night, religious, and even political meetings, center around a similar "supper table," as well "dressed" as "money runnings" permit.

A master of ceremonies proposes formal toasts. One of the most important moments comes when the cake is unveiled by the person who baked it. Traditionally, this is the bride's mother. The cake, a "she," has been "dressed" prettily with white icing and cake decorations and, like the bride's face, waits covered by a veil (which keeps off flies). After making a short speech, the mother lifts this. While men as fathers provide and present brides, women as mothers provide and present food. Next, the groom and bride cut the cake together.

Jamaican wedding cake is dark, heavy, and full of dried fruits, red wine, and rum. Cake ingredients are expensive, and baking without refined sugar, ovens, or electric mixers is a task indeed. Cake signifies money and having money symbolizes and buys prestige. The wedding cake's symbolic importance goes beyond this because of the significance of sharing food. Rich in spirits, raisins, preserved cherries, and candied peel, it resembles oversweet, "well ripe" fruit just about to ferment: fruitcake occupies a precarious position on the border between the edible and the foul. And it can conceal poison easily in its dark, moist interior. Accepting such fare without question is a true act of good faith.

Unwary food-sharing demonstrates and demands a solid relationship of trust. The bride and groom feed each other in front of their guests without the mediation of a fork, "bird style" (mouth to mouth). This, people say, symbolizes the way they keep each other fed in life. He gives her (money for) food to cook, she cooks it, and feeds it back to him. He signals his trust and his dependence by eating her cake, incorporating into his "structure" something as dark and moist as a mother's fetus-building blood. Similarly, with her "food mouth" (and her "buddy mouth") a wife ingests what a husband offers from the "work" his body does. All this binds newlyweds by symbolizing kinship as Jamaicans construct it, through shared substances and interdependencies.

People who "taste piece cake" witness the marriage contract, for if seeing is believing, eating is too. They "prove" for themselves that each intends well and they approve the union. Marriage is not something for the lazy or the manipulative. It must be worked toward honestly and marks a relationship's culmination, not its beginning. While few comment on how pretty a bride looks, many will say that she certainly "deserves" her wedding.

"Tasting" cake also signals a positive, kinshiplike affiliation between newlyweds and their guests who, if unsociably wary, would not partake. One young couple was overheard boasting that they would not invite any villagers to their hypothetical wedding because they did not want any "dirty naygur" to eat of their wedding cake. They said this to each other, asserting their unity by figuratively segregating themselves from other villagers.

Wedding gifts also link guests and newlyweds and pieces of cake are sent as acknowledgments and in thanks. A "madman" who lived in the village proposed marriage to me and spoke "plain" about what "righted" (sane) people do not publicly admit, promising to invite "pure rich people" to our wedding. That way, we could be sure that in exchange for the expense of our feast we would get nice gifts such as toasters, which are imported and carry high prestige value. Our return gifts of food would only get sent to and ingested by "respectable," upper-class villagers—people of the class with whom we would want to ally. The statements of the "madman" and the couple above expose the purpose of a wedding: "social uplift." It is no coincidence that more than one person called the last wedding I attended a "coronation."

CHOOSING NOT TO WED

With age, many realize the futility of hoping for "uplift" through a marriage to someone of high "station." After spending years together, lower-class couples may decide to marry, and many try to raise the funds. Without riches to be handed down to heirs or insurance benefits to be paid out, marriage contracts bring few bonuses except church approval and, through that, a little "respect" for attempting to "uplift" and "live clean."

Others are content with common-law status and prefer the flexibility it allows to the shackles of married life. As the next chapter shows, the obligations entailed in contracts of any sort, whether broken or appealed to, give many Jamaicans cause to fret. There is a tension between individual desires and the demands of others. Many resent interdependence and desire full freedom. Often, resented obligations and ambivalences are worked out through one's own body or on the bodies of others. Sexual relations are one area in which intergender argument takes place.

Chapter 11

Gender Tension
and Sexual Expression

The male and female spheres in rural Jamaica do not overlap very much, and with the exception of courtships, men and women rarely do things as couples. Sexual intercourse, a previously noted example, is thought of as an exchange rather than a joint activity. It is also used for the expression of hostilities and ambivalences held toward the opposite sex. Intergender tensions and power struggles are symbolized in the treatment of bodies.

Ideally, conjugal partners imaginatively create "one love" between themselves, modeling their relations on kinship, which involves shared blood and the altruism shared blood should engender. But coupled lovers are not kin. Unions have an underlying pragmatic basis. Each partner worries about the other fulfilling his or her part of the conjugal bargain. Wariness pervades gender relations, and defensiveness or selfish desire sometimes gets the better of both men and women.

THE DRAWBACKS OF MARRIAGE

People say marriage seals the death of a relationship; a wedding is often referred to as a "funeral" and death itself as the "wedding supper." Legal marriage tests relationships: "When the ring goes on, the devil slips in." People joke that one woman gets the ring but another gets the man. A ring is said to attach a ball and chain and, like a curse, is easier put on than taken off. The ambivalences that these jokes indicate appear wherever marriage does. They are less or more intense depending on the types of marriage a culture recommends and on the sociocultural contexts of those recommendations.

Jamaicans view marriage as an unbreakable lifelong commitment that each spouse must feel sure s/he wants to make (see Clarke 1957, 74). Partly in reaction to the legacy of slavery and also because of resentment toward kin obligations, people dislike the sense of being bound or indebted by contracts of any kind and hesitate to sign them. Legal divorce is not easily had (for example, a separated couple must stay so for at least five years and must publish costly and embarrassing public announcements). While nonkin relations should be voluntary, after a marriage tie is made, a spouse cannot easily break free.

Men understand that, even while coupling with them, women of their class seek men of higher "stations." They know that legal husbands must fulfill some heavy financial expectations. Cultural and socioeconomic conditions dictate that many just cannot rise to them. Men who cannot marry, like those who do not wish to, may denigrate marriage in self-defense.

Unmarried men are often happy not having to fulfill marriage obligations. They need not so carefully divide their loyalties between mothers and wives. They need not "hear" or abide by demands for fidelity nor listen to diatribes against spending long hours at the pub. Legal wives can make these more often than common-law wives because they have the backing of both the law and the customary expectations held for married men. Married men know that if they wish to maintain "respect" they must maintain appearances.

Women know how men "stay." They do not marry young men because, besides having no wealth to offer, impetuous youths cannot carry on affairs as surreptitiously as marriage recommends. Unmarried women spare themselves the shame that a misbehaving husband can bring. They also avoid exploitation, they say. Not legally bound, they need not put up with men who are "strict" and "mean," which many become after marriage.

RECREATION SEGREGATION

Couples live but do not socialize together. This is part of the "dissociated conjugal role pattern" R. T. Smith (1988) describes. One woman, Matrise, demonstrated an ideal union with two rocks. First, she placed them close together on a railing before us. She described the stress one partner brings the other by keeping too close a watch. Women must be given leave to walk "up street" to the shop or water "stand-pipe" (public spigot) as they please and to "live life independently." Men must be free to sit at the pub, drink, and play dominoes if they like. Too much jealousy stifles and embarrasses the guarded spouse, whose "jailer" provides villagers a "puppy [puppet] show."

Matrise moved the stones apart, demonstrating the proper distance partners should maintain. Men and women prefer different types of recreation and pass their time apart. Men often move out of their yards alone toward trees under which they gather to rest, sharpen machetes, tell tales, cut each other's hair, and smoke *ganja*. More established men walk to the rum shop or pub to gamble, drink, and talk.

Men spend more time with other men than with their women. But male homosexuality stays, for the most part, latent or hidden. Jamaicans feel that heterosexual unions are proper and believe homosexuality so aberrant that those engaging in it should be killed, as a popular song says, "without mercy." People realize that men need sexual release, but even when women are not "plenty," homosexuals bring "disgrace" to their communities. They signal to the world that the women there reject village men and denigrate them "cuz they can't do the work," that the women themselves are not sexually up to standard, and that "carelessness" abounds there (lesbians bring disgrace for similar reasons). Nonetheless, men spend lots of time with men and do harbor aggressions for, identifications with, and ambivalences about women and about their own masculine identities.

Women relaxing stay in their yards, watching the children and sometimes chatting with a neighbor as they shell peas or sew. They help each other wash, comb, and plait (or sometimes straighten or dye) their hair. Those who have access watch the single television station in the country. Women leave their yards only "'pon mission." They either go to the shop, where they may meet some people they know and stop for a short talk, or to church. Church membership consists mainly of women: it is one of the few places where they can sit and relax without being harassed or having their right to "respect" questioned. Only "rebel" women congregate at the bars.

Men and women must have freedom to move as separate individuals. Symbiotic fusion does not figure in the Jamaican idea of conjugal unions; people do not overtly desire to be incorporated by even their spouses. Affection is not displayed publicly (except during weddings or by courting youths). One couple did not as much as hug each other when they reunited the day after Hurricane Gilbert destroyed their house (the woman was caught in another village by the storm).

Many men in unions do not socialize with their women because "they don't rate them" (i.e., the men do not think highly of their women). A villager explained candidly that many keep women only to cook, wash, and provide sex. It is more acceptable for men than for women to act instrumentally (recall that only men can solicit sex), so male egoism gets exposed in more contexts and with more impunity. Plenty of men do "rate" their women but fear other men's intentions. One villager said he would never bring his common-law wife out because he did not want other men to touch or "wind up against her." He would stay by her side if he did take her out, not leaving her even to fetch drinks. He trusts her, but trusts no other man: he knows how men "stay."

Many women do not like the pub or dance hall anyway, as men there "take set 'pon" them. What may at first look like affection to an outsider is superficial and related to efforts to arrange sex. Longtime intimates very rarely even hug in public or dance together, but most men touch women whenever they can, resting a hand on a thigh or clumsily grabbing a breast. One woman complained that many men who frequent bars do not bathe and rub their "stinking" bodies up against women as they try to "take step" or make advances. Many women see men as "too terrible," "too trick," "too liared," and "too plague," although they still rely on them for money and other types of aid.

THE DRAWBACKS OF MEN

Men are often seen as good-for-nothings who, because of their sexual voraciousness, "promise you downtown and parade and give you neither." Women warn young girls, "don't turn fool-fool over a boy and ruin things for yourself," especially if he is one of the many that "can't give you nothing." "Don't let nobody spin you round," warned one grandmother who knows that men are always "bugging in your earsholes" promises never meant for keeping.

Although only 1.3 percent of the women Brody spoke to reported having no regular mate (1981, 187), many women would if they could quite proudly say (like Aunt Belle did), "No man hold fork and knife at my table." A full 70 percent of Brody's subjects felt negatively about men, over whom 56 percent preferred their own mothers (1981, 192). The tendency to label men "irresponsible" increased with age, number of children, and years of cohabitation (195). Life experience increases the negative perception women have of men.

Many women desire to reach a "stage" when they can say, "No man master me." The privilege of manlessness is generally reserved for older women who have already built families and have been able to make themselves independent. Home-owning women, for example, can order men out. Some women report purposely getting receipts for beds and other furniture made out in their names; when they and their men split, they can claim these. To many, being manless by choice epitomizes "bigness."

One self-proclaimed "independent" women said, "No one can't push me around" (note that "push" has sexual connotations; during intercourse, women's vaginas and cervixes get "pushed back" and "pushed around"). In a separate incident in front of a market, one older woman boasted to another that she could hold her head up because "no man rugoo-rugoo me" (uses her sexually). This "boasy" woman has worked very hard and has had the luck to become truly independent. She "can look any man in the eye" as she owes nothing to any man. She is also the owner of a very "clean" body as she has no need to "dirty" herself through sexual intercourse, a thing that one "deep" in the Christian church, she said, must avoid.

Back in the village, Nelle, whose children supported her well, asked rhetorically why she should want some lazy man to sit on her veranda, mess her bed with his "big dirty foot," and demand sexual favors. Her children would stop sending money as they would expect her hypothetical man to support her. She would lose her freedom to come and go. A man would question her about who would cook and wash if she went off to visit a child's yard, which she likes to do to "fe rest my body, eat good food, and sleep." "A man?" she laughed, "fe what?"

DIVIDED LOYALTIES

Nelle's friend told of the split loyalties men feel for their mothers and their wives (whether legal or common-law). Clarke discusses the role the mother plays in creating a sense of indebtedness (1957, 162–164). Often, a mother resents her son's wife for commanding a good portion of his money and services; sons, for their part, have trouble choosing whether to honor their mothers' or wives' needs more. One woman, Effie, jokes, whenever asked about her husband, that she has finished with him and sent him back to his mother—the source of their marital discord.

Joking disguises the seriousness of Effie's complaint. Her husband, the "babyfather" of her three children, had problems deciding who should get his money. His mother believed the better part of it belonged to her. "Grudgeful," she stole some of Effie's clothing, cursed her through it, and magically brought sickness upon her so she could not fulfill her part of the implicit labor contract with her husband. This gave him a culturally legitimate excuse to leave.

Women, no matter how upset with their men and no matter how cold or obnoxious they may act toward them, must always cook dinner and otherwise maintain their mates. As long as they fulfill the labor bargain the union involves, their men can "have no complaint." Emotional unfulfillment is not cause for abandonment but poorly done wash or forgotten dinner is.

Because she did not look after him, Effie's husband had a culturally valid complaint and a reason to leave, which she could not appeal. He abandoned her. She cannot seek another legal husband because she is still legally married. She does not despair, however. Trained as a health aide, Effie was able (after her recovery) to support her small children, and although not well off, she has shelter, food to eat, and only feels glad to be free of the problems men bring.

COMPETING WITH "OUTSIDE" WOMEN

Mothers-in-law are not the only people who can sap a man's monetary resources. "Outside" girlfriends and "baby-mothers" compete with a man's mate for his money—assuming he has some. "Wives" are troubled when others get money which, by rights, should be theirs to maintain their households and children. "Outside" women who "eat out" a "husband's" money take some sexual pressure off of his "wife" (and for that she may be glad), but they also cause financial strain. This is more important to most women complaining about their men's exploits than infidelity (except when men act with blatant indiscretion, bringing "disrespect").

Women compete for desirable (e.g., financially solvent, "respectable," and "kind") men. They warned me that a "next woman" would surely "steal" my man while I was away. Many women, even one's girlfriends, will "dance with your man and sleep with him as well," especially if "his pocket deep" (money-filled). During a "tracing," a woman defended herself against the accusation that she had lured another's man into adultery, citing the man's insolvency: "Me no want fe your man," she said, "him no have nothing."

Men who do have the money for it rationalize their infidelity. "Man can't eat chicken every day," they say, bolstering this argument with the traditional justification that male "nature" runs "high." Their "loving" is supported by the culturally constructed notion that for each man, seven (to ten) women exist. Men claim to selflessly provide their services to extra women, who would otherwise not "find relief." Freilich's (1968) argument that resources are reallocated through extramarital sex resembles this idea.

While there is some truth to the economic argument, the traditional idea that women outnumber men is pure fabrication. Women do live longer than men, but the number of old widows notwithstanding, about equal numbers of men and women live in Jamaica. In fact, the village in which I lived had more men. 406 males and 394 females are registered in the 1982 census, meaning 1.04 males exist for every female. The parish did have more females than males, but only by a ratio of 101:100 (STATIN 1982).

The entire island had only 1.04 females for every one male in general and only 1.07 women might have required the services of any one man if we consider only those ages twenty to forty-nine (and assume them interested in heterosexual liaisons) (STATIN 1988a, 6–7). The parish I lived in had only 1.03 women for every man in this age group. These figures are far, far lower than those that promiscuous men promote.

CHARACTER AND CLASS

Women with "ambition" comport themselves "respectably" in social interactions, while others "go on careless," seeking instant, instead of delayed, gratification. A "careless woman" will often "look another woman's man" because he already has someone washing and cooking for him. "Careless" women "cheapen" themselves by cavorting with many men. They do not think about the future, people say, and they get the blame for ending up low in "station" and with "nothing to show."

One man had his wife quite piqued because he committed adultery with a very "common" woman. The wife, irately "tracing" this woman's deeds for her sister and husband as they sat on the veranda, called her (among other things) a "dirty bitch" ("bitch" and "slut" retain direct connections with female dogs and their sexual behavior). She observed that villagers known to "carry tale" said the girl was pregnant, and all laughed at the thought that the man, nearly eighty, might get "named" "babyfather." He asked with a chortle if the two women thought him a "stallion." His sister-in-law jokingly advised that he, like her dog, should be "cut" (castrated) so he would not, like the dog had been doing, "rub up" against his "nasty, stinking girlfriends," "breed" them, and carry "raw" scent back to her yard.

The husband laughed, but thought it especially unbecoming for women to "chat" and berate other women less fortunate than themselves. He noted that women, not men, judge women harshly. Some, he said, simply have bad luck with men who "breed them up with pickney and leave." He offered his sympathy for "the girl" (his ex-lover) with "her pickney them dead fe hungry." Then he addressed his wife's sister, claiming her own daughter would have had to "drop her drawers like anybody else" to stay fed had the "babyfather" not "owned" and "responsed" for her.

The sister retorted that his ex-lover's "bad character" put

her in her dire straits. Women who act like "tramps" and "disgrace" themselves, letting "any and any man climb on top" even when experience has proven these men irresponsible as "babyfathers," are simply "stupid" and "careless," she argued. The husband defended his ex-lover as a woman unlucky enough to be born with "high nature," who "just love sex too much."

The women pointed out that the ex-lover confirmed her own reputation as "careless, dirty trash" by not keeping silent about the liaison—"ambitious" women know to remain secretive. The ex-lover's own mouth did her (and the husband) in. By boasting about having him for a "boops," she drew attention to the affair, and publicity killed it. Not even the husband's colleagues cheered him on. Many tried to dissuade him from ruining his "reputation" and losing much of his hard-won "respect" by cavorting with "that dirty gal."

The wife noted that the "girl" did not even own a mattress, and said she was so filthy that upon her death she would surely rot with abnormal speed. "Good thing they have fridge for dead. That heggs up [uppity], nasty gal couldn't keep twenty-four hours." The wife also observed that if her husband had taken up with a "respectable" woman, the news would have never left the yard.

MALE "TRICKS"

Traditionally, male adultery has a physical cause: "nature." But since men "know what they would do" and because they feel women are always looking for "something" (money), men often suspect their women of adulterous behavior too. Some say men make women "wicked" by offering money. Whatever prompts female infidelity, it suggests that their men "can't do the work" and do not provide well. Men cannot stand this type of assault on their pride. They hate to be called "soft."

A man "owns" his woman and demands exclusive rights to her labor and her body. Traditionally, it is he who will "put her in a room" and pay her bills; therefore, he should "rule." If he is going away he can rub an herbal concoction, often mixed with chemicals from the pharmacy, on his woman's lower abdomen to "sick" any man who "interferes" with her. The poison rubs into the trespasser and his penis becomes inflamed. Richard joked about drawing a ram goat on his wife's belly: if any man rubbed it out while he was gone, he would know of his wife's infidelity.

Women are privately "owned" sperm receptacles. The meanings of no. 8, used for "drop pan" gambling, reflects this association. Villagers said no. 8 means "bellywoman." It also means "bag" and "hole" (Chevannes 1989, 48). A woman provides the "hole" in which a man plants his "seed," and as a "bellywoman," she carries his baby in her "baby bag." If she aborts or does not conceive, her "baby bag" becomes a "grave" (another no. 8 meaning), a "hole" containing dead sperm. She becomes a "walking cemetery." Men would rather their sperm survive.

Men, concerned with self-perpetuation, want to control women's wombs and fidelity. They fear being duped into supporting a child who should actually be another man's responsibility. They know that people hearing that their women have gone "outside" will assume them financially and sexually "useless." They often have "confederates" spy on their women. Women know that mercenaries often carry back lies just to keep jealous mates' money "running" to them or to break unions apart.

But men say they can tell when reports are true: women who have had "outside sex" return to their husbands with their vaginas "pushed around" (reshaped). They are harder to satisfy as their regular mates' penises no longer "fit" and also because they may have been introduced to better sex "outside." Women who complain about their men's skills, like women whose vaginas change in shape or "size" (as all do, over both the menstrual and the life cycle), are often accused of keeping "outside friends."

A well-endowed man is always the first suspect when another believes someone has "interfered" with his mate.

Normally, then, only men who wish to "hurt" others express concern with large size. A well-endowed, "dangerous" man can inflict pain and can spitefully ensure the exposure of a woman's adultery when he "push her back." Women with extensively "stretched" vaginas become "useless" to their men. Because they no longer "fit," they cannot provide as much sexual pleasure nor can they easily conceive. They are said to have no use to men.

Men can harm women by spreading venereal diseases, which many say people do on purpose (some women try to routinely check the penises of men they have sex with for signs of infection; they think this common sense). A man can also "trick" and "sick" a woman by placing the membrane of a boiled egg—the thin white veil which lies between the shell and the egg white—on his penis before intercourse. As noted earlier, people say the membrane stays behind with the semen and "sicks" the woman by rotting or blocking a "tube."

Men also "trick" women by impregnating them while using condoms. A man merely "pinches," cuts, or pricks the condom he intends to use so his semen flows through. Women know men do this, and many would rather have unprotected intercourse with a "conscious" man who promises to withdraw before ejaculation than with a condom user. One young girl routinely searches suitors' wallets, "looking money" but mainly for condoms. Finding them, she infers a man's deceitful intentions.

Men say they "pinch" condoms "for joke." Women call this "cruelty." Most men say that "most" have tried this "trick," and they give three reasons for doing so. First, they believe that impregnating a woman who thinks herself safe is funny. It makes her look like a "tramp" because she cannot "name" a father. Secondly, it proves virility. Third, and more importantly, it "cuts a jacket" for another man. That is, if a woman with one steady partner gets a "belly" from a "next man," her partner will be "fooled" into "owning" it (she could never admit to the "outside" affair).

One young man testified that "the majority" of men have "pinched" condoms and told me of another "trick": gang rape.

One man at a bar asks a woman for sex. When she agrees, he takes her out back or to a room, has his way, and then the "trick" begins: a parade of males rape her, single-file or all at once. The young man estimated that one of every five women who go to bars has been gang-raped and said many men participate. The latent homoeroticism of the act may be as attractive to men as expressing aggression toward women is.

Some men pay bartenders to add aphrodisiacs like Spanish fly to the drinks they buy for women; others do it themselves. Men believe this a way to maintain "reputation" by showing colleagues that they can get women. They also claim that this heightens the possibility that targeted partners will be "ready," "willing," and easily sated. Women know full well that men will do this and never accept opened drinks. They learn how to use their teeth to pry off caps because only by opening drinks themselves can they be sure of no tampering. They also refuse to finish drinks left unattended, for "anything can happen."

FEMALE "TRICKS"

Women also have "tricks." Some, especially "whores," have their own "confederates" who go through men's trousers for money while they engage them with sex. Others do it themselves while the men nap afterward. Some say women can put laundry bluing inside their vaginas to harm men's penises. This may have little to do with the bluing but lots to do with the fact that the women using it are probably menstruating (and menstrual blood is dangerous). Prostitutes who need work think that bluing erases menstruation. Perhaps this has to do with its regular use for bleaching clothing stains.

Some women ask for money before sex and pretend to find menstrual blood on their underclothes so that intercourse cannot take place. These women sometimes paint their panties with streaks of red-brown floor polish. Women can also, people say, stick a pin through any piece of their clothing, magically rendering the men they would bed impotent and relieving themselves of having to "do the work." One woman admitted that this "trick" failed when she tried it.

As long as no one has explicitly stated that money handed over was for sex, especially when an exchange occurs between people already known to each other, men and women collusively agree that they are not dealing in prostitution. Because "trickify" women who endeavor to avoid sexual labor are not prostitutes in the pure Jamaican sense, men cannot ask for their money back. To do so would insult the women, classing them as prostitutes, and it would expose the baser, instrumental aspects of sexual liaisons.

DEMANDING WOMEN AND MALE FEARS OF IMPOTENCE

Pea tells of a man who came to her for sex but could not maintain an erection. He wrongly accused her of playing the pin "trick" and insisted on searching her clothing. Most Jamaican men fear impotence. They feel badly when others can tell them they "have no use," are "soft," or are otherwise as unmanly and inadequate as an overripe, inedible banana. "Softness" and "uselessness" connote poverty, passivity, a lack of virility, and the inability to satisfy women (as the penis always and only the penis should bring pleasure).

Men want to be known as capable sexual partners. Despite the stereotype of women as paid-for sexual receptacles with little libido and no need for pleasure, an alternative portrait exists: the insatiable woman. Both depictions carry some truth. The first one makes sexual activity a simpler, self-oriented act for men. The second scares them.

Over the years, Jamaican men have encountered more and more adventurous white women from "foreign." White women supposedly have "higher natures" than black ones, although Jamaicans know that some "dangerous" "white liver" or "high nature" women exist among their own. The links between the color white and ideas about "white" blood or sexual effluvia and dryness and wetness are strengthened by Jamaicans' beliefs about the sexual behavior of white women.

UNFULFILLED WOMEN

The image of the insatiable woman comes, in part, from the real woman left unfulfilled. This is partially due to the cultural construction of sex, wherein purely genital contact is permitted and other types of sexuality warned against. To "suck titty," for example, suggests incest and childhood dependence. Although many do manipulate breasts, they are not culturally constructed as sexy and do not figure in ideals for sex. That Jamaican album covers rely almost exclusively on the female backside when seeking to titillate illustrates this.

Although "plenty" women have fine sex lives, because so much is proscribed many finish "the work" with physical "feelings" unabated. Kerr comments on the "split between sex and tenderness" (1963, 90). This might overtly aggravate things when affection is expected, but if not expected, affection may not be consciously missed. Still, the lack of affection expressed sexually adds to the functional nature of sex while lessening the emotional satisfaction it offers. The economics of sex and this lack of affection promote the objectification of women's bodies by women as well as by men (see Blake 1961, 126) as things that exist for men's pleasures. Women's workhorse or donkeylike image is exacerbated by the tendency men have to "jump on and grind," which in turn makes sex even worse for women. The lack of privacy keeps things prototypical, hushed, and speedy, ruling out play, experiments, and anything that might start a scandal.

Letters to newspaper and tabloid advice columns constantly contain queries about women's distaste for sex, their experience of pain from dry penetration, and feelings of unfulfillment. Women who "know" orgasm say that others are "directly ignorant" of the fact of sexual climax. They see themselves as passive receivers and simply feel glad when their men come to them to "discharge." Some know something is missing but do not know how to find it or are afraid to try. Women say that they rarely touch or explore their genitals. Some would in secret, but privacy is scarce. Self-exploration is often out of the question, as is masturbation.

HOMOSEXUALITY

Ideas about lesbian couples, in which one must be the "man" and penetrate the other during sex, follow and perpetuate the cultural model for heterosexual interaction in which "the penis is a great thing" and one for which nothing can truly substitute. Because "two pot lids can't close," a "man" lesbian uses a special stretching oil on her external genitalia to make it like a penis or mounts her woman with a "false." The vagina and penis but not the clitoris receive attention, even in talk regarding lesbian relations.

In addition to adopting top and bottom, penetrant and receptacle roles, lesbians or "sodomites" and gay men or "batty boys" ("batty" refers to the buttocks) also assume male and female subsistence roles, the "top" supporting the "bottom," economically, as s/he can. They enjoy "plenty" sex and are very "selfish," jealous people. The Jamaican tabloids are always full of voyeuristic tales of gay and lesbian passions, and village gossip constantly concerns them. Stories illustrate what happens when self-centered sexual "cravenness" or "puppy shows" of egoistic jealousy get out of hand.

As with abortion, the frequency of homosexuality is hard to ascertain. Such behavior is scorned, and admissions would bring ostracism and even murder. Because of the stigma, I made no systematic inquiry. But at least eight village women I knew took most of their pleasure homosexually. The village had 134 women between the ages of fifteen and forty-four (STATIN 1982), which means that at least one of seventeen women and probably many more have had homosexual experiences. I have no figures for men, and it appears that their homosexuality comes out much less often due to complexities in the male identity-building process (see Chapter 8).

The village woman most infamous for lesbianism, Sarah, was well liked by many young men and by some young women. Other people scorned her, but Sarah was never beaten or strongly accosted. Occasionally (and rarely in public), people might "pass remarks" about her masculine and jealous personality (while she kept many intimate "friends" she allowed her "inside" lover no one else), but Sarah made it a point to "live good" with others so no one had cause to "trace" her experiences. Sarah conversed with men often and held an intermediate position between the male and female worlds, often making asked-for "friending" introductions and answering queries about how women "stay."

Although Sarah did wear pants more frequently than dresses, her appearance had nothing to do with her sexuality. No uniform "sodomite" or "batty boy" style exists. One woman dressed in a particularly masculine fashion, but villagers explained this as showing men her independence and toughness; her heterosexual drives were not in question. Similarly, a man who preferred plaits and one who kept his nails long were not "chatted" as "batty boys"; these affectations were considered simply "a style." The thing most likely to give homosexuals away (short of being caught in the act) is the fact that "sin" eventually wreaks havoc in and on the body. Resultant ill-health bespeaks antisocial deeds.

THE ABILITY TO "KILL" DESIRE

Some women turn to other women for "outside" fulfillment, but most stick with men. Men, however, may fear their inability to "kill" a woman's desire. A man must "kill it" for his woman, or she may malign him as "soft" and might seek another more satisfying lover. She may "shame" him when he cannot fulfill her demand that he "stand 'pon it long." His "uselessness" may become known—she may spread malicious "chat" to undermine his "reputation." Men fear impotence and seek to protect what fragile self-esteem they have created.

Economic conditions keep many men from holding jobs, keeping them from becoming "big men" with houses and beds and wives. For a man who has none of the traditional trappings of the "big man," the penis, especially in its erect state, serves as a natural and economical symbol of masculinity. Some people lamented that circumcision, which makes the penis look a bit as if continually erect and most manly, is seen less often, now that the operation is no longer free. Circumcised or not, erect or flaccid, the penis is ultimately what makes men not women.

The aggressive connotations of the phrase "kill it" and the slang terms for male genitalia that associate the penis with weapons ("wood," "brief knife," or "big bamboo") express the male need to negate the feminine in order to create and sustain their own masculinity. Thus, they "cut" the "panty pudding" and "push the wood." A woman forced onto a bed (in a video shown at the pub) drew audience comments full of bloody imagery: "He got her 'pon cutting board now!"

Women will insult a man for lacking money, a house, and a bed as well as for lacking virility. They generally feel negatively about men and devalue them as people. Most of Brody's respondents called men "all alike," and despite patriarchal teachings, most did not feel themselves less worthy than men (1981, 193). Men resent these sorts of things. They can retaliate for slights anticipated or received by seeking to "hurt" women: men feeling insecure try to outlast women sexually— to "give the agony."

All men guard their fitness, taking precautions to keep their vital "natures" strong and insure against premature ejaculation and impotence. Quick "discharge" is (except when "caused from witchcraft") physically normal, but tonics and such can counteract it. People believe that without potency aids, most men "can't do the work" for more than "five or ten minutes" because sexual intercourse is very taxing. Some resort to magical (and illegal) means to sustain firmer erections for long lengths of time so that even the most demanding woman cries "Cease!"

POTENCY AIDS

Traditional potency medicines are well known and widely used. A variety of modern, imported, chemical substances are also available. Villagers say that perhaps only one in twenty rural men resort to chemical means, but many urban dwellers do. Urban women are more apt to try to "shame" men, rural people said. Besides, urban women more often have "well-stretched" vaginas because they are more "whorish" and supposedly work as prostitutes more often than women "in country." With large vaginas, people reason, city women are hard to satisfy; they ridicule their partners as "useless." Men see large penises, otherwise "dangerous," as necessary in such cases. Through the use of modern chemicals, men can try to fill and outlast the most experienced of women, "hurt" them physically and emotionally, and cause them pain and "shame."

Some potency boosters like "Chiney brush," a concoction of mostly mixed barks made in China, are smuggled in from "foreign." Others are made in laboratories and kitchens within the island. All are expensive by Jamaican standards— "Chiney brush" costs about $45 to $65 (about $10 U.S.)—and can be bought on the streets in Kingston. Some erection nostrums can be purchased in specialized pharmacies. One man told of a trip to a certain pharmacist in a nearby market town. He handed her a small bit of paper on which he had written the name of the substance he wished to buy. He advised me that speaking the name might call what he assumed to be an illegal transaction to people's attention.

People purchasing Obeah oils and other accoutrements for magic and healing also avoid uttering the names of the things they purchase. Obeah has been outlawed since 1898, but many oils, powders, lotions, and the like are legally available. Healers, or "physicians," write "prescriptions," which mystify the procurement process and bolster their power claims. If people think they need a "prescription," they are more likely to patronize healers. If they believe they are engaging in illegal exchanges, they guard their actions, adding to the mystique and so the power of Obeah. Besides, handing a pharmacist a slip of paper hinders others who would "fasten inna you business."

The man above could not raise the full price of purchase, but the pharmacist agreed to sell him half an order for half the full cost. Buying pills "one-one" and not by the bottle is common, as most people have little ready cash. The man bought half of a pellet of "Stone," a brownish chunk or tablet used by rubbing with a damp finger and applying the substance so picked up onto the penis. He paid $30 (about $5.50 U.S.) for what he said would last about three months.

Besides the "Stone," oral pills such as "Boom," a type of amphetamine athletes take and which makes men feel "strong" and "ready," are available. Men, like lesbians, can buy a topical oil for "stretching." Ointments and powders with names like "Bull" and "Stud" may also be purchased.

THE DRAWBACKS OF CHEMICAL PREPARATIONS

Some people fear chemical stamina boosters. Pills like "Boom" leave men with headaches and other aches, feeling very spent. One man confided that using chemicals leads to a physical dependency on them. Others spoke of the danger of finding no outlet for the vital energy induced. They warned of the embarrassment and pain of having to be "cut down" from an erect state by a doctor and spoke of cases in which men's enlarged penises got "stuck" on insertion. A man and woman so bound up must be taken to the hospital where the doctor supposedly must kill the man to save and set free his poor partner.

The fear of everlasting, endangering erections does have some biomedical basis. For example, "Stud 55" and "International" contain Tantaradine, a drug for stud horses. When a man ingests Tantaradine to boost his potency, priapism, a painful condition characterized by a prolonged and rugged erection, can result. The tabloids now and again carry stories about and photos of affected men and their engorged genitalia (see *Weekend Enquirer* 1989a).

NATURAL "TONICS"

Many men choose traditional, homemade, natural "roots tonic" (discussed in Chapter 3) instead of directly aggressive chemicals. The word *roots* refers to nature, the bush lands, the earth, and her bounties. Anything "roots" is "real" and "natural" as opposed to things made of chemicals or grown with fertilizers. "Roots tonic" is prepared from things set on this earth for human beings by God, so it is both good and necessary. And "roots tonic," from nature, is for "nature": it promotes vital libidos by enriching, cleansing, and strengthening the blood.

Jamaicans subscribe to an ethnophysiology in which rich, healthy blood means a strong libido. "Fit" individuals have strong "natures," bespeaking healthy blood. The fortification concoctions they make for their blood and essential vitality are, like those of the Europeans, called "tonics." Any pharmaceutical blend bearing the title "tonic" is understood to function similarly. Many of these are iron preparations which do enhance strength, relieving anemia. For "nature," though, natural "roots tonics" are highly preferred.

AMBIVALENT GENDER RELATIONS

Men claim a dominant social status but cannot live up to the standards they have set because of socioeconomic constraints. Cultural beliefs and values that encourage laziness, duplicity, and spending sprees exacerbate this. So does the "obsessive" dependency mothers promote (Clarke 1957, 163–64) and the expectation that men will have many sexual partners; these factors lead men to disperse resources among several households rather than fully supporting any one.

For the most part, women find men "too terrible" and "irresponsible" and devalue them as a group. Men often do treat women unkindly and abusively; part of the reason for their irresponsible behavior is compensatory. Lacking self-esteem and harboring aggression toward women, men compete for ascendency even in sex, an arena in which satisfying women can pose quite a challenge because of cultural ideas surrounding it.

Both men and women are ambivalent about intergender relations. Men know that they are essentially meal tickets and capitalize on this. Women capitalize on their own bodies. Men fear being used economically while women fear sexual and reproductive abuse. Conjugal unions are ultimately justified economically, but because of the value placed on enduring solidarity and selfless sharing, the idea of buying and selling sex is distasteful. This reality is concealed through references to moral, kinshiplike bonds. These function ideologically, promoting sociability and stable reciprocal relations that endure over time. If the pretense crumbles, so can the relationship. Economic concerns are then exposed and become topics for negotiation until the instrumental health of a relationship is resolved (or the relationship is ended).

The culturally promoted mystification of the instrumental dimension of sex creates a situation in which women become dependents and debtors, because the sex they trade is made to seem like an owed gift given in return for "supportance." Henry and Wilson note the prevalence of the "theme of the dependent woman and her offspring in constant search of a male on whom they can rely" (1975, 172). Because women's work has less monetary value than men's (see Massiah 1988; Senior 1991), they must accept gifts from men graciously. As mates, women must be monogamous since men "own" them. Men fear both having to support the children other men sire and living up to the sexual expectations other men may engender in their women.

Jamaicans feel ambivalent about relationships because they fear that instrumental motives are behind them. For men this fear is stronger because, even though male power is allowed overt expression, often with physical force, women have more magical potency and greater power to "tie" than men. The following chapters explore how this is so.

Digging a grave

PART
FIVE

"Bad Bellies"

Chapter 12

Menstrual Taboos and Binding "Ties"*

Ambivalence about relationships and the motives of others is neatly revealed in the fear of being "tied." The custom of "tying" is built on notions about kinship, procreation, and parent-child relationships. Frightening for all because it raises questions about independence as well as egoism and altruism, "tying" scares men more than women. Because of their reproductive role, women have access to the most potent means to "tie" and so to compel action. Menstrual taboos stem from this "natural" fact.

INTERGENDER DEPENDENCE AND VOLUNTARY RELATIONS

People resent the façade of altruism demanded by traditional kinship ideals, although they are quick to call on it in

---

*This chapter is based upon Elisa J. Sobo's essay ""Unclean Deeds': Menstrual Taboos and Binding 'Ties' in Rural Jamaica" in Mark Nichter's *Anthropological Approaches to the Study of Ethnomedicine* (© 1992, New York: Gordon and Breach, Science Publishers) and is included by courtesy of the publisher.

self-interest. Ambivalence, resentment, and suspicion of the egoistic underpinnings of relationships surface in fears about the poisons through which "unclean" individuals initiate self-serving relationships or alter healthy, mutually beneficial ones to suit themselves. Men have deep concerns about being poisoned and controlled because, according to cultural ideals, they hold money and others seek it. They are particularly concerned about being taken advantage of by women.

Cultural ideals make men providers and women the dependent receivers of men's support. In reality, as seen in the previous chapters, many men have problems providing and many remain dependent on women. Childrearing practices that engender strong bonds help bring about this dependency. Traditions such as the "free mentality" and the expectation of male irresponsibility deter men from seeking secure jobs. So does the bad economy.

Women resent having to keep up a conjugal bargain (by cooking, washing, etc.) when male financial obligations are not fulfilled. They resent being treated as beasts of burden and as "seed" receptacles when resources are given to their men's "outside" girlfriends. Woman seek the devotion of employed, responsible mates. A partnership with such a man is enviable as it eases a woman's daily struggle and enhances her status accordingly. If one woman "grudges" another, chances are it will be for her man and, ultimately, the financial "supportance" and social "respectability" he provides her.

Men know that they often undercompensate or take advantage of women, and many do feel badly. Through talk of the female practice of "tying," men can deny their shortcomings as breadwinners and can project their exploitive tendencies back onto women. Moreover, the discourse on "tying" allows men to express their resentment of kin and kinlike demands.

While kin are involuntarily bound to and obliged to one another through irrevocable blood ties, conjugal partners are not kin: their bonds are elected. Sociable partners do ask things of each other, but they do not "take advantage" or seek control. Good people do appeal to the understood rights and obligations that inhere in relationships, but a good relationship sours when partners feel that they have forfeited their freedom. When "tied" by a woman, a man's autonomy is stolen so that his resources and devotion can be secured. His sense of obligation toward this "wife" is then not really his own, and his "willingness" is taken advantage of.

Any "tie" arrived at by "unclean" means and meant solely for the benefit of the other is "unnatural" and undesirable. The fear of lost liberty and the resentment of forced actions that surface in talk about "tying" reflects ideals for nonkin relationships that are not only a foil for kinship expectations but are also a reaction to the legacy of slavery. This fear and resentment was discussed earlier in relation to binding contracts (like that which marriage involves). "Big men" are supposed to call in debts, not pay them off. Sexist expectations exacerbate the male fear of "tying": "big men" rule their women, not the reverse.

WOMEN'S "TRICKS" AND THE "POWER IN THE BLOOD"

Men see women as connivers. Recall the comments "passed" about women politicians "tying" constituents and using old bath water for cooking when they want to "fix a thing." Female expressions of power are culturally curtailed. Men may make demands; women must manipulate. The experiences each gender has of the other's power differ accordingly.

Men may use brute force, as in rape. They can also exercise jural power and give orders. When they wish to impose their desires inconspicuously (as when "turning" the "minds" of others in an "unnatural" way), they generally seek the help of a sorcery specialist. Women, however, because of cultural expectations and an ethnophysiological advantage, can "fix" many things by themselves—with their own blood. Like any poison, this is secretly added to people's food. Women prepare the food men eat and men hold the coveted money, and so men have reason to fear women's power.

Women are harder than men to poison orally. For one thing, many women rarely take drinks in bars, where anyone might drop something in. For another, cooking is women's work. As women cook, they rarely eat from others. A woman knows what goes into her "family pot." She "shares out" food, sees it move from pot to plate, and need not fear magical additions. But a man can only trust the woman who cooks for him not to add "magic" or avert her eyes long enough for another to do so. "Anything could happen," people say; "bad mind and grudgeful" endeavors are rampant.

Traditionally, menstruating women do not cook and are considered "unclean." This is due to more than mere hygienic fears: menstrual blood provides the most potent means of "compellance." Men must rely on Obeah and other forms of magic to compel, but women can "tie" men to them and thus secure their love and money by collecting their own menstrual blood for use in preparing food.[1] This is easily done by squatting over a steaming pot. The hot steam helps gravity to ease out some of the menses. Sometimes, used menstrual rags are soaked in water to loosen the blood which is then "queezed" (wrung out). Quantities can be collected and stored for later use.

The most commonly adulterated food is rice and peas, a reddish-brown dish. A woman can steam herself directly over the pot as she finishes cooking this. Red pea soup, carrot juice, "stew-peas," and potato pudding are also known as potential menses carriers. All are the correct color and are commonly eaten. Some men are so frightened of ingesting menses that they refuse even red herring, a dried fish which they say takes its color from having been killed when menstruating. As careful as men are, menstrual blood diluted in food cannot be tasted. As one woman said, laughing about the small amount needed to compel, "Cho—you think that little bit can flavor pot?"

Behavioral changes can indicate "tying" but not everyone can sense these. A small overdose, however, or the continued ingestion of menstrual blood signals itself in a "bad belly" that seems to have no cause and looks "funny" (owing to its shape, accompanying symptoms, persistence, etc.). Massive overdoses can bring death. Women must exert care when trying to "tie." They take comfort in knowing that, because of its "natural" quality, ingested blood evades the biomedical doctor's or coroner's detection.

UNCLE'S CASE

Menstrual rhetoric is often used to confirm or legitimize claims concerning preexisting, problematic conjugal relations. One man, Uncle, sensed strife in his relationship with his common-law wife and soon became alarmed by chronic "belly" pain. In the kitchen, he stumbled upon a vial of dark, viscous liquid. A visit to an Obeah specialist confirmed his suspicion that, because she loved him so much and with such jealousy, his "wife" had been trying to "tie" him to her by cooking with her menstrual blood. This explained the strife (not being fully "tied," he felt "contrary") and the "belly" pain and justified Uncle's concern. Had he not put a stop to things, the buildup of menstrual toxins in his "belly" would have killed him.

It seems that Uncle's long-time "wife" had become too demanding; Uncle felt that their relationship had ceased being mutually beneficial. The "bad belly" physically represented his sense that too many demands were being made of him. Indeed, his partner's desire to control his decisions regarding what he would do for her brought the sickness on to begin with. Before Uncle's "bad belly," he had no palpable reason for deserting his "wife": she had cooked and cleaned well and had never "slept out." But her "trick" gave him just cause to leave her. In her rush to "bend" his "mind," the man's "wife" had administered too much of her poison, so exposing her own dirty deed.

BLOOD "TIES"

As babes are bound to mothers through the intake of mothers' blood both in the womb and at the breast, so too are those men who unknowingly eat blood-infused food bound to the women who provide it. The sociable mother-child kin-bonding model underlies the powerful connotations of blood. It adds to the significance of sharing food and accounts for "tying's" mechanism.

Real kinship is substantial: it is based on shared blood. People of "one blood" share "one mind" and are of "one accord." The kinship bond between a mother and a child is "tied" with her blood which, incorporated into the body of the child, physically compels seemingly altruistic actions. Fed to and incorporated into the bodies of desired husbands by aspiring or insecure surrogate mothers/wives, menstrual blood works as it does for the biological mother who uses it to "grow" her fetus. It "ties" the man to her just as it "ties" a child to its mother. The ambivalence men feel for their mothers resurfaces in "tying" and, because now they really are having sex with the women who feed them, incest is implicated. Moreover, men ingesting menstrual blood selfishly (even if not through their own volition) eat what should have nourished their own offspring, an idea that causes more distress.

All this helps explain the traditional taboo on a "babyfather" eating food prepared by his "babymother's" postpartum helper. Traditionally, a new mother's mother takes over for her during her baby's first nine weeks or so, giving her time to "knit up" her loosened joints and safely "close" her stretched "tube." Childbirth and the need for support it entails can motivate a woman to "tie" a man, and afterbirth blood could work as an especially strong "tying" agent. Its connection with procreation and fetal nourishment is patent. The helper would have this blood on her hands from washing the "babymother's" clothing and maternity "clat" (blood rags) and might, with or without intent, contaminate food as she cooks.

MENSTRUAL TABOOS REINTERPRETED

As Buckley and Gottlieb point out in their review of the study of menstrual taboos, anthropologists have too quickly attributed menstrual taboos to the "inherent pollution of the female principle" (1988, 39). Since the "pollution theory" used to illuminate menstrual taboos has itself been fashioned on data concerning these, past work has "tended toward redundancy" (4). Another shortcoming of past scholarship identified in Buckley and Gottlieb is the reliance on universal, monocausal explanations for what is more likely to be "overdetermined by a plethora of psychological, ecological, and social facts."[2] But "menstrual taboos are cultural constructions and must first be approached as such" (24).

The positive meanings of menstruation and the fact that women may benefit from certain menstrual taboos has generally been ignored. So has the idea that the meanings of menstrual blood rest on ethnophysiological explanations regarding its reproductive function.[3] Rural Jamaican notions about the power of menstrual blood are certainly tied to its procreative role and so to its kinship function.

Men refuse to eat from the pots of "unclean" women because of a fear of "unclean deeds." It is a mistake to equate this kind of "uncleanliness" solely with simple pollution. Menstrual taboos are more complex than that. Although temporal uncleanliness does figure in menstrual beliefs, the scrupulousness with which cooks wash hands indicates that "slackness" during menstruation would have to be intentional. The possibility of having and acting on this intent in order to "tie" is central to menstruating women's "unclean" state, as "unclean deeds" means sorcery. The label "unclean" expresses the ambivalences and resentments many people have about the power mothers exert over children by virtue of their blood, exposing this power's potentially self-centered, instrumental, "unclean" dimension.

Calling menstruating women "unclean" mystifies women's power and at the same time shames them. It moves attention away from their "natural" abilities to the fact that menstrual blood emanates from their lower regions, where waste leaves. It associates menstrual blood with "dirt" and so lowers women's self-esteem, highlighting women's "nasty" state and "trickify," antisocial character. Rather than celebrating the positive aspects of their powers, it associates them with those "unclean" people who deal with black magic.

Only those who "live clean" and act out of pure altruism can have socially sanctioned power. So references to "uncleanliness" may be employed to check women's claims to ascendency. If a woman gets "bright" (uppity), one need only "remind her of the last thing she wore": her "raas clat" or "pussy clat" (her menstrual cloth or pad).

"RAWNESS" AND MENSTRUAL PROSCRIPTIONS

The temporal "uncleanliness" of the menses supports the idea that menstruating women should "stay a yard." On menstrual days, women have a sense of smelling "raw" and "nasty." They used to rely on "clat" (cloth) to absorb their flows and, upon leaving the yard, had to carry another "clat" and something to hold the used one. They feared others might notice the stink (heightened by the tropical heat) and think them "nasty." Although women today use disposable sanitary napkins (not tampons, which involve touching the genitals and arouse ideas related to intercourse), worries about odor, inconveniences, and unwanted attention live on. Schoolgirls speak of the humiliation of having to "beg" permission to use whatever toilet facilities exist and fear they smell "raw" while menstruating. As children they learned the importance of bodily cleanliness; many prefer to stay home.

MENSTRUAL BLOOD'S POLLUTING CONTENTS

Menstruation's "rawness" stems from its role in washing old semen and lingering "discharge" out of the female reproductive organs. The blood of menstruation, like the water of sweat, is itself pure and clean; "dirt" is what it carries. One old woman used an analogy in explaining the menses: the river is clean but the mud at the bottom is dirty. The vagina is a river-like conduit in which water equals clean blood, and mud semen.

Unused, semen symbolizes death and social breakdown as it does not get transformed into a child and does not help reproduce society. Moreover, like other potentially toxic or physically polluting things, semen can rot and become a source of contagion. Women can handle this because of how "God made they." Men try to keep clean, taking tea to purify and drinking "plenty beer" to flush out poison just as women do through menstruation. But the male body was not made to deal with defiling semen.

Between monthly cleansings women's bodies harbor male "discharge." Most of the stuck semen is far up the "tube," but men can come in contact with a little bit of semen during sex. Since it is not "plenty" and does not penetrate into their "bellies" it does no harm to their health. But as cunnilingus (also called to "eat under the two-legged table" in reference to woman's food-giving role and the link between sex and eating) involves the ingestion of sexual effluvia, with oral sex some semen from a woman's last sexual encounter can enter the male gut.

As with anal sex, effluvia discharged during oral sex has no "natural" destination in the recipient's body, and procreation is impossible. Sex can be recreational, but the possibility of procreating should be inherent in the act. The ethnophysiological dangers of cunnilingus (and fellatio) are used to justify proclamations of its ascribed immorality. Semen and the other waste passed out in vaginal "discharge" can "sick" if enough of it ends up in men's "bellies" or other body parts. A group of men attributed a (verified) rise in throat cancer to an increasing "slackness" with regard to oral sex. One man who worked in a nearby market town estimated that 10 percent of men now risk their health to perform cunnilingus, although they can never boast about it or even admit it. Others volunteer that the sorts of men who do this live only in urban areas and have experience with foreign women, who they say introduced oral sex to the island.

If men could menstruate—if their bodies were as efficient as women's at removing toxins and keeping clean—cunnilingus would not be such a problem. But men cannot menstruate and must rely solely on cleansing teas and "building" tonics for self-protection. These cannot keep men well if they insist on "carelessness." Oral sex with a prostitute or promiscuous woman (as opposed to with a faithful "wife") is one example of extremely foolish behavior: another's rotten semen is much more dangerous than one's own septic "discharge" because of its difference from one's own substances.

Old semen pollutes but cannot "tie" like menstrual blood. Neither can new: semen is a relatively weak obligating substance because father-child ties are never as highly charged as mother-child relations. Its other dangers notwithstanding, women can perform fellatio with minimal fear of having their "minds bent" by semen (men say that most men do not desire this service). And men do not worry that the little semen passed out when a girlfriend "discharges" or the mass passed out in menstrual blood can "tie" them to women's other lovers. The ideas of indirect bonding or homosexual contact seem logical, considering the cultural construction of consubstantial kinship, but prove far too frightening to exist anywhere but in the unconscious.

WHEN "WHITE" BLOOD "TIES"

The bit of rotting semen it contains can cannot "tie," but ingested female "discharge" itself can obligate just like menstrual blood. When carrying an egg—and many feel that female "discharge" always does so—female "white" blood can bind people just as tightly as red. A man performing oral sex can eat his lover's egg and incorporate it into his own body. All who give oral sex are "cannibals" and antisocial beings who invert the preferred order by "eating" potential children.

Having no womb, a man cannot "grow" an egg into a baby. He could, however, mesh with what would have been his lover's child, so becoming like her son as he would if he ingested her red (menstrual) blood. In this fashion, cunnilingus can "tie man like donkey" just as menstrual magic can. Because of this and because of the power of vaginal secretions to "sick," people were aghast at a tabloid account of a corporation where bosses searched women's vaginas for contraband in the canteen—a place where people must eat (*Weekend Enquirer* 1989b). They worried over this and not the unfair and exploitive aspects of the practice.

THE DANGEROUS VAGINA

Men can use talk of the perils of cunnilingus to promote genital sex. The following tale makes clear the dangers associated with vaginal secretions. A robbery occurred in which several "idlers" stole a large amount of cash from a woman who worked "in foreign" and had returned home to the village for a visit. One of the young thieves gave a big wad of bills to a lover, who decided to take a bus to Kingston. She hid the money inside her vagina, or so the story goes. On a tip, the police stopped the bus, took her in for questioning, stripped and searched her, and found the money. Thinking this a tale about corruption, I asked the storyteller if the victim got her money back. He looked at me with wide-eyed shock: that money, stored as it was, could kill a person, he said—no one would want that cash. Amazed at my naïveté, he declared it a good thing police found the money. Each dollar spent would endanger the life and the "mind" of the one who accepted it because of where it was stashed.

HEALTH, PRAGMATISM, AND MENSTRUAL TABOOS ON SEX

Even a "most high nature" man would never have intercourse with a menstruating woman—or at least he would never admit to having done so knowingly. Upon menstruation, the majority of muddying semen is washed down and out of the vagina, making sexual intercourse at this time "careless." Any contact with menstrual blood is dangerous because of the weight of compelling and sickening poisons it contains.

Taboos on sex during menstruation keep men from direct physical contact with harmful, polluting substances and the powerful, obligating blood of reproduction. Men know that only a fluke would allow it to penetrate their bodies but are still scared: "Anything could happen." It might seep in through "pulps" (pores) opened up by "the work," for example. By avoiding sex with menstruating women men also avoid the sight of blood on their penises, which can suggest castration. This terrifies men who, lacking other avenues to manhood, locate their very masculinity and social adulthood in their genitals.

Taboos give women a justification for refusing to allow men "'pon belly," whether their disinterest stems from cramps and other cyclical changes which can make penetration painful or other factors, such as fatigue, messiness (washing is women's work), or boredom with a man's technique. Taboos also protect women, "open" from the "heat" and "looseness" menstruating entails, from "catching up draft" and "taking up cold."

But even menstruating women may need "the work." Prostitutes can supposedly stop their periods by drinking laundry bluing diluted in water or by inserting it vaginally when they "see the blood." It seems that bluing whitens menstrual blood as it bleaches clothing stains. The belief that women put bluing in their vaginas to "sick" men probably exists as an extension of this: even "clear" (light-colored) menses must carry contaminating things and may still be able to compel action. Unmarked—not reddish—it might gain entrance to the "belly" of a man with his guard down.

People abstaining from sex during menstruation avoid subjecting themselves to culturally salient "raw" odors, associated with decay and death. Strong odors are vested with much meaning in traditional thought. Through scent, especially a "bad smell, like something old," one can tell that a duppy "deh about." And Obeah workers supposedly have a typical "pungent" smell (Barrett 1976, 76). Sexual sweat and effluvia can raise quite an odor—especially in the heat of the day or during or just before a woman's menstrual period (female villagers report that their bodily odors become "higher" then). People believe that the pungency of sex lingers and reveals their "business." During menstruation, the stench of sweat and sex would be "higher," "renker," and even more likely to bring shame. The maintenance of "respect" necessitates sexual abstinence during this period.

POSITIVE ASSOCIATIONS

Villagers who gamble on the "drop pan" lottery know that no. 4 means "monthly period" and "blood." It also signifies "wine," "egg," "breast," and "sexual intercourse" (Chevannes 1989, 48). Wine, blood, eggs, breast milk, and sexual substances are all potentially life-giving if not misused, "raw," or "nasty." Wine, associated with the "cleansing blood of the lamb" or Jesus also "builds" human blood, and blood is often called "wine." Protein-rich eggs which, if left under brooding hens, hatch into living chicks, also "build." Menstruating or seeing one's "health" is itself a precursor of new life because of its preparatory cleansing function. When sexual substances—sperm and egg—mingle, "God bless the womb" with a baby. The breast and mother's milk provide a life source for the newborn (and breast milk creates or augments consubstantial kinship). With additional members, society reproduces itself and carries on.

As "drop pan" associations reveal, even though menstrual taboos highlight the "unclean" and negative, menstruation has a "clean" or positive dimension too. Its socially and physically beneficial functions include preparing the body for childbearing and keeping it clean. Menstrual taboos also have positive aspects. They can be used by women to protect power positions within the yard and also to safeguard their conjugal relationships. They perpetuate ideas about female abilities to manipulate, which on one level empower women.

WHEN WOMEN SUPPORT MENSTRUAL TABOOS

Fearing women's power (and intention) to "tie," men promote taboos that keep menstruating women away from their food. This requires the collusion of women, and collude they do—when they see the benefit. A shopkeeper would not close shop, nor would a woman with no one to help cook put away her pot. Taboos can easily be broken because people cannot always know who is menstruating: women do not advertise their cycles. Also, malnutrition, conception, lactation, depression, and other conditions can suppress ovulation. Regular four-week periods are far from inevitable.

Miss Reeny laughed when asked if menstruating bothered women: "If anything, they glad to see it. Means they can left from fireside." The ban on cooking during menstruation allows women a period of rest from this chore. Most rural Jamaicans do not say, as U.S. women would, that menstruation brings relief by confirming nonpregnancy. Nor do they dwell on the bodily irritations that can accompany menstruation. Women do have aches, as folk knowledge shows: marigold (*Bidens reptans*) tea eases cramps and sinkle bible (*Aloe vera*) tea or a drink made by soaking its scrapings in water eases nausea and other small "belly" troubles. But Jamaican women do not think about dysmenorrhea until reminded and, even then, not much unless they experience unusually severe discomfort. Instead, they think about the pleasures and drawbacks that accompany being "unclean."

Menstrual taboos have social uses beyond those that stem directly from the ethnophysiological ideas underlying them. Old women can exercise power over younger ones by demanding they submit to the taboos. The high status postmenopausal women enjoy rests, in part, on their "cleanliness," which they highlight by emphasizing the "uncleanliness" of young women who might otherwise usurp their positions. Moreover, by keeping girls ignorant of all but the barest details of menstruation, older women invest it with the sacredness that accompanies secrecy, making knowledge of it a valuable tool for bonding between older females.

Women can make use of the power their vaginas and vaginal secretions contain in other ways, too. A woman stepped over a pan of food and exposed it (and its owner, her brother) to the "unclean" power emanating from her vagina, rendering it unhealthy (not to mention potentially obligating), and sending a definitely aggressive message to him. (He did not eat it.)

By making men aware of the threat inherent in menstrual blood, women try to reduce the chances of their men taking food (and sex) from unknown women who might steal them away by "tying" them. Even without blood and for reasons stated in Chapter 4, food-sharing symbolizes relatedness. A woman sharing food with an unrelated man indicates the likelihood of intimacy. A man expects to give a woman something useful in exchange for cooking and sexual services, but that woman can "tie" him to ensure that this happens. It is women's hope that the fear of this will keep their men coming home for dinner and keep them from readily creating new relationships (and so incurring financial obligations) by sharing a "next woman's" food. Ideally, the fear of menstrual "uncleanliness" helps keep a man's money flowing to his regular conjugal partner.

Women have a vested interest in men believing in their power for it promises to help them control and "hold onto" their men. Talk of the danger of menstruation mobilizes the male anxieties mentioned earlier and so promotes the female ideal of male sexual and financial fidelity; the threat of "tying" should work like the threat of menstrual irregularity that helps keep women faithful. But the structural function that menstrual symbolism should serve in advancing conjugal stability and so ensuring the continuity of resource allocation is undermined by other cultural factors such as the expectation (upon which male reputations depend) that men have many lovers.

While they may not be able to stop adultery, women at least can lower the social standings of their competitors through gossip about "nastiness" and "bad habits." They can try to ensure that their rivals be excluded from female reciprocity networks and social circles by convincing members that these rivals are dangerous and will try to usurp their men. Attempting to protect their interests and manipulate social relations, women use menstrual rhetoric against each other. While ruining others' reputations, women represent themselves as morally upstanding and respectable; they make the claim that, unlike the maligned rivals, they pose no threat to other women and so are worthy of social support.

In using talk of "unclean" female power to control members of their own gender and gain status women unwittingly participate in a system of oppression and male dominance that limits their authority and leads them to consider "tying" men to begin with. But this dimension of menstrual discourse generally remains unseen, overshadowed by the more immediate and practical benefits that menstrual taboos bring women and also by the psychological value of the belief in female power. Women's talk of their power can fuel a sense of independence from men. Seen in this light, women's support of menstrual taboos perpetuates "ideas of self-management and autonomy" that substantiate women's "collective self-representation" as powerful social actors (Brody 1985, 176)—actors who are, in certain circumstances and to a certain degree, able to control their lives.

MEN'S VESTED INTERESTS

Its health and social benefits notwithstanding, menstruation confirms that semen is being washed out instead of "ingrafted," and this upsets men. They like the thought of reproducing more than women do: on the average, men beginning their reproductive careers desire 2.8 children while beginning women want only 2.2 (Powell and Jackson 1988, xv). Menstrual taboos reinforce female shame about their genitals and help instill in them a lack of willingness to even think about their reproductive organs. This means many women do little to guard themselves from pregnancy, which benefits men who want to impregnate them. It also means that many women do not think to ask for sexual gratification, which benefits men unable or unwilling to comply. Indeed, taboos gain most support today from men.

Taboos guard men from unhealthy or dangerous "raw" things and from having to acknowledge their lack of procreative power, which semen washed away confirms. More importantly, taboos protect men from being "tied" by women who would add their menstrual blood to cooking pots. This is why men are so adamant about keeping menstruants from preparing food. Women who gain by maintaining patterns of resource allocation also support this belief.

Knowing a mate's cycle helps a man stay undefiled (and un-"tied"). But many women do not bleed punctually. Noticeably irregular schedules are attributed to infidelity (and men can justifiably abandon women for this). The body, confused by so much different foreign matter, purges itself irregularly. Knowledge of this keeps many women faithful; none want to risk having their sins physically announced with each capricious period.

Fear of having intercourse during menstruation is private business. To admit and to speak openly of the "bad belly" that "tying" can bring would expose a belief in "superstitions." People claim these ideas are outmoded, but they are still widely held. The next chapters explore explanations and solutions for another "bad belly," the unwanted pregnancy, which can be either humanly or "unnaturally" induced. Both this and the "bad belly" of "tying" reflect and express inter-gender tensions rooted in a cultural system that pits "family" against "strangers," altruism against egoism, and society against the individual.

Chapter 13

To "Dash Away Baby," "Wash Away Belly"

While men fear the unwelcome obligations of "tying" and the dangerous "bad belly" it brings, women fear the "bad belly" of an inauspicious pregnancy: the unwanted baby. "Belly-women" might be pregnant "for" duppies as well as "for" humans, and babies may be "troubled" in the womb so that monsters no mother could love are created. There are ways to "wash" such pregnancies away.

"CLEAN" AND CAUTIOUS LIVING

"Clean" living is "good" living—altruistic living which perpetuates the social and moral order. Those "right with God" have been washed of the self-centered sinfulness that the "unclean" wicked retain. Because "sin" would undermine the social and moral order it is denigrated and targeted for purges. "Sin" also undermines physical well-being, as do blockages and other disagreeable substances; purging such matter from the body is essential to health. Incorrigibly wicked individuals are sometimes "run" from a community.

245

PART FIVE

Like "dirt" they should get swept away by the broom of social morality. Individual physical pathologies and social pathologies—and their cures—are homologous (Taylor 1988).

Antisocial leanings often gain covert expression. Childhood training promotes the rechanneling of antisocial aggression from superiors toward other targets (see Cohen 1955). It also engenders ideas about manipulating would-be bosses so that one's own wishes can be realized. Children learn early that the very food that "builds" a person can be used to covertly convey "unclean" substances. Uncomfortable about their own antisocial feelings, people project them. They know that despite an overt belief in the value of altruism, "bad mind" wishes of others are rampant. As a result, people are wary of nearly everyone but their closest kin (and at times, they are even wary of them).

Menstruation's "uncleanliness" has to do with belief in the ability and inclination of women to use their menstrual blood wickedly as "compellance" poison, to "tie" others to them. "Uncleanliness" indexes antisocial possibilities in the menstruating women themselves, not just the connections between "raw" menstrual blood and sepsis, rot, or death.

Women do not fear "tying" like men do because, unlike men, women cook for themselves, lack the male's role expectation of independence (although they can and do attain it), and are not very vulnerable to semen as a binding poison. Women do talk about being "tied" through Obeah by men who have nothing to give them but beatings. Many take precautions, such as not drinking from opened bottles and guarding their underclothes which, if ritually buried in a man's yard, can compel a woman to stay with him. But because women are seen as plentiful "like rice grain" and since men tend to overtly express power, the likelihood of this scenario is low, and people know it.

THE VAGINA AND THE PENETRATION OF EVIL

What women fear is the vaginal penetration of undesirable matter. The vagina is the orifice that receives things from men.

Gifts or exchanges, including those of sexual substances, involve rights and obligations. And since social relations generally exist in an unegalitarian fashion (as opposed to idealized, selfless, horizontal parity), occasions for exchange, including sex , can be used to inflict harm just as easily as to establish or renew trust.

The "buddy mouth" takes in male "discharge." "Discharge" is a kind of food: it "grows" babies, as does female blood, and it ends up in a woman's "belly" (where the "baby bag" is). In the "belly," substances mingle, and good food gets converted into bodily components. Foul substances, however, generate sickness. Just as such substances may reach the "belly" through the "food mouth," they may reach it through the "buddy mouth" too. Foul substances include semen from irresponsible or otherwise contemptible men and "bad" air or "discharge" left by spirits. Such dangerous matter—and the babies and ties it can entail—must be "cut" to restore one's physical health and to maintain one's social well-being.

THE GENERAL CONTEXT OF UNDESIRED PREGNANCIES

The "discharge" of a "natural," living man is a disagreeable intrusion if it "catches" in a woman who does not want a baby. She then experiences pregnancy as a form of "bad belly," and she may seek to end it. If she does, she must do so covertly: abortion is not condoned.

Consubstantial kin circles are strengthened and recreated with the addition of children. With no procreation, networks would crumble. People who abort do not add to their family circles. Instead, they "wash away baby" or "dash away pickney" with abortion techniques that follow the general purgative model for health.

To "dash away" something means to spill it or spoil it. Children who spill milk or drop food are often scolded as they "dash away" valued, life-supporting things. People who have not met in a long time often accost each other, asking "Why you throw me away?" or, "So, you dash me away!" To "dash away" anyone means to ignore a relationship and its ensuing obligations. To really do so could be foolish: survival depends upon maintaining network links.

Procreation is also important as it is the basis for social adulthood. Without having children—and without caring for them responsibly—self-esteem and the respect of others cannot be attained. The social value of responsible parenting is paramount: adulthood is confirmed through the assumption of responsibility for others. Having children allows for this because children require care.

Measured against the general cultural ideology of altruism and kinship obligations, abortion is not an acceptable option: it represents opposition to the social and moral order. Indeed, it is (with few exceptions) illegal. But abortion is practiced, and the laws against it are "rarely if ever enforced" (Smith and Johnson 1978, 242).

UNPLANNED PREGNANCIES AND THE FREQUENCY OF ABORTION

Unplanned pregnancies are frequent because people are reluctant to use contraceptives and because, not properly informed, they misuse them. Three out of four pregnant women surveyed in 1989 by government agents reported their pregnancies to be mistimed (55 percent) or actually unwanted (20 percent) (Althaus 1991, 32). Although most would never admit to it, many villagers, clinicians, and folk-practitioners claim that the majority of women have had or will have abortions. One person, for example, estimated eight out of ten, another guessed three of four, and one other said 95 percent had done so. The latter estimate seems inflated yet it was not given flippantly; however, the Jamaican tendency to suspect others of carrying out self-centered, evil missions might explain this and other grand figures reported to me.

Most authorities officially oppose the view that abortion is common. A family planning nurse, for example, claimed only one in one hundred islanders would "do that thing." In another typical instance, two workers at family planning headquarters in Kingston told me that no Jamaican woman would abort.

We had been talking for about five minutes when one of the woman looked intently at the other, then locked her eyes with mine. After nervously apologizing that theirs was a family planning and not an abortion association and clarifying that these were their personal and uneducated opinions, she and her colleague began to share their experiences. They cast at least one out of two women as aborters. Their estimate was low in comparison with rural guesses; schooled and well-off, these women are likely to have known more people who opted for (and knew how to use) "the planning" than most villagers did.

Nurses and midwives believe that illegal abortions are more common than miscarriages (Smith and Johnson 1978, 250). MacCormack refers to the "large" proportion of "septic abortions" seen by clinicians (1985, 281). Husting (cited in Smith and Johnson 1978, 251n) estimates that 15,000 to 25,000 abortions were performed in 1972. Brody refers to but does not specify the source(s) of "estimates of illegally performed procedures" that "range up to 25,000 yearly" (1981, 51). As there was an average of about 60,000 live births each year during the 1970s (STATIN 1988a, 35), it is possible that between 20 and 30 percent of all pregnancies—or about one out of four—were aborted. So, although most of the estimates I was given were probably too high, the available data supports assertions that abortion happens often.

ABORTION IN SPECIFIC CONTEXTS

Many women terminate pregnancies illegally, and many more may long to do so but do not act. The village abortionist, who befriended me before she knew what I was in the area for and far before I knew that this was one of her many occupations, would vouch for that. Despite its general cultural meaning, certain circumstances make abortion a desirable option and exceptions to the rules are made.

As Schlegel (1990) notes in reference to inconsistencies in the intracultural meaning of gender, seeming contradictions make sense when the context in which meanings are assigned is considered. Following Schlegel's model, the general abortion ideology must be viewed within the context of the total ideology of the culture. But a specific abortion's meaning—as opposed to the meaning of abortion in general— is arrived at within a specific context: what Schlegel describes as "a particular location in the social structure or within a particular field of action" (24). This helps to explain why abortions are sometimes performed even though they are, in general, not condoned.

Villagers told me of many situations in which abortion is justifiable. Often, "babyfathers" refuse to or cannot support their progeny, leaving "babymothers" very burdened. While some men simply abandon their "babymothers," those who pay for intercourse directly have no obligation to support the offspring to begin with. With no financial help, a woman might try abortion. She might also try it if she has been raped or beaten by the "babyfather," or if he simply changes for the worse. In such situations, a woman may not want to ally herself with a man through a child.

A woman involved in a long-term union who gets pregnant while her man is away can abort to preserve the integrity of her marriage and to increase her chances for receiving continued support from her mate. An employed woman who gets pregnant often tries to get an abortion so that she can keep her job. Jobs enable women to feed the children they already have. Another child can increase a woman's responsibility to the point where she cannot bear or fulfill it. Villagers' views support Brody's suggestion that women's use of abortion increases with successive pregnancies (1981, 51).

Often, a mother-to-be is herself a child: Brody found a median age of sixteen for first pregnancies (1981, 153). One-fourth of all live births are to girls nineteen or younger (STATIN 1988a, 48). Even though pressure to prove one's fertility is great, many girls would rather stay in school than have a baby (school rules bar pregnant girls from classes). They believe that education improves their future ability to care for children well. Many know that their own caretakers cannot help them to shoulder the burdens of motherhood. People dislike abortion, but many reasons can lead girls and women to think of a fetus as a kind of "blockage" to be rid of.

With abortion, undesirable matter is cleansed from the "belly" of a woman "sick" with child. Potentially draining obligations to a baby that would impede rather than enable the flow of resources between kin are removed. The "blood tie" taken in through the "buddy mouth" (vagina) that would have bound "babymother" and "babyfather" is undone. This releases the woman from kinship obligations she cannot fulfil and that might endanger already strained networks. In this sense, abortion actually supports cohesion, preserving the solidarity of existing circles of kin.

Abortion's beneficial uses notwithstanding, wasting blood that should be recycled back into society in the form of human beings who will reproduce the kin network is, according to the general ideology, a sinful, instrumental, and self-centered assertion of egoistic power. In light of this, abortion can be an aggressive act: the symbolic murder of a man who refuses to uphold his obligations, as a fetus contains part of his substance and so represents him. It can also symbolize the vengeful destruction of men in general. Brody links abortion with the fantasy of autonomy or personal control in the face of male domination (1985, 176).

Abortion denies men control over their route to reproduction, deprecating their potency. They do not like it. Men say that abortion "pollutes" and wastes their blood and essence. In a sense it turns men into "mules." Women feeling particularly oppressed by men may take comfort in this.

The possibility of women redirecting hostility meant for irresponsible men can be pursued. "Passing on" children—sending them off to be raised by relatives—can also be a way of destroying ties with and expressing destructive wishes concerning their fathers (Brody 1981, 182). Abandoning them could express hostility against their fathers even more strongly. Brodber (1974) found that matrifocally raised boys are particularly prone to be abandoned (see also Sargent and Harris 1991). This need not be unconsciously driven, however; economic destitution and a lack of other options may motivate it. Also, girls are easier to "pass on" than boys because they can provide more of the kind of help and companionship that would-be foster caretakers seek.

Importantly, real material, structural, and historical concerns (often linked to colonial and patriarchal domination) underlie women's hostility and their need to cut free of particular men and particular obligations. Discussion of abortion's psychological, expressive dimension is important, but it must not divert attention from abortion's pragmatic functions and the specific reasons women give for needing it.

WAYS TO "DASH AWAY BABY"

When beneficial social ends can be found to justify the means, pregnancies can be terminated. Babies grow in women's "bellies," occupying food space, blocking the rectum, or otherwise causing "belly" troubles, so like other "blockages," they can be purged with "washout." Birth itself is a big "washout" that "cleanses" women by expelling children and the sperm that went into their making. It rids women's bodies of the "nasty" waste that had been physically blocked from exiting. The logic of catharsis underlies abortion and the restoration of menses, just as it does birth, blood purification, and the regulation of appetite and bowel action.

Because of how they think their bodies work, Jamaican women never try extraction with knitting needles or wire hangers inserted through the vagina. It makes no sense to pull out what can be washed through—a process much less likely to cause death from a uterine or vaginal perforation. Rural Jamaican women's distaste for touching their "privates" notwithstanding, there is fear that one might poke the wrong bag or go up the wrong tube, or that the invasive tool might get stuck or get lost inside. Purging makes more cultural sense; also, it does not lead to septic infection at the rate inserted hangars and such do.

Sometimes, women "hackle" (stress) their bodies with hard work or heavy "romping" to break loose the tiny fetus; they use strong purgatives afterward to help pass the fetus out. One girl dislodged a pregnancy by carrying heavy cement blocks; another, by diving off of a high rock into the sea. If miscarrying this way causes problems that force a woman to seek medical assistance, she can claim she had no knowledge of what her "belly" did contain. Sometimes, this is true.

MENSTRUAL REGULATION

The frequency of amenorrhea, subfertility, and infertility from disease, malnutrition, and hard physical labor means that missed periods do not necessarily indicate conception. Pregnancy tests are not commonplace, and a woman might not know that she is pregnant until her second trimester, when the fetus begins to "form up" and move. Fertility is not certain, and a woman may conclude that "cold" or other matter has clogged her "tube(s)." She can "take washout" to clear whatever blocks the menstrual path. This can be done as a cure for barrenness: by unblocking the "tube(s)," a woman can better the chances that "discharge" will find its way to an egg. It can also be done to remove a blood clot.

Medicines to bring back the menses are common cross-culturally (Erasmus 1977; Newman 1985; Nichter and Nichter 1987). While pregnancy is a yes/no condition from the Western point of view, many cultures recognize it as the end result of a lengthy process (Newman 1985). In Jamaica as elsewhere, that recognition provides a woman with flexibility in interpreting her state and in deciding on and explaining a course of action. As a blood-clot conceptus is different from a baby, a woman washing out a lump of blood is practicing menstrual regulation, not abortion. The fact that matter which washes out during the early and ambiguous stages of pregnancy resembles menses—not babies—often gets used to prove that an abortion has not taken place. And indeed it has not, according to traditional notions.

If a woman who views her condition as a pregnancy decides to "take washout" and her conscience needs soothing, she can convince herself of her ignorance, just as "bad minded" others can convince themselves that an enemy purposefully used "washout" in an "evilous" effort to abort. Unsure women can focus on relieving nausea or other "belly" complaints, the source of which they do not care to know but only to be rid of. One "bush doctor" explained that women often rationalize successful purges by claiming that if a pregnancy had caused the symptoms, God would have "made it stay."

AMBIGUITY AND "WASHOUT"

Emmenagogues restore the menses, while abortifacients "make baby turn into blood and wash out." While abortifacients are similar to medicines intended to bring down the menses, they are often stronger, and their acknowledged end differs. Still, although people readily explain that certain purgatives have certain effects, there is no common English or patois word to denote abortifacients or emmenagogues in particular; all purgatives are classified generically as "washout." The ambiguity inherent in this system makes privacy possible and allows for the covert transmission of abortion and other information about women's health.

Women interested in abortion but in need of total secrecy can ask their close relations about "washout." Or because menstrual regulation and abortion differ but both involve purging, people can talk about concoctions that "unblock the tube(s)," "bring down menses," or restore "the health" by washing out "cold or clot" when they do not want to discuss abortion openly. An herbalist working in a Kingston shop recommended tea of pennyroyal (*Micromeria brownei*), a known abortifacient, for just this—after insistently disclaiming any knowledge about abortion.

Polysemy and ambiguity facilitate veiled information-sharing but can also be turned against people. "Washout's" all-purpose nature and menstrual regulation's relation to abortion leaves observers room to draw conclusions and manipulate them in a socially damaging fashion, whether through strategic insinuations or by overt accusations concerning abortion.

One day, as I picked my way up a path to visit with Aunt Gret, I happened to pass a young woman, Patsy, vomiting behind her small house. She looked up and I inquired about her health. She had been feeling sick, she said, so had taken a very strong "washout," one of the few which cause vomiting on top of easing the bowels. She knew this would make her feel "strong" later. But Patsy "took sick" for a week. Two months later, it became apparent that "she a breed."

People began to talk about Patsy's pregnancy. The man for whom they thought she "carry punkin" had a wife. They found out he had stopped giving Patsy money, food, clothing, or any other kind of help. They also knew that Patsy and the "bush doctor" "move good together." "Look how she shabby," they said with glee, using knowledge of her relationships and of her new poverty and lack of male-provided capital to support their hindsighted contention that the bout of sickness Patsy had experienced earlier was really a failed abortion attempt.

Lucky that her baby came out fine (botched abortions or strong "washouts" can cause birth defects; disabled babies often get used as proof of their mothers' "evilousness"), Patsy contended that she had no clue to her pregnancy when she took her purge. True or not, the villagers saw her sickness as evidence of an abortion and thus of her bad character. Patsy was known as a "rebel" before, and those bothered by this felt good to "pull her name down." Perhaps Patsy had no awareness of her state, but it is also possible that she tried to hide her intention by claiming "washout."

ABORTIFACIENTS

Abortion identified as such usually occurs later in the first trimester than those purges intended for menstrual regulation; sometimes it occurs in the second trimester. When the fetus is older and firmer, stronger "washout" concoctions are needed, and abortion causes more physical trauma. There are side effects to these traumatic "washouts," such as a "softening" of the body through the loss of plumping fluids. Although this accompanies maturity, women with breasts that no longer "stand up" and fat that is "soft" or "bad" and no longer firm can get accused of "taking" abortion. People "can tell you about it" by observing a woman's "shape." They point to physical qualities to "show" that accusations are true.

Commonly known abortifacients include Dragon brand stout boiled down with "cobweb" (the black soot that gathers on kitchen ceilings), castor oil, and "salt physic" (epsom salts) in cream soda. Epsom salts is a purely modern purgative. Castor oil can be bought or made from the seeds of oil nut trees (*Rincinus communis*). These nuts or seeds can also be used directly. Dragon stout may have replaced dragon plant (perhaps *Zebrina pendula*). These three methods can be used in combination, alone, or with other cathartics. What gets mixed for a case depends on what that woman's body can "take."

When big or tough enough, a "belly" clogging offender is broken down or tenderized so it can get flushed through. But some matter cannot pass: many report that for each fetus aborted, especially when late, a "headskull" or "head cup" remains. A "headskull" might embed itself in the next conception or cause sickness in the "belly" or wherever it may lodge. Many women avoid abortion until they have produced at least one child because they fear such problems and fear they may not "get" more children.

Iron tenderizes flesh. People often look for rusty nails (that is, iron ones) to stick in gristly meat to make it tender. They know rusty nails also tenderize, "poison," or "rotten" human flesh, as when stepped on. So for abortion, particularly late in gestation, they boil rusty nails with marigold plants (*Bidens reptans* and *Wedelia trilobata*), themselves good for purifying blood, making a purgative tea.

"Cutting rust" involves softening and loosening hardened substances. Having sex after abstinence is "cutting rust," as

is easing arthritic stiffness: both involve warming and freeing "white" blood or "sinews" that has "slept up." Old iron and
so old blood (which iron "builds") can rust. People believe
Pepsi Cola "cuts rust" in the body as well as out (it can dissolve certain metals). A Pepsi and two Phensic pain tablets
turn a fetus back into blood that can be "cut" or expunged.
One Phensic tablet contains 380 mg of aspirin and 50 mg of
caffeine, and a maternity nurse explained that aspirin (and
other medications) can indeed induce abortion. But a woman
in her thirties confided that the Pepsi and Phensic combination does not work. She tried it when sixteen and still had to
carry that pregnancy to term.

Theoretically, anything that induces a physical catharsis
(whether a laxative, diuretic, blood-cleanser, gas-easer, sweat-
inducer, or any other type of purgative) can spur the body to
"dash away baby" if taken in quantity. For abortion, people
recommend teas brewed from senna leaves (*Cassia occiden-
talis* and *Cassia obovata*), a powerful laxative for men and
horses that is not to be taken by pregnant women, or from
corkscrew (*Helicteres jamaicensis*), its name indicative of its
nature. A dangerously strong "tube"-clearing abortifacient can
be made by roasting an immature paki or calabash (*Crescentia
cujete*), scraping off its blackened outer layer, and squeezing
the remains for juice, which is boiled, cooled, strained, doc-
tored with honey and castor oil, and drunk.

Abortifacients are usually brewed in combination with
other things like Dragon stout, the popular blood detoxifier
cerrasee (*Momordica charantia*), John Charles (*Cordia glo-
bos*) which loosens "cold" and cures gout, and vervain (*Stachytarpheta jamaicansis*) which washes out worms and "cold."
Some concoctions call for wild "basley" or basil (*Ocimum
micrantham*), "nuttenegg" or nutmeg, and guava buds. Any
cathartic agent that stimulates excretion should help. People
recommend drinking "plenty" water as well.

Jamaicans know many pharmaceutical agents that bring
on cathartic and abortive expurgations. Villagers who have
lived in "town" and those who have had experience "giving"
(or giving advice on) abortions—worldly people less afraid of

touching the genitals than the average rural woman—told of douches made from carbolic "soap-water" mixed with laundry bluing, or quinine pills (the pills taken alone orally should also work). One woman douched with the mixture during her fourth or fifth month (her guess), and the fetus came out "right in the bag." Anything which "operates" (removes or "cuts" offensive matter, as in surgery) or "runs belly" can be used. People mention Indian Root purgative pills and the now unavailable cathartic "black pill."

One woman seeking an abortion some years back looked all over Kingston for the "good" kind of "black pill" after they had become rare. "They doesn't make black pill like first-time," she complained, adding that, "red" and small, even in large doses the new ones "can't work." The "black pill" of old, which used to be sold under the name of Cathartic Pill, was discontinued in the early 1980s. Pharmacists said that its replacement, Alophen, which contains 60 mg of phenolph-thalein and is so-called "red" in color (a North American would probably call it "brown"), still brings complaints from people who prefer the stronger action of its black predecessor.

Some women go to family planning clinics for "injection" under the pretense of needing contraception when they actually seek the abortions "injection" can induce. Some overdose on birth control pills, eating them all at once, thinking they work (as cultural logic would have it) by purging the fetus instead of by preventing ovulation.

Prevcon, a nonprescription postcoital contraceptive containing the hormone levonorgestrel, was introduced in May 1989. It was not referred to as an abortifacient because of the understanding that conception is a process and that fetuses are not abortable babies until they "form up." Although Prevcon had been available by prescription since 1987 as Postinor (which pharmacists would continue to carry) the "flood" of requests for Prevcon in Kingston led officials to suspect that women would "abuse" the drug, causing themselves "serious damage." The ad campaign for the pill was halted by the Ministry of Health less than a week after it started (*Gleaner* 1989b; DaCosta 1989).

Prevcon's quick popularity, which contrasts with the poor reputation of other available modern contraceptives, reflects the eagerness of Jamaicans "take wahshout" to cleanse "blockage"—blood-clot fetuses included. It shows that women's interest in procuring abortions (biomedically defined) is actually quite high.

GETTING HELP WITH ABORTIONS

Although abortion can preserve particular relationships that the arrival of a child would unduly try, in keeping with general ideals that posit altruism, sociability, and reproduction as the aim of the individual in society, abortion is branded "evil." This (and its related criminal status) explains the secrecy surrounding it. While many women use what they know of "washout" ingredients to concoct emmenagogues on their own, for abortifacient recipe suggestions they generally consult with trusted female relations. But being "traced" for one's abortion or being seen to "boil burn pan" (that is, to brew an abortifacient) can ruin a woman's social standing.

Fear of gossip and even future blackmail leads some women to turn to sympathetic biomedical doctors for abortions; villagers knew of several who performed the procedure (one doctor famous for it is reportedly suffering a grave skin disease "cause from sin"). Doctors do not talk, people say, describing what they see as a growing preference for clinical procedures. But conclusions can get drawn about women seen waiting in one of these doctors' surgeries. Still, many feel that the chances the deed will get found out are smaller this way than with a "bush doctor."

Biomedical abortions cost about $100 U.S. dollars—one-tenth of the average yearly income. So, unless a woman is wealthy, in dire mental or physical danger, agrees to a tubal ligation, or gets pregnant while being a family planning program participant (the government promises abortions in such cases), a clinical abortion is not an option.

Inopportunely pregnant women can seek out traditional "bush doctors" for help. Scattered among the villages live people secretly famous for their expert ethnomedical knowledge. Their numbers are shrinking as new generations reject the "bongo" and "tribal" ways of the "old heads," but some do remain. In public places, "bush doctors" willing to help with abortions meet a mixture of respect and disdain, the balance of which depends on how covertly they ply their trade and how "good" they live with others. To live otherwise would incite people to expose them as antisocial and wicked by "tracing" their deeds.

Most patients are wary about letting others see them traveling to and from a "bush doctor." But even those who cover their tracks most carefully show health-related changes both in body and behavior, from which others draw conclusions. Patients often malign their healers in attempts to hide their associations with "first-time fool-fool business" or "superstition." By dirtying healers' names, patients distance themselves from their "bush doctors" and lessen the suspicions others may have that they consult them. One woman famous for her skill reports that many of her patients act "ungrateful." They forget to pay for her kind help and "carry" her name indiscriminately. Folk-healers of all sorts commonly complain of "ungratefulness." A pair of church-associated healing "mothers" bemoaned the fact that their names got linked with the Poco religion and "iniquity" or evil by "ungrateful-like" patients—ungrateful, like children.

One local "bush doctor" has a "mind" to give her practice up but "now and again" someone comes for help. She provides it, advising them about the methods for washing clean and getting free from too-constraining obligations. She no longer performs abortions herself, as she fears legal trouble and social problems. Sometimes people misunderstand her instructions and complications arise. One "young miss" brewed her "washout" mix too strongly, and after she "dropped" the fetus in its "bag," she began to pass "tripe" (probably placental matter). Panicking, she cut it off, "damaged herself," and had to be hospitalized. The "bush doctor" complained that "the girl lack sense" as she did not send for her help. Such complications made this "bush doctor" decide to withdraw from practice even more completely.

Unfortunately, the decreasing status of ethnomedicine and the increasing reluctance of experts to share their knowledge for fear of the social and legal consequences means more young women must simply improvise, following the menstruation-like logic of the "belly wash." They use what they know of cathartics and what they have heard second-hand concerning abortifacients, but often guess wrongly about effective combinations and proper dosages. In numbers sure to increase unless abortion is decriminalized, girls and women end up dehydrated and hemorrhaging dangerously, often in clinics and hospitals. They often hinder their own treatment by concealing the cause of their condition.

USING SICKNESS DISCOURSE TO COVER ABORTIVE INTENT

While women can use menstrual regulation and simple "washout" in an honest fashion, they can also use them to bring on abortions. But a woman who needs to conceal her intentions completely, whether from others or from herself, may decide that a frog and not a fetus occupies her "belly." Mrs. Brown, who was about fifty years old and already the mother of seven dependent children, sought help from a local healer for just this problem. Her husband put her on their last donkey (the rest had died of overwork and lack of food, as the couple had come upon hard times) and "carried" her over the hill to a healer

Mrs. Brown's healer prescribed what another healer, Mother Jo, told me was a purgative. Mother Jo knew this because Mrs. Brown's daughter paid her a visit, seeking help for her mother's predicament. Mother Jo advised the daughter to fetch Mrs. Brown before she took the prescribed "washout."

After listening to Mrs. Brown's story and "sounding" her body by laying on hands and by groping it, Mother Jo declared talk of frogs "pure foolishness." According to her, Mrs. Brown did not think her "belly" held a frog until after having a discussion with a neighbor who convinced her this was possible. Her "belly" held a "natural" baby, Mother Jo said, so to take "washout" would be to "dash away pickney," an evil deed. Mother Jo promised to help the family through their hard times and to pray for them, so Mrs. Brown decided to have her baby after all.

In her attempt to justify "washing out" a conceptus that she would have had no means to support, Mrs. Brown made use of a cultural tradition in which women are impregnated with frogs. She may have done so unconsciously to ease her guilt about abortion. But chances are that she knew full well what she sought to do and also knew that without a cover a healer might not have given her advice. Mother Jo lived closer to Mrs. Brown than the first healer did, but it was known that Mother Jo would never have colluded in an abortion—even when disguised. Had the abortive "washout" been carried out, proof that Mrs. Brown had indeed "gotten" a frog would have been found in the aborted matter. Women know that aborted fetuses often resemble frogs, just as they believe that witchcraft can cause them to deliver frogs and froglike creatures.

The lack of explicit references to abortion by women seeking or giving them does not mean that the intention is not there or that everyone remains unaware of it. Jamaican conversational style and rules of conduct in regard to others' business demand that speakers leave much to listeners' imaginations. The silence regarding abortion occurs as a culturally provided discourse that justifies and actually calls for cleansing the "belly" of unwanted matter. The strategic use of this discourse further diminishes the need for direct abortion talk. This allows people to act in collusion and hide what is ideologically unpalatable (abortion) when by doing so they can profit.

One "first-time" midwife, 102 years old, reported that many women came to her for abortions. "Me no business with that wicked something," she said, claiming that she sent them on their way. She claimed to "hate that thing." But this midwife used to make a cure-all that can "bring down the menses," "clear the tube" and ease out afterbirth, enhance fertility, and speed delivery. It consists of one long sinkle bible, a handful of senna, and half of a lime cut from a tree (the other half must remain attached), all boiled until "well red," cooled, bottled, and taken in small glasses before and after sleep for three days and nights. The ingredients sound familiar because they also figure in abortifacient and emmenagogue recipes mentioned earlier. Blood, often dark, clotted, and stringy, washes out of the woman in three days. "She happy—she well want fe see it! When the blood come down 'pon him [the woman], you fe charge nuf, nuf money!"

Chapter 14

The "False Belly," or "Witchcraft Baby"

Opinions about kinship and gender relations—and the social and economic implications of such relations—are expressed through talking about (and trying to cure) the "bad bellies" caused by "tying," blocked "tubes," and aberrant pregnancies. Beliefs about frog babies are part of a larger discourse on "witchcraft babies" or "false bellies": undesirable or "funny" pregnancies brought about by "unnatural" means. Traditional ideas about ghosts and their connections with living people and with "Obeah" (sorcery) are used to explain "false belly" and to express individual and interpersonal tensions and concerns, in both general and specific terms.

DUPPIES

The social world includes ancestors. Their continued existence complicates obligation. No one ever disappears completely, and relationship tensions are projected onto the dead (see Goldberg 1979). "Duppies" (ghosts) can demand recognition or favors. They can easily trouble things, undetected, and bring sickness. This increases the need for and complexity of protective measures taken in defense of one's health and so one's social standing.

Committed Christians claim that duppies are not ghosts but evil spirits. Whether ghosts or demons, duppies can act as people who were once part of a network of obligation. Sometimes duppies come of their own accord and "interfere with," "trouble," or—to "talk it straight"—rape women as they sleep. During the forty days and nights after a death when "dead must walk" before "cooling" and settling down, any lover might return for sex. Duppies do not understand that they are dead and so, although they should settle into their graves and rest, they try to do the things they did in life. Duppies who lived "good" generally mean no harm.

On meeting a duppy, one's head "raises" or feels big. One may feel warm or cool drafts, and smell a stink. People who encounter duppies feel "different," whether they see them or not. Only some have the "foresight" of "four eyes," which allows them to "see" duppies: they are people born with a caul, a veil-like portion of the birth sac, stuck to their heads.

A "raised" head and the other sensations that are interpreted as "cause from" a duppy's nearness might be somatic manifestations of anxiety attacks, triggered by the circumstances of actual living. The symptoms also could indicate misfiring neurons, perhaps due to fatigue. Of course, dark nights, the shadow of a banana plant set to sway by the breeze, and mysterious noises in the bush provide the right conditions in which to meet a duppy.

Duppies visit less these days, people say, because we "cool" new "warm" dead on ice and in mortuary refrigerators, rendering them less active. The association between cool temperature and sluggishness seen in descriptions of how "cold" or blood can "sleep up" repeats itself here.

AVOIDING DUPPY TROUBLE

Every "dead" walks about for a bit, but those people known for wickedness in life persist in making mischief long after their deaths. Promiscuous, "girly-girly" men are certain to return to their lovers' yards as duppies. So along with women with "fresh dead" mates, those whose men were known as sinners must take precautions. Sometimes, the dead get "planted" when buried: survivors take magical steps to keep them from walking, burying them with fetishes to do this. Another way is to stick common straight pins in a corpse's feet and hands so that walking and touching things forces them deeper; the pain deters the duppy from action.

The living do things with themselves to "keep off dead." Wary women, particularly those with dead mates, must not sleep on their backs (a vulnerable position) and must wear red or black panties when they sleep (panties are barriers, and these colors scare duppy rapists). Surviving lovers must move their beds and can rearrange other furniture and paint their houses or veranda stairs to confuse the dead.

It is as easy to outwit and "rule" a duppy as an "idiot" or "dunce"—names children get called in disapproval. Maintaining that duppies lack "sense" equates them with children, who also make demands, impinge on caretakers' freedom, and bring trouble; it allows mortals some legitimate command over them. Only in certain vertical relations, such as parent-child, can people exert overt control over others. Otherwise, they must only advise, offering caveats: "You must know your mind" or "must know what fe do." With proper techniques, however, people can control duppies, easing the distress that belief in them brings.

Although people do not like to appear "superstitious," many take open precautions to "run" duppies back to their graves. A myriad of methods for exorcising duppy intruders exist. Those who fear intimate visits wear measuring tapes around their waists. The tapes remind duppies of being measured for their coffins. Some say they stop to count the lines, wasting time, forgetting their original intentions. Open Bibles further deter duppies. Women lay them in bedrooms. People cast their urine around their yards and along their borders as a duppy repellent, as dogs mark territorial boundaries. Some say urine is offensive because it is waste. Others

claim that duppies hate its saltiness. They explain that salting food heavily keeps duppies from "playing" with it, dou-
bling the "sin" of those "mean" with their salt and allying
them further with the antisocial. Some say salt makes duppies "heavy." Hurston's informants told her it keeps them
from flying (1938, 62).

The ever-present threat of duppy interference increases
at night. At sundown, all but the "rebels" and real "big men"
come off the streets and withdraw to verandas or indoors.
Inside, all portals are shut tight and locked for fear that "cool
night dew," "cool breeze," and duppies might enter and make
people sick. My landlady's two young grandchildren always
begged me to shut my windows when visiting me in my room
at night, lest duppies float in and harm us, even indirectly,
with their breath or air currents created as they passed. It
helped keep mosquitoes out (like duppies, they carry disease), but I liked the breeze.

Friends asked me to at least "lock down" my shutters
before I went to sleep. If things that can stress the body, such
as simple thermal changes or the "breath" of duppies, hit the
body in its "hot" and permeable sleeping state, pores will be
penetrated. Disagreeable intrusive substances can cause one
to "collapse" and "draw" or "drop down" in size through prolonged or "funny" sickness. Chamber pots are kept under beds
so that no one need venture outside to the toilet at night.

I was also instructed not to sleep on my back, as this often
brings nightmares and leaves the "privates" vulnerable to
duppy rape. "Gal pickney" learn to sleep on their bellies, and
people always wear nightclothes to bed, even in midsummer
heat. The teenaged neighbor girls always slept in panties,
bras, and slips. Praying before sleep helps, and dispensing
with this precaution is said to cause bad dreams.

DIVISION OF DUPPY LABOR

Women must always beware of men: dead or alive, men
constantly seek sex. Female duppies may visit for sex but

rarely do. For one thing, the mechanics of intercourse with a
uninterested man make this tricky (uninterested women simply get raped). For another, traditionally, women do not desire
sex as men do. Because of this, one man confided, he and many
males ignore recommended precautions concerning dead
mates. Men do not fear sex from living women, either, except
those known for antisocial behavior. Female duppies prefer to
"trouble" babies and food, reflecting their roles in life.

BABY STEALERS

Some duppies lay in wait under the beds of women in
labor, intending to kidnap or to kill their babies as they are
delivered. They taint the babies with their "bad" air or
breath, which can penetrate any orifice and "melt out" these
infants, or they "suck out" their flesh or blood. Generally, the
duppies who do this are dead mothers who do not like their
daughters' "babyfathers" or feel threatened by their daughters' becoming adults and mothers. They may even "grudge"
their daughters their male "friends," as mothers are believed
to do in life. However, when attacks are "cause from grudge,"
the duppy under the bed is more typically a dead relation of
the "babyfather"—a lover or even his own mother.

These attacks, described to me during discussions about
births in which babies and/or mothers died, bespeak the tensions womanhood involves. Young women feel ambivalent
about "coming up" and taking on adult responsibilities in a
harsh world. They fear and resent competition with other
women for power or men. Daughters know that they threaten
their mothers when they become mothers themselves and
may feel guilt and resentment. Children embody the union of
male and female and so attacking them is, by extension,
attacking that union. Someone might do so to retain power
over a dependent, to rid a loved one of a mate, or to break a
rival's hold on a man. These things happen in real life, and
the tradition of baby violation by female relations provides
an idiom in which the problems they cause gain expression.

People told me that others, women especially, steal unguarded "pretty" babies. This belief reflects a general distrust of others' intentions. It affirms the value of children to women in particular and confirms the importance of physical characteristics. Even maternity nurses, people contend, steal "pretty" children. A pregnant nurse must leave her job, one woman explained, asking rhetorically how I thought nurses got their families. So even one's motherhood, one of the few sources women have for self-esteem, can get stolen away by competitors in the guise of altruistic helpers (which even kin may pretend to be). Women compete for social status and "lazy naygurs" steal children to gain "ownership" instead of putting in their own labor.

Baby-hunting monsters appear in some tales, but people talk of these "witches" or "demons" as "foolishness" and "fairy tale." The "pitchy-patchy" way they construct the identities of these monsters and the infrequence of references (including covert ones) indicate that this tradition is fading. "Long Titty Susan" most fully embodies the traits people attribute to these "witches." She is mortal but sheds her skin at night, walks out raw, and sucks the blood of babies. Her breasts sag low, resembling those of women who have "dashed away pickney" or are finished bearing children. If one comes across Long Titty Susan's skin, one must salt it so she cannot get back in. Salt draws blood from meat and hurts when it gets in a wound. It also dissolves seemingly skinless creatures such as frogs, which in Jamaica can be as large as squirrels. People find frogs frightening; if a pregnant woman is scared by one, she can give birth to a frog-child. Brave individuals are often implored to pour salt on frogs' backs to "melt" and kill them. By trying to slip on her salted skin, so too can "Long Titty" meet harm.

Long Titty Susan's form embodies her antithetical nature. Her breasts invert the cultural ideal for "titties" which "stand up." Moreover, they are empty of milk. Instead of giving, Long Titty Susan—a true egoist—only takes. She sucks out babies' blood (like rats suck or "eat out" eggs and mistresses "eat out" men's money). Women should, however, create and "grow" babies, nursing them with their own life fluid. Long Titty Susan takes back life, refusing to recreate society by bearing children.

Like the dead whose skins rot away, Long Titty Susan's flesh lies exposed and her insides unguarded. "Careless" of her body, she walks at night, the time of duppies and a time when "cool night dew" easily "sicks." Yet, she gets no "lick"; she comes through fine. All this attests to her identity with the antisocial, the "raw," and the dead and rotten. Long Titty Susan, normal by day, becomes a cannibalistic "vampire" by night and "walks out" as a symbolic inversion of the ideal Jamaican woman. In talking about her, people can express their ambivalences about their mothers and their fears of being deceived by supposedly trustworthy others.

TO "SET" A DUPPY

Spirit pregnancies may be "cause from" someone "setting" a duppy on a woman to "trick" her and bring her down. Vengeful people seek out Obeah specialists who, alone or with the aid of demons, command duppies and "set" them to work "iniquity." Obeah" work is facilitated by duppies' lack of "sense." The less "sense" an individual has, the more s/he gets ordered about and the more likely s/he is to follow commands. Adult mortals cannot be ordered about, as they have developed the ability to make decisions "sensibly." They also have the right to autonomy. This is not the case with duppies. Infant duppies, doubly lacking "sense" (being both babies and dead) are easily compelled.

People who "set" duppies break moral rules. They do dealings privately, without a church and sometimes even without keeping patrons informed. Patrons themselves fear sorcerers, and also fear what others may say if they are seen to be employing them. Everyone knows that those rising early or on the first bus (which runs before dawn) have evil in mind.

Obeah workers traffic at night and with spirits of the ground, as Pocomania churches do. Religious specialists who are healers and "don't business" with evil, such as church-associated "physicians," deal with God and sky-dwelling spirits to bring "good" to the world. They generally work in the daytime. The form for dealing in the supernatural or "created" world is similar for both types of work, as both grew from one African root. But while sorcerers separate themselves from society, healers ally themselves with it.

Sorcerers are generally men. In Africa, sorcery had legitimacy and commanded respect, and in a system in which men cannot "uplift" or effectively control others, it is not surprising that they seek power as Obeah workers. The sorcerer's "unclean deeds" bring good pay and people fear his power. Wedenoja explains, "Men monopolize public positions of wealth and power, and leave the less lucrative positions to women" (1989, 87). Healing, women's work, pays much less.

Women are responsible for their families' health and women healers exploit this. Childhood experience leads people to seek mother figures for healers, and healing women or "mothers" serve and guide "children," who obey, respect, and idealize them as perfect mothers. "Mothers" build their legitimacy through social ties and also through the church.

Women join churches more than men, mostly because church is "the very source of respectability" (Wilson 1973, 100), which interests women more than men. It is also the one place they can socialize without risking their good names (102), and it allows them to ease a nurturance deficit: women—mothers—do not get sufficient mothering themselves and seek it in the church. This bolsters their resolve to attend and secure "respect." Church membership constitutes a first step toward "receiving the gift of healing."

There is a typology of "negromancy" workers, which include "professors," "Obeahmen," and "scientists." Seaga (1969), Barrett (1976), and Wedenoja (1988) trace the historical differences between branches of folk religion like Myalism, Revival, Pocomania, and Obeah. "Scientists" instruct themselves with mail-order books and favor the written; Obeah workers have usually been apprenticed and use mainly performance. "Scientists" draw on demonic forces detailed in their books. Obeah workers deal with ancestors. "Professors" stand somewhere in between. Jamaicans actually use all labels interchangeably, lump all types of "workers of iniquity" together, and oppose them and the "Poco people" to "children of God" who deal only with "good." The opposition between good and evil is what matters.

Each sorcerer has a distinct method to "capture" and "set" duppies, but most (for large sums of money) use incantations and props such as cat bones and graveyard dirt for their "negromancy" (this word combines the idea of "dirty black naygurs" with necromancy). Some use imported instruction manuals (such as those from the DeLaurence Company in Chicago); others rely on traditional knowledge. Sometimes, sorcerers ask clients to provide property belonging to the intended victim (such as hair or dirty clothing) or to carry out tasks (such as burying a bundle of props and reading prayers) to strengthen the spell. For small "iniquities," duppies may not need "setting" and acts as simple as inserting a paper with a name written on it into one's shoe and walking on it will do.

The dread Jamaicans have of rotting things has an empirical basis. Dirt from graveyards is contaminated by rotting corpses, and can poison; its use is not based on "pure foolishness." Hurston (1938) noted that Pasteur himself wrote of the graveyard's danger. Germs for yellow fever, scarlatina, typhoid, and other diseases have been found in cemetery topsoil. Many other seemingly harmless substances still in use (including alligator gall bladders which contain poison, chopped horsehair which, ingested, can irritate and puncture intestines, and fur brushings which can carry germs from animal skins) can kill (251–53). "Scientists" and women who would "tie" with their blood know that organic matter is less easily detected than other types of poisons.

Obeah (I use the term generically, as do Jamaicans) usually involves oils or "medicines" purchased in towns at special shops. Colored and often fragrant or stinking, oils and perfumes called "Oil of Deliverance," "High John the Conqueror," "Protection," "Evil," "Compel," "Dead Man's Bones," "Success," and so forth ("Oil of Stand Tall" and those with similarly suggestive names being used for potency) sell for about $1.50 U.S. for a two-ounce bottle. Sorcerers often mix oils. Sometimes, the intended victim's name is written on paper and wrapped around a bottled concoction, which is then buried. This works through sympathetic magic, as does the name-in-shoe "trick" or as using someone's old clothes as floor rags keeps him or her from "uplift."

One local Poco woman (who was actually a Revivalist) was accused of "negromancy" after the sudden death of a follower who had given her land. Villagers say that the dead woman's "people" reclaimed the land and ripped down the church that "that Poco lady" had built. Below the floorboards, they say, were vials of destructive oil, each with a different name written on paper bound to it by an elastic band. The accused, a modestly successful healer and preacher, told me "nothing no go so," but villagers insisted she was wicked. She said that the villagers are the "naygur" ones, always asking her to bring down their neighbors and kill off their mates. They "bad mouth" her, she said, because she will not help with "evilous intentions" and "they know what they will do": they project their "bad mind" onto her.

Like the oils, clothing is useful. Once worn and perspired on, it can be "fixed" or treated and shown to a duppy, buried at a grave, or otherwise used (another reason to worry about theft). Underclothes are preferred. Sometimes, the article is prayed over and sprinkled with magical powder (for which, as for oils, the Obeah worker supplies a "prescription") and returned. Knowledge of this practice saved one middle-aged woman from trouble: she noticed her favorite frock missing and announced that the first one to see that dress must burn it. It turned up behind a barrel. She destroyed it, believing that wearing it would have been dangerous.

Candles (often black) and incense are lit and incantations made by those intending evil. Sorcerers also rely on modern props. One "professor" I visited used flash powder, a plastic light bulb which glowed when its base was pressed on the pot-metal "high power guard ring" he wished to sell to my friend for about $375 U.S. (these rings are worn by many), Egyptian-style Tarot cards (not read in a very Tarot-like style) and a "Magic Eight Ball," a children's fortune-telling toy widely available in the United States. Most Obeah workers do not use as many modern props. As long as they have charisma, their "performances" will impress, and their pronouncements will seem cannily applicable.

Most Obeahmen have favorite duppies. "Coolie" duppies work hardest; they persevere when dead as when alive. Most Obeah workers also have "confederates" who bring them customers, inform them of social rifts and squabbles, run ahead and bury things in a potential customer's or victim's yard, and dispense poison unseen. One man explained that "invisible stones" thrown by "unseen hands" (almost everyone has heard such tales and many have seen it happen) are really ice cubes, which make a great racket against zinc rooftops and then melt away leaving no trace.

SPIRIT INTERFERENCE WITH THE "BELLY"

Sorcerers can "set" duppies to rape and impregnate women. "Witchcraft baby" refers to a pregnancy resulting from this sort of premeditated rape; "false belly" is a more generic term that includes "bellies" brought on by duppies of their own accord. The phrases, however, are interchanged regularly, as with sorcerer labels.

A spirit pregnancy can mimic a regular one so well that a woman might think it "natural" until the time of delivery when only clots of "cold," "sinews," and "bad" gas or air come out. If she was already pregnant before the attack, or if an attacker's leavings "catch" one of her eggs, a monster baby can develop. People told of froglike creatures, memberless torsos, and children resembling monkeys. Miss Amelia, who lived up the hill, gave birth to a cow head.

Some villagers argue that "witchcraft babies" cannot come from "discharge" because "duppy cocky rotten off, don't it!" But all agree that it can come from the "unclean" "bad" air that spirits "troubling" women's bodies leave behind. Whether odious air or "discharge," duppy leavings penetrate a woman through her vagina and move to her "belly," sometimes "catching" an egg and moving to the womb, always making the "belly" swell (quickly or slowly) as if the woman is pregnant.

A duppy can insert a small creature into the body through the vagina, by hand. A duppy can also place a tadpole, say, on the tip of his penis and "shoot" it into the victim. One old woman passed a large, "natural" lizard which spoke up and told her healer, "I been there since a tot." A duppy must have inserted that lizard years ago, a cousin explained.

Sometimes, a duppy "troubles" a woman's food. Some of its essence enters her "belly" as she eats, and impregnates her or affects a previous conception. A polliwog or any other small creature could likewise be ingested. A woman can take active precautions, such as always using salt and hot pepper (which duppies hate) and never leaving her food unguarded.

A duppy might punch a pregnant woman in the "belly," although this is often its childish reaction to being knocked into or ignored, not an act of malice. But women fear unwanted vaginal penetration far more than this or "troubled" food. Sleeping people cannot actively protect themselves from anything. Locked doors do not always deter human rapists; they can never stop duppies intent on doing harm.

EXPRESSING GENDER TENSIONS

Jamaicans combine their cultural model of how the body works with social and moral understandings so that social causes can be found for "funny" sicknesses like "false belly," making them manageable, meaningful, and useful for discourse concerning social and moral affairs. Culturally perpetuated intergender tensions are among the issues that spirit pregnancies allow people to discuss or express.

The substances men give women can turn to poison, both figuratively and literally, just as the food women give men can poison them. Men "breed and leave" so frequently that almost any mysterious swelling of the female "belly" gets attributed to some man—alive or dead—having left a baby of some kind. An "owner" will be "named" unless the healing process itself brings sufficient mental relief.

SORCERY AND TENSION BETWEEN WOMEN

While male duppies do "trouble" women on their own initiative, "witchcraft babies" are frequently instigated by living people. A neighbor may want the victim's man for herself or her daughter. A mother-in-law may want her son back. Someone may believe that the victim has "uplifted" too high. Now and again, a man seeks to punish another man by hurting his wife, or tries to remove a woman who has gained a promotion at work over him (expressing the ideal that pregnant women do not "work out" or compete with men for jobs) or to hurt one who rejected him. But instigators are normally women.

People listening to tales of "false belly" always surmise that the woman attacked had been suspected by another of "carrying on" with her man (generally, other transgressions—such as usurping promotions—are revenged with other types of "tricks"). A teenaged girl explained it this way: "Supposing that I have a boyfriend and you saw him and get acquainted, and I found out. I can hurt you for it. All I have to do is go to an Obeahman. So I tell him I want to give you a false belly, and I'll pay him the amount he ask for. And then he'll send the spirit to your house and get you pregnant and you are going to say it belongs to my boyfriend." This breaks up the affair, probably at once, but certainly later, when he sees what gets born. The "false belly" woman (in this case, me) delivers a frog or "something funny," or will "just have that stomach for the rest of your life—until you die."

Misfortune often follows "careless," antisocial behavior. An instigator is wicked and "bad mind" for "dirtying" her hands with "unclean business" but a victim is wicked, too, for "taking up" another woman's man and "mashing up" a union. Since she is immoral, she forfeits God's protection.

In addition to highlighting the social tension between two women, "false belly" also expresses those larger tensions created by role expectations inconsistent with socioeconomic reality. For example, a lack of resources may have forced a victim to "look a next woman's man." Male gender expectations for "reputation" encouraged his complicity. And the idea of relations who continue to "interfere" even when dead reveals the ambivalence generated by kin obligations.

NIGHTTIME VISITATIONS

People do experience what they interpret as molestation by duppies at night. When many share one bed, any movement against one's sleeping body can trigger this experience. One woman, Sam-sam, who had probably never done so in her life, told me that sleeping alone is one way to be sure about intrusions. She had been sleeping with her small son and unfortunately mistook duppy mischief as her son pressing her left breast. Sam-sam woke and, realizing that her boy was sleeping at the foot of the bed, grabbed her Bible and rebuked whatever duppy had come to "trouble" her that night.

"Some duppy they smart," Sam-sam said, explaining that this one tried to outwit her by easing onto her as if he were her son. A duppy may change shape, come as one's lover, and press for sex. The victim believes herself having intercourse with her mate. One woman's dead lover did this to her. She conceived a spirit child made of "cold," "bad" air, and "sinews" that threatened her life, giving her great pain and "a salt provision and a half" between her legs (a swollen, suppurating vagina). She survived, but her condition led to her legal husband's discovery that she had cheated on him.

JUMBLED SLEEP CYCLES AND NIGHT VISITORS

Hufford (1982) reviews the literature concerning nighttime visitations and reports that the experience itself is universal and remarkably uniform. As Hufford shows, many people in many societies have had the experience of being awakened by an anthropomorphic presence that commonly exerts pressure on the chest. About 15 percent of the general population in North America has experienced a nocturnal visit (162). Knowledge of such a cultural tradition has no causal link to the experience of visitation. Hufford cites Ring's work concerning a similar tradition in which experiences and knowledge of their possibility are actually negatively associated (255).

The consistency of the phenomenological experience itself (Hufford 1982, 162) and the lack of any correlations between these and psychopathological or socially deviant people whom psychoanalysts call sexually repressed (80) rule out a psychodynamic explanation for night visitations. This does not cancel the psychodynamic aspects of the content of culturally constructed interpretations of such events; it simply suggests that actual causes may not be psychodynamic. Hufford locates them in the biological basis of sleep itself.

According to Hufford, the event interpreted as a nighttime visitation occurs when rapid eye movement (REM or dream) sleep intrudes on presleep hypnogogic or postsleep hypnopompic consciousness—states in which regular consciousness is partially obscured. That is, nighttime visitations are a type of hallucination (called an HH because it occurs hypnogogic or hypnopompically)—a waking dream that occurs when the sleep cycle gets jumbled. This can happen when noise, whether misfiring neurons or bumps in the night, disrupts sleep. Crowded sleeping arrangements make for many nocturnal disturbances.

Sleep paralysis (SP) often accompanies REM HH attacks, and Hufford reports that Mack has associated this with the motor inhibitions that accompany sleep (1982, 145). SP explains why, in their terror, some people cannot move. REM HH (whether with or without SP) is most frequently seen with extreme fatigue (63), which may overtax the sleep cycle. The hard labor rural Jamaicans do and the impediments to undisturbed rest with which they must deal often leave them overtired. Hufford did not explore the additional possibility that sleeping on one's back—the most common position for a nighttime visitation (11), the position Jamaicans warn about and one linked with snoring—may distort air intake and so trigger REM HH attacks, nor did he look at the link between eating and REM HH dreaming (Jamaicans notice that late suppers can generate nightmares, or "foolishness").

DISEASE AND "FALSE BELLY"

While nighttime visitations are most likely related to disturbed sleep cycles, the complaints and outcomes that can accompany "false belly" are not so easily rationalized or explained. Their variety and the fact that any disease that causes swelling can appear as a pregnancy means that "false belly" is not simply a gloss for one biomedically recognized abnormality. A dead fetus might cause "witchcraft baby" symptoms. A fibroid tumor can seem like "false belly"; more common among black women than among whites, these tumors can grow quite large without the discomfort people expect from disease. So can some ovarian cysts and some cervical or uterine cancers.

Another condition that can mimic pregnancy occurs when fluids seep into the abdominal cavity from inside the baglike membrane that holds the viscera. This is generally painless unless swelling is extreme. Usually, an equilibrium state comes about because fluid also moves out of the cavity, being absorbed through its walls and reintegrated. Fluid seepage from the intestines or stomach, however, would carry bacteria and bring infection, and so this particular type of leakage would probably get brought to a clinician's attention.

Genetically well-adapted to temperate and tropical zones, blacks are more prone than whites to retain salt and thereby to suffer from hypertension and edema (swelling caused by fluid retention). Blacks also suffer more frequently from sickle-cell anemia, which can induce "belly" swelling. Protein deficiency diseases such as kwashiorkor, commoner among the poor than the rich, also could cause "false belly." Simple obesity can resemble pregnancy too.

"False belly" can accommodate a range of biomedical conditions; however, it is not merely a way of labeling symptoms. The experienced meanings of bodily perceptions are paramount, as are the uses to which they are put.

PSYCHOCULTURAL EXPLANATIONS

The biomedical model assumes a mind-body split (see Ots 1990), so if a doctor can find no biomedical reason for a "false belly" s/he generally diagnoses it as a hysterical pregnancy, interpreting its symptoms as somatic manifestations of a psychological crisis—usually the desire for a child. But most sufferers described to me and those I met already had children. The first victim I encountered (we met at a healing or "balmyard") was about forty-five and had long since built her family. It is likely that "false belly" does not represent the wish for another child but is, instead, a strategy for dealing with or giving voice to the problems entailed by social relations.

Knowledge of "false belly" could bring forth symptoms in women sensitive to the tensions it expresses, especially if they have experienced an intrusion during the night, as emotion and bodily states are related (see Ots 1990, 23–35). It can also be used to explain and deal with the otherwise mystifying symptoms of any number of diseases by relating them to commonly known gender and kinship tensions and a known, treatable syndrome. Or, as mentioned before, real pregnancies might get cast as "witchcraft babies" to ease the procurement of abortifacients and to justify abortion "washouts."

SEEKING HEALING

Some women approach healers directly after experiencing night visitations; others wait until symptoms show. Not all women with "false belly" recall an intrusion so not all attribute a social or "created," spiritual dimension to their conditions. But when the "bellies" of women who know they cannot be pregnant "rise," they usually seek help. When doctors cannot cure them, these women join their duppy-visited sisters in seeking spiritual healing.

Healers normally make sure that patients have consulted clinicians. This assures that, should anything happen, no accusations of practicing medicine without a license or inquests into the circumstances of death need be made. The healer generally insists on a pregnancy test. Mother Geddes, however, got ahead of herself once and, in an excited state during a public service, advised a young woman visiting for the first time that day against buying diapers, as her "belly" held no baby. An observant church member commented that even though Mother had not "sounded" the woman (felt her body and "belly"), anyone could tell by looking that the "belly" held no child: its shape gave that away.

The patient, a mother of three, agreed. Her common-law husband had run off with her neighbor and, although they had had sex recently, she believed that no fetus had "started." She had no money to feed the children she already had and no man to support a new baby. She proposed that the neighbor had "set" this "false belly" to make sure that the man, who held a well-paying job, did not return to his rightful "wife." Whether the pregnancy was "natural" (that is, her "husband's" progeny) or "created," diagnosed with "false belly" the woman now had a moral right and physical necessity to "dash away baby."

Another pregnant woman was beset by the prospect of giving birth to a "witchcraft baby." A neighbor had accused her of having sex with her Chinese mate, claiming that the baby was "for" him. The "bellywoman" said it was not so. But at the clinic, she was told that the baby was "not right," and given tablets. Suspecting her neighbor had "fixed" her, the woman consulted an old midwife (who told me the tale). She advised the woman not to eat the pills but to see a certain healer. The "bellywoman" did, and through prayer, anointment with blessed water, and the laying on of hands her condition improved; her doctor credited the tablets. "Yes, sir," she said. Her delivery went well and her child's facial features were taken to prove that no "jacket" was "cut to fit" for her mate by the neighboring Chinese man.

ANTISOCIAL OBEAH
OR THE IDEALISTIC CHURCH

With "false belly" as with other social sicknesses, a person wishing to "set" a "turnback blow" (which returns a "trick" to the original attacker) consults an Obeahman. Sometimes, the sorcerer moves the offending thing from the victim's body to the attacker's, symbolically empowering the patient and crystallizing her projection of "bad mind" onto her supposed persecutor. At other times, a new "trick" is "set." If a victim cannot name her attacker the Obeah worker, through supernatural communications, helpful confederates, an informed neighbor, or through the story told by the patient herself, can find out. "Turnback blows" help victims release anger and assuage feelings of powerlessness.

Church-associated healers keep people from directly expressing anger. The Obeah system thrives on revenge (and perpetuates a climate of interpersonal anxiety over others' intents), but the church leaves vengeance to God. This is not to say that churchgoers never seek revenge or consult sorcerers—they do—but church teachings discourage hate and destructive confrontations. While healers sometimes know how "a thing" got done (through information brought by messenger angels, "confederates," neighbors, etc.) they work only to heal. They work to "build up," not to "break down," pacifying people in the process.

One villager, who helps with the "healing work" at a Revival "mission" and often gets taken away "in the spirit" and "shown" visions of people "fixing" others, told me, "God is not the author of confusion." What one learns from "the messengers" cannot be revealed to the patient. This would cause "hatrage" (hate and rage) and encourage acts of revenge. The church promotes "one love" and not cycles of vengeance. But a spirit pregnancy not attributed to a specific duppy, a partic-

ular social crime, or a certain enemy's instigation, still comments on social tensions because the mechanism of spirit
impregnation itself and so its cure implicates them.

DELIVERING A SPIRIT CHILD

"False bellies" become apparent when labor comes early
(as for a miscarriage) or at nine months when no babies show.
A wizened midwife who had delivered many monsters (like a
"so-so" or plain head, a "so-so batty," an alligator, a monkey,
and a plethora of frogs) explained that she normally inserted
her hand into the vagina to check for a head during labor. If
no head was found, she knew to expect a "witchcraft baby."
Sometimes these "babies" took no form at all, often being
"just a bunch of gook." She buried them, usually in the yard
where the birth took place, although anywhere would do.

Upon determining the nature of a case, Granny (her
methods typical of "first-time" midwives and current-day
healers) promptly lit a white candle. To hasten and ease
delivery, Granny would pass this lit candle "under the foot"
(between the legs) of the patient and over the head three
times, "chanting" the eighteenth Psalm. Once she used any
color, but changed to white after being dragged to court,
sometime in the 1920s she thought, for using black candles.
Her competitors, she claims, many of them male biomedical
doctors, "grudged" her the trade and miscast her use of colored candles as an (illegal) Obeah practice.

Fumigation with smoke is common in healing rituals.
Like the duppy's air entered the vagina and "belly," now so
too does the air of the flame. It heats and melts out evil matter, or drives it away as smoke drives off mosquitoes and
forces rabbits and snakes from their holes.

Granny then washed the "babymother" in cold water (perhaps to force the warming and "opening" of her body for
birth, maybe to cool evil forces), and anointed her, usually
with "Oil of Virgin Mary" and "Oil of Conqueror." Next,
Granny had the candle placed at the gate and gave the

patient a big spoon each of castor oil and white rum. Now labor began.

Granny had to "work" to drive "destruction" away. Though her instructions seem specific, rituals retain a plasticity that allows for improvisation and substitution depending on a patient's or midwife's immediate needs. Bible passages differ between midwives as do the types of oil named, but "sounding," praying, anointing, fumigating, administering purgatives, and the like always occur.

Granny mixed oils of "Conqueror," "Devil," myrrh, cinnamon, and thyme in a saucer and carried it to the gate after the delivery. She rebuked the spirit of the "witchcraft baby" and any duppy intent on hindering things: "I beseech you to leave this gate immediately." Then she buried the mixture, right at the gate. To ease out what remained in the uterus, the "babymother" drank tea boiled from sinkle bible, senna, and one half of a lime cut on the tree. This mixture is identical to a tonic for amenorrhea previously described.

Now that midwifery is under government control and most "babymothers" give birth in hospitals, most "witchcraft baby" purging gets done by healers instead of midwives. Sometimes a healer must "work" a hospitalized case from her yard. One healed a woman so sick with "false belly" that hospital doctors had given up, leaving her on intravenous "life drip." That was when the distraught husband sought the healer out. She made him fetch his wife's nightdress, which she "fixed." She told the man to go to his wife, take off her hospital gown, and dress her in the nightdress with no one else's help.

The woman was released from the hospital yet had little relief. She still carried her "false belly" load and could hardly climb the hill to the healer's yard where she "gave birth." The healer boasts of "delivering" that "witchcraft baby" in the pit toilet after a grueling day of praying over, anointing, fumigating, "sounding," and feeding purgatives to the patient. She worked to "cut and clear destruction" from her charge and this seemed to bring benefits biomedicine could not offer, for the would-be "babymother" now feels fine.

Through temporal and spiritual cleansing, the substances that bloated the woman's "belly" fell into the pit with other waste. Whether the fetid, gaseous air, gelatinous clots, and toadlike "something" (toads being tiny and much slimier than frogs) that came out was the remains of a fetus or the effluvia of a cyst did not matter. The woman found relief through her purge, not only for an otherwise unintelligible, unmanageable physical condition, but also for those existential and situational tensions engendered by male-female relations.

Through her "false belly," the woman—and those who talked about her predicament and those who participated in curing it—acknowledged feelings about the constant sexual pressure that men subject women to. The specific meaning of this "false belly" had to do with the particular duppy who "started" it: this was the woman whose dead ex-lover came to call while her husband was away. Her "witchcraft baby" exposed her earlier sin of adultery, allowing her to work through her guilt. Happily, her husband forgave her and felt only glad that her life had been saved.

SWEEPING EVIL AWAY

Healers literally sweep out "evil," physically removing and deterring demons, ghosts, and other invisible, malevolent things. Besides using purgatives to bring inner cleanliness, sometimes banners are waved, flagging away evil spirits, and some healers spin or "turn the roll" themselves or with their charges to "spin off destruction" like a centrifuge. Some shake and then break open soda bottles or pierce their lids with ice picks and use them like sandblasters to "drive off evil," showering people with carbonated beverage in the process. Some speak in tongues. "The angels" often send "messages" "instructing" receivers how to remove or wash away "destruction" so the patient can be purified and healed. Spiritual as well as temporal ("bush doctor") healers know that good health depends on driving debris from the body and avoiding social trouble and immoral actions.

THE SUBVERSIVE AND CONSERVATIVE NATURE OF "FALSE BELLY"

"Bad belly" pregnancies and the understandings that accompany them can be used in discourse to support and to challenge the status quo, as can "bad bellies" created by "tying" and the understandings this and menstruation entail. In addition, people use "false belly" to work through gender tensions and antisocial feelings, such as resentments of men and familial obligations, as well as sex-related affect such as guilt over adulterous liaisons or over lusting for them.

While women's "bad bellies" often symptomize disease, they can also be real pregnancies. Sometimes, because abortions of "natural" pregnancies are socially unacceptable, unwanted babies are recast according to cultural traditions as unhealthy, socially "created" "false bellies" to justify aborting them. Regular abortions overtly challenge social traditions yet are often covertly "taken" in order to maintain a lifestyle and so social stability. Abortion and childbirth techniques (whether for "natural" or "created" pregnancies) follow the purgative model provided by the ethnophysiology of menstruation.

Jamaican beliefs about the body construct as well as represent the phenomena they purport to describe. They help people understand and so manipulate their bodily workings. And as people discuss their bodies, they discuss society, often challenging, supporting, subverting, and maintaining the status quo, all at the same time. The flexibility of "meaning systems" allows for this sort of multilayered action. It allows human beings as social actors, through discourse, to announce their social and moral opinions and standings.

Cultural inconsistency also leaves room for real change, which occurs when enough people come to invest revisionary cultural constructions with "naturalness"—with unquestionable validity. Things anchored into the body are easily spoken of as "natural," so anchoring a thing in the body is a simple route to promoting a particular ideological stance. Gender relations and even ideal gender-linked attributes (such as male promiscuity) are maintained by ethnophysiological beliefs. These beliefs can be manipulated for definitional and subversive purposes as, for example, in procuring abortions by crying "duppy."

Chapter 15

Making Use of Culture

Traditional health beliefs guide people's attempts to deal with problems their bodies present, providing explanations for sickness and suggesting solutions (sometimes thwarting biomedical interventions). They also provide guidelines for maintaining health and fitness.

In addition to their practical applications, understandings that inform the body's cultural construction reflect happenings in other subcultural realms and so serve as commentaries on them. Understandings are not merely repeated but used, often creatively, as people minister to their bodies and as they attempt to inform one another about social and moral opinions and standings. In this, the body serves as a symbolic medium for the expression of ideas about the social and moral order and, ultimately, about one's own position within this order.

Douglas observes a general "concordance between symbolic and social experience" (1982, 64); even "the cosmos is seen through the medium of the body" (18). "Concordance" cannot mean simple recapitulation. Ideals notwithstanding, social experience is too complex to lend itself solely to templatelike transfers. Cultures are not wholly integrated but instead contain many oppositions, inversions, and exceptions. People, being perceptive and creative, use symbolic discourse to express awarenesses of these inconsistencies, whether to deny or legitimize, support or challenge, submit to or resist, exacerbate or alleviate them. In doing so, people make tactical use of ambiguity and the multiple meanings with which symbols can be invested. They do not necessarily do this in a consciously strategic fashion.

Cultural meaning systems do not simply represent but also partly create a reality (D'Andrade 1984, 96). For example, health beliefs are used to interpret bodily states and so play a part in their construction (see Ots 1990, 39). Other kinds of beliefs are also used to shape experience. The imposition of ideological meaning systems in any subcultural realm allows individuals to deal with the threat that ideal expectations will not be met and to adjust for the strain felt when the incongruity between an expectation and its realization cannot otherwise be encompassed or explained (Geertz 1973).

The imposition of understandings about the social and moral order (contained in traditional health beliefs) onto the body provides individuals with a chance to express thoughts and sentiments that, addressed directly, would expose the questionable nature of the social enterprise (and implicate the speaker as subversive). Ethnophysiological discourse provides a way to make political—ideological—assertions when legitimate means to do so are not available (as in the "gas" of hunger), when subtlety is called for (as when that which one asserts—a desire for an abortion, for example—cannot be explicitly stated because its very secrecy supports an important bit of ideology), or when "symbolic capital" (Bourdieu 1982), which can be used to gird one's social position, must be accrued.

Although the body is but one arena in which such imposition and expression takes place, it is a privileged one because it mediates between the individual and his or her social reality and also because of the ease with which, in its inherent physical capacities and various states, it lends itself to symbolic manipulation. Those things cast as "naturally" inhering in biology are agreed upon to form unchallengeable support bases for ideological stances, such as ideas about what sort of work each sex is fit for.

Because ideological discourse relieves strain, either by legitimizing it, challenging it, or denying it, such discourse helps ensure that the wholesale disintegration of a culture from such straining or its complete revision through revolution is avoided. Indeed, as Bourdieu points out in his discussion of "habitus" (which he defines as "a system of dispositions" [1982, 214n.1]), ideological discourses often serve to "reproduce those objective structures of which they are the product" (72). For example, the social divisiveness of habitually taking food precautions to prevent poisoning is part of what necessitates them in the first place.

Even when overtly subversive, ideological discourse couched in ethnophysiological language can support and preserve the perceived order because good health is modeled on that order. In allowing people to express their feelings about others, as by accusing a duppy of "interfering" with one's health, such talk can release tension and so dissipate it. It can also explicitly highlight the unacceptable or "unnatural," as when social and moral causes (such as "carelessness") are identified (see Turner 1979). At the least, it reinforces belief in the ethnophysiology that gives it shape and in the particular set of relations captured in that piece of ethnophysiology.

Abortion, for instance, is subversive in rural Jamaica when viewed against the general cultural emphasis on parenting and kinship obligations. While it therefore creates certain social and moral tensions, it also releases the tension inherent in specific, nonideal situations. It can allow for adjustments in the unhappy mother-to-be's relations with her household, her possible child, and its father. And, moreover, ideas about how to abort, how a baby is conceived in the first place, and who should have babies reflect certain aspects of social and gender relations, casting them as "natural."

Not all is "habitus"; not all is the un-self-conscious result of what Bourdieu describes as unreflexive yet system-recreating, structurally predetermined dispositions. Individuals can consciously use the body as a mouthpiece for opinion and a bargaining tool, manipulating others and rationalizing their own beliefs or bodily states through arguments cloaked in the ethnophysiological idiom and supported with reference to their "naturalness" or inherence in the body. For instance, a man can warn a woman who does not want to have intercourse with him that she will get sick.

Despite the fact that cultural inconsistencies help to generate ideological discourses to begin with, culture's innate incongruities and inherent flexibility provide room for debate or "bases for leverage toward change" (Levine 1985, 31) where fully integrated and therefore rigid and fragile cultural systems would shatter. So if, for example, enough people argue that a certain quality does not inhere in the body, they can undermine the ideological system based in that assertion, altering—but not destroying—their culture.

BORROWING METAPHORS

Understandings from one realm applied to another, directly (as in metonymy and metaphor) or formally (as guidelines for construction or parallel-shaping) have illuminative as well as strategically manipulative and structurally reinforcing, socially reproductive value. They help people to bound, understand, and manage otherwise incomprehensible and uncontrollable things (see Lévi-Strauss 1979). Naming and assigning a thing a mechanic or mode of operation brings it into one's meaningful world.

The Jamaican construction of the body takes its characteristic form from several culturally predominant motifs. Those most overtly obvious concern the life cycle of fruit which, when overripe, has outlived its moment of potential use as something to be incorporated into the body and begins to rot. Once firm and good, now it softens, decomposes, and its sweetness sours. "Soft" things "have no use" and, like rotten things, must be eliminated. Similarly, feces and other wastes must be swept from the body. Death—unused sperm included—must be washed away, as contact brings sickness.

While excessive moistness is linked with the fetid suppuration of decomposition, excessive dryness is linked with death, too; both deluge and drought can kill. Generally, light, dry, thin, husks are associated with infertility, greed, stinginess, and antisocial behavior. Firm fat and a suitable amount of ripe moistness signal fertility and sociability. But too much of a good thing is as bad as too little.

For example, when there is a surfeit of fruit that is not shared, some must rot. One rotten fruit can quickly contaminate and ruin the rest if not swiftly removed from the pile. Excess resources such as fruit are—like feces—only good when passed. Antisocial urges to hoard and antisocial individuals must be kept in check. The health of the reciprocity network, like that of the body, depends on unimpeded flow and the expurgation of bad elements.

The healthy, fertile individual has firm fat, sufficient moistness, and inner cleanliness, while the sick are any of a combination of soft, thin, dry, overmoist, husklike, oozing, and infertile. They are likened to the newly dead (and to decomposing fruit) or to those so long since gone that only their bones remain. They are like dirty vessels which, full of filth, contaminate anything put in them for storage.

Healthiness itself is sociable while sickness, like infertility and (societal) decay, is not. The "concordance" between formal, organizational metaphors, metaphors used to describe the processes by which the body becomes sick, and social reality is apparent in the comparisons Jamaicans make between fruit, the body, and healthy social life. While fruit-body metaphors easily represent binary value judgments and add color to bodily discourse, metaphors involving the skin as a boundary and those that emphasize internal balance and cleanliness are more directly representative of the unresolvable social tensions Jamaicans must live with.

Maintaining the Jamaican body depends upon maintaining its equilibrium. This can be done by guarding its portals and making sure that offensive substances do not gain entrance, just as society must (at least in the eyes of committed members) be protected from antisocial or evil intruders.

It can also be done by cleansing toxins from the body, much as members of a society would expel subversives, and just as individuals must repel evil others who would take advantage of and destroy them. Orifices can be protected mechanically and offensive substances can be guarded against; if they gain entrance, they can be washed out. People can also take moral and social precautions to defend their health, since physical health is tied to the state of one's social and moral affairs.

People who follow health customs have bodies "fit" enough to withstand minor insults. They do not, anyway, place themselves in positions in which harmful matter might enter; they would not walk into cool rain from a hot room. They are relatively safe from asocial sickness as they respect and abide by traditions, being sociable and moral. They take purges to purify their bodies, "don't business" with evil, and try to "move good" with others.

People who "live good" cannot, ideally, be caught by socially precipitated sicknesses: sickness instigated in response to perceived affronts by an animate being (a neighbor, a demon, God, or a duppy sent by a "science man" hired by a "grudgeful" villager). In an ideal world, a moral, sociable person could never anger anyone enough to attack. And should anyone really want to "sick" a physically and spiritually "clean" person (a "bad mind" individual might), God and his angels provide protection. When sickness strikes, then, the moral and social well-being of the victim appears to others to be in a questionable state.

THE BODY AND THE SELF

Mortality applies to the body and not to the person, who continues to live as a ghost after death. Nonetheless, the Jamaican self is physically informed. Adina, accustomed to caring for her younger siblings, pointed out that before small children "know" their own selves they may walk off the edges of verandas; they do not yet know the limitations of the bodies they have been given. The Jamaican body both carries and equals the living self. One's body connotes and denotes one's identity; it is a social symbol thereof. This fact underscores the importance of bodily wellness in Jamaica, where like one's status one's body must be protected.

THE SOCIAL ORIFICES AND THE DANGERS OF TRUST

Jamaican bodies must eat, drink, rest, work or exercise, rid themselves of waste, and express "nature." Cleansing the body remains in the control of the individual and does not involve others. Rest is also essentially asocial, although others can impinge on it, making it a social event in specific instances. Nourishment and sex, however, are at once social events and specifically intergender events. In this they differ from other equally necessary bodily functions.

While an unrested, "unclean" (in both senses of the word) body is a vulnerable one because not "fit," the body and so the self is most prone to attack during eating and during sex because these activities involve others (and others are always potentially self-centered and destructive). Moreover, those involved must be of opposite genders. The interdependence necessitated by the division of labor and sexual dimorphism makes intergender relations fuller and more balanced than intragender ones in the sense that all culturally necessary tasks can be accomplished by a heterosexual pair but not by two people of one gender. But at the same time, each gender has differing goals, and this adds to the volatility of intergender relations. Heterosexually social, the arenas of eating and sexuality have a kind of significance that resting and purging lack.

Social occasions by definition involve the demonstration of relationships, whether between close and trusted allies (real or fictitious kin), wary acquaintances who have not yet fully cloaked their instrumental relations in an expressive idiom, or full enemies with no altruistic bonds whatsoever and so no trust. People continually reaffirm, redefine, and regroup their relations. However, the same things that demonstrate trust and relatedness, such as sharing food and having sex, can easily be interpreted as hostile presentations because trust itself is known to be a pretense in many situations. Jamaicans pretend that relations are fully altruistic (and many truly are) but a well known, subversive cultural tradition holds that most relationships are exploitive. With this in mind, trust becomes very hard for people to establish and maintain except with closest kin.

Eating and having sex are among those social occasions in which trust gets tested because relationships are being put into action. On these specific occasions more than on others, the body (and so the self) can be attacked by a person pretending to act altruistically. People fear the instrumental and manipulative base of gestures made in these idioms, so the arenas of eating and sexuality become especially meaningful settings for calling "fitness" into play. Rest and purging can be seen as personal, preparatory antecedents for an upcoming and interpersonal match or "big game" in which one's teammate—one's sex partner or food-giver—may become one's enemy and betrayer. The "bad belly" can signal that this has occurred.

"BAD BELLIES"

The "belly" is where negative reactions caused by offensive intrusions actually take place. Improper mixtures produce toxic or health-threatening substances, such as "cold," gas, "boil," and so on, much like improper social mixtures "bring problem": incestuous marriages, for example, end in trouble; liaisons between respected "big women" and "common" men of "low station" bring scandal; pastors cannot drink, and thieves cannot attend church. Excess "cold," gas, and "boil" can clog the system and "cause problem," much like people can block others' progress by depleting their resources, taking up too much of their time, or making other draining demands. Irritations and blockages can be "washed out" of inner tubes, but real-life hurdles cannot be cleared so easily. Neither can sorcery-induced blockages meant to impede life-progress, usually by harming health, be easily cleared.

To attack the health is to attack the livelihood and so to block another's success. People wishing others harm tend to use edibles because, in addition to the thrill of inverting the meaning of food, otherwise a symbol of trust and a vehicle for nurturance, this is the easiest way to get poison into the "belly" where it can cause bad reactions.

Men are more likely than women to ingest poison as they must eat others' cooking. They most fear poisons capable of "bending the mind" and undermining their (already precarious sense of) independence, leading to behavior that would otherwise—or so they can say—never even be considered. Men dread menstrual "tying," in which women use their blood to recreate and inculcate or—and here I borrow a term used by several men as they described productive insemination—to "ingraft" the sense of altruistic obligation inherent in kinship by virtue of consubstantiality. This is one of the main reasons for menstrual taboos.

Women do not generally eat others' cooking, but since they must have heterosexual intercourse to survive (that is, for the sake of finance and the sake of health, not to mention "reputation" and "respect"), they do incorporate others' substances through their vaginas. The vaginal "mouth" is thus a focal point for female fears. Unincorporated sperm—sperm taken in but not "ingrafted" in a fetus—can defile and sicken; moreover, men can introduce poisons vaginally. Babies produced by mixing bodily substances are threatening when unwanted, harmed through witchcraft, or fathered by duppies. They represent unwanted social ties, involve unwanted social responsibilities, and place unwanted limits on freedom. They are often gotten rid of, like too many demands or obligations.

Both men and women, then, can contract problems through the incorporation of others' bodily substances and the ensuing creation of undesirable ties. Both men and women can suffer "bad belly" when the obligations inherent in sharing "one blood" are "unnaturally" forced upon them or, as in the case of the irresponsible babyfather, unrespected. "Bad bellies" can be used to comment upon social reality. One of the most troubling inconsistencies for Jamaicans is the tension between the ideal of altruistically motivated interdependent relationships and the understood reality and dangers of manipulative, deceitful, self-centered social actors. This tension pervades gender as well as many other relations.

Because they can be created so easily through sex and eating, the two main arenas for gender interaction, "bad bellies" are especially useful in arguments concerning gender relations. These arguments can be made by the sufferers themselves or by those observing their conditions. They can be subversive or supportive of those relations on which they remark. Regardless, they comment on the state of a person's social relations, for if there were no tensions within these they would not have come about. The same symptoms might then have been grouped and labeled differently.

Generally, arguments couched in the idioms of the "false belly" pregnancy and the "bad belly" of "tying" express resentments engendered by the demands of others upon the individual and the ambivalences surrounding dependency needs. Fears about duppies stealing babies and cunnilingus do the same. Others' demands cause tension because it is culturally unacceptable to refuse them. That to "look something" from others—to take advantage of them—is culturally promoted makes this more problematic. People can be kept from getting ahead when those around them keep depleting the resources they would have to save to get ahead. So people "beg" not only out of neediness but also to avoid humiliation through others' success. And to make matters worse, even the dead, surviving as duppies, can make demands on living persons.

"Tying" and "false belly" comment on these things as they pertain to gender relations in particular. Menstrual "tying" creates consubstantial, "one blood" kinship bonds (which, ideally, require a selfless fulfillment of obligation). These are too much like mother-son ties for men's comfort. Male independence is highly promoted yet hard to attain because of socioeconomic and cultural conditions, and this exacerbates men's concern over it. Women also wish for independence, but because men continually "breed and leave" them as sole supports for families, women have few options other than trading sexual favors for survival. That women as mates and mothers must nurture others but receive little nurturance themselves increases their resentment of others' demands. Both men and women use "tying" and "false belly" beliefs to comment upon these situations.

PROCREATION ENVY

Prostitution, infertility, female infidelity, birth control, and abortion can all be understood (and expressed) as self-centered actions or arguments against the importance of recreating society through procreation. They also challenge patriarchal ideas about controlling women's sexuality, the attribution of the right to solicit sex to men only, and the male right and ability to procreate. For when women control their reproductivity, they can dispose of progeny males might desire, denying men a procreative role. The cultural significance of these indigenously made connections is shown in the talk surrounding these things in rural Jamaica.

To overcome their own inability to get pregnant, whether consciously or not, men seek to usurp and control female procreative power (Bettleheim 1962; Gregor 1985). The cultural construction of male "nature," the casting of women as mere vessels, and the belief that a male God is the ultimate "creator" exemplify this (Weigle 1989).

MENSTRUATION: A MODEL FOR PURITY

Menstrual blood is welcome in Jamaica and menstruation is considered healthy. The same is true in other cultural contexts (Browner 1985, 105; Newman 1985, 15; Skultans 1988, 159). The "washout," modeled on menstruation, is key to health in Jamaica and indicative of a gynocentric (as opposed to

androcentric) construction of wellness. People follow the principles they understand menstruation to work by, using
"washouts" for prevention and cure. Certain "bush" teas and
pharmaceuticals, for instance, cleanse the blood or "belly" by
catharsis. Bodily processes such as sexual "discharge" and
childbirth are understood as types of purges. Even abortion
techniques are modeled on the purifying menstrual "washout."

A bodily catharsis of offensive matter can be construed as a
metaphor for ridding oneself of unwanted and cumbersome
obligations that can block progress much like "cold" can block
impregnation or bowel action. It can also be seen as a symbolic
denial of burdensome demands and requests for aid. Although
many relationships are genuinely moral (as opposed to pragmatic) and many sacrifices are altruistically made for well-
loved kin, people often resent obligations to others, and
"washouts" provide individuals with ways to express these
resentments and symbolically exorcise them, and those who
engender them.

The "washout" of menstruation physically rids women of
defiling old semen. The belief that semen is polluting has been
documented for a few other cultures (Eilberg-Schwartz 1990,
chap. 7; Gregor 1990, 103 and 145; McClain 1989, 75), but the
belief's connection with menstruation's "uncleanliness" and
menstrual taboos has gone virtually unnoted.

In Jamaica, the notion that aged semen sickens reflects
understandings about decay and also the primacy of reproduction because "ingrafted" semen does not pollute. Contamination with death, however, does. This has practical reasons—rotting things such as corpses often carry disease—as
well as symbolic ones.

In addition to its significance for personal catharses and
its meaning for health, the concern with rot and purification
can be seen as a metaphorical expression of a desire to maintain order within society: to get rid of decadence and evil
antisociability, to vent antisocial frustrations, and so to protect one's society (as one would protect oneself). It is no coincidence that bothersome individuals and those who offend
are referred to by people who "cuss bad word" as "blood clot"

(menstrual rags) or "one bag of shit"; they are referred to as being full of and equal to dangerous matter that can contaminate and poison.

The "washout" is a social and an antisocial act. As a symbolic medium, it promotes the health of society even as it allows for antisocial expressions. The flexibility of meaning systems allows for alternate arguments. Yet these need not destroy social and moral order. When consensus changes and different values are vested with ideological "naturalness," this same flexibility and tolerance for inconsistency allows the meaning system to change without breaking apart. Meanwhile, individuals continue to use the current culturally constructed idioms of health and sickness to describe the states of their relationships and to mark their places within the social and moral order.

Notes

INTRODUCTION

1. Few full accounts of Afro-Caribbean ethnophysiology exist. Laguerre, who reviews the literature in *Afro-Caribbean Folk Medicine* (1987), could fill only eight pages with information on how the body is thought to work; the dearth of written resources drove him to set aside his interest in medical anthropology (personal communication 1989).

2. See, for example, Bordo (1990), Douglas (1982), Farmer (1988), Jordanova (1980), Kleinman (1986, 1980), Laws et al. (1985), Lock (1990), Martin (1987), Scheper-Hughes (1988), and Taylor (1988).

CHAPTER 1

1. A succinct description of the island nation is found in Hudson and Seyler (1989).

2. Of all Jamaicans, 85 percent are poor (M. G. Smith 1989) and about half reside in rural areas (STATIN 1988a, 10). But many urban dwellers are migrants from the countryside. Brody found that three-fifths of his urban subjects were born in truly rural areas and one-fifth had been born in small towns (1981, 101). As Brody points out, urban residence "does not necessarily mean a modern world view... [Urban dwellers] often continue to perceive themselves as rooted in the country" and lack the "sense of self" typical in industrialized nations (69). This suggests that my findings reflect the attitudes of the majority of Jamaicans.

3. A full discussion of higglering is found in Durant-Gonzalez (1976); see also Katzin (1960).

4. See Rubin and Comitas (1975) and Dreher (1982) for full discussions of Jamaican *ganja* use.

CHAPTER 2

1. Descriptions of "bush" or herbs traditionally used for medicinal purposes can be found in Asprey and Thornton (1953–55), Campbell (1974), Lowe (1972), and Robertson (1982).

CHAPTER 3

1. People may link venereal disease transmission to a transfer of germ cells during sexual intercourse, as the "poisons" that cause sexually transmitted diseases are sometimes called "germs" (see Mitchell 1983, 843).

CHAPTER 4

1. Bailey (1971) discusses the importance of maintaining control over personal information by keeping to oneself; Cohen (1953) provides a classic description and discussion of paranoia and suspicion in the Jamaican context.

CHAPTER 6

1. The fear of external control by others is also seen among African-Americans and they, too, report feeling great anxiety about adulterated food and others' evil intentions (Snow 1974).

2. See Barrett (1988, 1976), Seaga (1969), Simpson (1970), and Wedenoja (1980, 1988) for more information on religion.

3. Liebow (1967) discusses the hopelessness poverty generates among African-Americans.

CHAPTER 8

1. See Cohen (1953, 1955), Kerr (1963), Patterson (1969), and Phillips (1973) in regard to Jamaican personality. See also Kardiner (1963) or LeVine (1982).

2. Liebow (1967) describes a similarly "self-serving" "theory of manly flaws" used by poor "streetcorner" men in the United States to explain marriage failure without undermining claims to manhood.

CHAPTER 10

1. Increased exposure to the notion of romantic love through television and other media, much of it imported from the U.S.A. and Britain, promises to change this.

CHAPTER 12

1. No woman I knew admitted to doing this herself and all the information I have is hearsay. Whether or not "tying" occurs often or at all, its island-wide cultural salience and the fear that it inspires make it "real" enough to warrant discussion.

2. Examples of such "monocausal explanations" are seen in the cross-cultural studies of Bock (1967), Montgomery (1974), Paige and Paige (1981), Stephens (1967), and Young and Bacdayan (1965).

3. There are a few exceptions. Women's benefits are discussed in Skultans (1988) and Lawrence (1988). Feminist appraisals are found in Golub (1985) and Laws, et al. (1985). Martin (1987) and Wright (1982) discuss the links between menstruation's meaning and its ethnophysiological function.

Bibliography

Althaus, F. 1991. Three in Four Jamaican Pregnancies Are Either Mistimed or Unwanted. *International Family Planning* 17(1):32–34.

Asprey, G. F., and Phyllis Thornton. 1953–55. Medical Plants of Jamaica: Parts 1 to 4. *West Indian Medical Journal* 2:233–52, 3:17–41, 4:69–84, 4:145–68.

Austin, Diane J. 1984. *Urban Life in Kingston, Jamaica: The Culture and Class Ideology of Two Neighborhoods.* New York: Gordon and Breach Science Publishers.

Bailey, F. G. 1971. Gifts and Poison. *In* F. G. Bailey, ed., *Gifts and Poison.* New York: Schocken Books, pp. 1–27.

Barrett, Leonard E. 1988. *The Rastafarians,* 2nd ed. Boston: Beacon Press.

———. 1976. *The Sun and the Drum: African Roots in Jamaican Folk Tradition.* Kingston: Sangster's Book Stores.

Barrow, Christine. 1988. Anthropology, The Family and Women in the Caribbean. *In* Patricia Mohammed and Catherine Shepherd, eds., *Gender in Caribbean Development.* Mona (Jamaica): The University of the West Indies, Women and Development Studies Project, pp. 156–69.

Bettelheim, Bruno. 1962 [1954]. *Symbolic Wounds: Puberty Rites and the Envious Male.* New York: Collier Books.

Black, Clinton. 1983 [1958]. *History of Jamaica.* Kingston: Longman Jamaica.

Blake, Judith. 1961. *Family Structure in Jamaica.* New York: Free Press.

Bock, Philip K. 1967. Love Magic, Menstrual Taboos, and the Facts of Geography. *American Anthropologist* 69(2):213–16.

Bordo, Susan. 1990. Reading the Slender Body. *In* Mary Jacobus, Evelyn Fox Keller, and Sally Shuttleworth, eds., *Body/Politics.* New York: Routledge, pp. 83–112.

Bott, Elizabeth. 1971 [1957]. *Family and Social Network.* New York: The Free Press.

Bourdieu, Pierre. 1982 [1972]. *Outline of a Theory of Practice,* trans. Richard Nice. Cambridge: Cambridge University Press.

Brodber, Erna. 1989. Socio-cultural Change in Jamaica. *In* Rex Nettleford, ed., *Jamaica in Independence.* Kingston: Heinemann Publishers, pp. 55–74.

———. 1974. *Abandonment of Children in Jamaica.* Mona (Jamaica): Institute of Social and Economic Research, University of the West Indies.

Brody, Eugene. 1985. Everyday Knowledge of Jamaican Women. *In* Lucile F. Newman, ed., *Women's Medicine: A Cross-Cultural Study of Indigenous Fertility Regulation.* New Brunswick, N.J.: Rutgers University Press, pp. 161–78.

———. 1981. *Sex, Contraception, and Motherhood in Jamaica.* Cambridge: Harvard University Press.

Browner, Carol H. 1985. Traditional Techniques for Diagnosis, Treatment, and Control of Pregnancy in Cali, Colombia. *In* Lucile F. Newman, ed., *Women's Medicine: A Cross-Cultural Study of Indigenous Fertility Regulation.* New Brunswick, N.J.: Rutgers University Press, pp. 99–123.

Buckley, Thomas, and Alma Gottlieb. 1988. A Critical

Appraisal of Theories of Menstrual Symbolism. *In* Thomas Buckley and Alma Gottlieb, eds., *Blood Magic: The Anthropology of Menstruation.* Los Angeles: University of California Press, pp. 3–50.

Bush, Barbara. 1990. *Slave Women in Caribbean Societies.* Bloomington: Indiana University Press.

Campbell, Sadie. 1974. Bush Teas: A Cure-all. *Jamaica Journal* 8(2&3):60–65.

Cassidy, Frederic G. 1982. *Jamaica Talk: Three Hundred Years of the English Language in Jamaica*, limp ed. London: Macmillan Education.

Chevannes, Barry. 1989. Drop Pan and Folk Consciousness. *Jamaica Journal* 22(2):45–50.

Chodorow, Nancy. 1978. *The Reproduction of Mothering: Psychoanalysis and the Sociology of Gender.* Los Angeles: University of California Press.

Clarke, Edith. 1957. *My Mother Who Fathered Me: A Study of the Family in Three Selected Communities in Jamaica.* Boston: George Allen and Unwin.

Cohen, Yehudi. 1955. Character Formation and Social Structure in a Jamaican Community. *Psychiatry* 18:275–96.

———. 1953. A Study of Interpersonal Relations in a Jamaican Community. Ph.D. diss., Yale University.

Comitas, Lambros. 1973 [1964]. Occupational Multiplicity in Rural Jamaica. *In* David Lowenthal and Lambros Comitas, eds., *Work and Family Life: West Indian Perspectives.* New York: Anchor Books, pp. 157–73.

DaCosta, C. 21 May 1989. Controversy over Prevcon. *The Sunday Gleaner* (Kingston), p. 3.

D'Andrade, Roy. 1984. Cultural Meaning Systems. *In* Richard A. Shweder and Robert A. LeVine, eds., *Culture Theory: Essays on Mind, Self, and Emotion.* New York: Cambridge University Press, pp. 87–119.

Davies, Omar, and Michael Witter. 1989. The Development of the Jamaican Economy since Independence. *In* Rex Nettleford, ed., *Jamaica in Independence*. Kingston: Heinemann Publishers, pp. 75–103.

De Cordoba, Jose. 28 December 1988. Jamaica's Drive on Ganja [Marijuana] Makes Peasant's Lives a Little Tougher. *Wall Street Journal.*

Douglas, Mary. 1982 [1970]. *Natural Symbols: Explorations in Cosmology*. New York: Pantheon Books.

Dreher, Melanie C. 1982. *Working Men and Ganja*. Philadelphia: Institute for the Study of Human Issues.

Durant-Gonzalez, Victoria. 1976. Role and Status of Rural Jamaican Women: Higglering and Mothering. Ph.D. diss., University of California at Berkeley.

Eilberg-Schwartz, Howard. 1990. *The Savage in Judaism: An Anthropology of Israelite Religion and Ancient Judaism*. Bloomington: Indiana University Press.

Emerick, Abraham J. 1915. Obeah and Duppyism in Jamaica. *In* Abraham Emerick, ed., *Woodstock Letters*. Woodstock, Md.

Erasmus, C. J. 1977 [1952]. Changing Folk Beliefs and the Relativity of Empirical Knowledge. *In* D. Landy, ed., *Culture, Disease, and Healing: Studies in Medical Anthropology*. New York: Macmillan Publishing, pp. 264–72.

Farmer, Paul. 1988. Bad Blood, Spoiled Milk: Bodily Fluids as Moral Barometers in Rural Haiti. *American Ethnologist* 15(1):62–83.

Foner, Nancy. 1973. *Status and Power in Rural Jamaica: A Study of Educational and Political Change*. New York: Teacher's College Press.

Foster, George M. 1971 [1965]. Peasant Society and the Image of Limited Good. *In* Yehudi A. Cohen, ed., *Man in Adaptation: The Institutional Framework*. Chicago: Aldine Atherton, pp. 298–311.

Freilich, Morris. 1968. Sex, Secrets, and Systems. *In* Stanford Gerber, ed., *The Family in the Caribbean*. Rio Piedras (Puerto Rico): Institute of Caribbean Studies, pp. 47–62.

Geertz, Clifford. 1973. Ideology as a Cultural System. *In* Clifford Geertz, ed., *The Interpretation of Cultures*. New York: Basic Books, pp. 193–233.

Gleaner (Kingston). 1989a (4 May). How AIDS Spreads in Jamaica, p. 1.

————. 1989b (21 May). Contraceptive Ad Withdrawn, p. 1.

Goldberg, Richard F. 1979. The Way We Were or Duppies: A Caribbean Phenomenon. *Journal of Psychological Anthropology* 2(2):197–212.

Golub, Sharon, ed. 1985. *Lifting the Curse of Menstruation: A Feminist Appraisal of the Influence of Menstruation on Women's Lives*. New York: Harrington Park Press.

Gregor, Thomas. 1990. Male Dominance and Sexual Coercion. *In* James W. Stigler, Richard A. Shweder, and Gilbert Herdt, eds., *Cultural Psychology: Essays on Comparative Human Development*. New York: Cambridge University Press, pp. 477–95.

————. 1985. *Anxious Pleasures*. Chicago: University of Chicago Press.

Hanna, W. J. 1988. Newspapers and Medicine in Jamaica a Century Ago. *Jamaica Journal* 21(4):33–36.

Henriques, Fernando. 1958 [1953]. *Family and Colour in Jamaica*. London: Macgibbon and Kee.

Henry, Frances, and Pamela Wilson. 1975. The Status of Women in Caribbean Societies: An Overview. *Social and Economic Studies* 24(2):165–98.

Hoetink, H. 1985. "Race" and Color in the Caribbean. *In* Sidney Mintz and Sally Price, eds., *Caribbean Contours*. Baltimore: Johns Hopkins University Press, pp. 55–84.

312 ONE BLOOD

Hogg, Donald W. 1964. Jamaican Religions: a Study in Variations. Ph.D. diss., Yale University.

Hudson, Rex A., and Daniel J. Seyler 1989. Jamaica. In Sandra W. Medita and Dennis M. Hanratty, eds., *Islands of the Commonwealth Caribbean: A Regional Study.* Washington, D.C.: Government Printing Office, pp. 43–160.

Hufford, David J. 1982. *The Terror That Comes in the Night.* Philadelphia: University of Pennsylvania Press.

Hurston, Zora Neale. 1938. *Tell My Horse.* New York: J. B. Lippincott Company.

Jayawardena, Chandra. 1963. *Conflict and Solidarity in a Guianese Plantation.* London: Athlone Press.

Jordanova, L. J. 1980. Natural Facts: A Historical Perspective on Science and Sexuality. In Carol MacCormack and Marilyn Strathern, eds., *Nature, Culture and Gender.* Cambridge: Cambridge University Press, pp. 42–69.

Kaplan, Irving, Howard Blutstein, Kathryn Therese Johnston, and David McMorris. 1976. *Area Handbook for Jamaica.* Washington, D.C.: The American University.

Kardiner, Abram. 1963 [1945]. *The Psychological Frontiers of Society.* New York: Columbia University Press.

Katzin, Margaret Fisher. 1960. The Business of Higglering in Jamaica. *Social and Economic Studies* 9(3):297–331.

Kerr, Madeline. 1963. *Personality and Conflict in Jamaica.* London: Willmer Brothers and Haram.

Kitzinger, S. 1982. The Social Context of Birth: Some Comparisons between Childbirth in Jamaica and Britain. In Carol P. MacCormack, ed., *Ethnography of Fertility and Birth.* San Diego: Academic Press, pp. 181–204.

Kleinman, A. 1986. *Social Origins of Distress and Disease.* New Haven, Conn.: Yale University Press.

———. 1980. *Patients and Healers in the Context of Culture.* Berkeley: University of California Press.

Laguerre, Michel. 1987. *Afro-Caribbean Folk Medicine*. South Hadley, Mass.: Bergin and Garvey Publishers.

Lawrence, Denise L. 1988. Menstrual Politics: Women and Pigs in Rura l Portugal. *In* Thomas Buckley and Alma Gottlieb, eds., *Blood Magic*. Los Angeles: University of California Press, pp. 117–36.

Laws, Sophie, Valerie Hay, and Andrea Eagan. 1985. *Seeing Red: The Politics of Premenstrual Tension*. London: Hutchinson and Company.

Lévi-Strauss, Claude. 1979 [1963]. The Effectiveness of Symbols, trans. Claire Jacobson and B. G. Scheepf. *In* William A. Lessa and Evon Z. Vogt, eds., *Reader in Comparative Religion*. San Francisco: Harper and Row, pp. 318–27.

Levine, Donald N. 1985. *The Flight From Ambiguity*. Chicago: University of Chicago Press.

LeVine, Robert A. 1982. *Culture, Behavior, and Personality*. New York: Aldine Publishing Company.

Liebow, Elliot. 1967. *Tally's Corner: A Study of Negro Streetcorner Men*. Boston: Little, Brown and Company.

Lock, Margaret. 1990. Words of Fear, Words of Power: Nerves and the Awakening of Political Consciousness. *Medical Anthropology* 11(1):79–90.

Lowe, H. I. C. 1972. Jamaican Folk Medicine. *Jamaica Journal* 6(2):20–24.

MacCormack, Carol P. 1985. Lay Concepts Affecting Utilization of Family Planning Services in Jamaica. *Journal of Tropical Medicine and Hygiene* 88:281–85.

MacCormack, Carol P., and Alizon Draper. 1987. Social and Cognitive Aspects of Female Sexuality in Jamaica. *In* Pat Caplan, ed., *The Cultural Construction of Sexuality*. New York: Tavistock Publications, pp. 143–61.

McClain, Carol Shepherd, ed., 1989. *Women as Healers: Cross-Cultural Perspectives*. New Brunswick, N.J.: Rutgers University Press.

McLeod, Joan. 1982. *Baseline Information on Nutrition Related Factors in the Canaan Mountain Area, Westmoreland, 1979.* Kingston: University of the West Indies, Tropical Metabolism Research Unit.

Martin, Emily. 1991. Toward an Anthropology of Immunology: The Body as Nation State. *Medical Anthropology Quarterly* 4(4):410–26.

———. 1987. *The Woman in the Body: A Cultural Analysis of Reproduction.* Boston: Beacon Press.

Massiah, Joycelin. 1988. Researching Women's Work: 1985 and Beyond. *In* Patricia Mohammed and Catherine Shepherd, eds., *Gender in Caribbean Development.* Mona (Jamaica): The University of the West Indies, Women and Development Studies Project, pp. 206–31.

Massiah, Joycelin, ed. 1986. Special Issue: Women in the Caribbean. *Social and Economic Studies* 35(2&3).

Meigs, Anna S. 1987. Blood Kin and Food Kin. *In* J. P. Spradley and D. W. McCurdy, eds., *Conformity and Conflict: Readings in Cultural Anthropology.* Boston: Little, Brown and Company, pp. 117–24.

———. 1983. *Food, Sex, and Pollution.* New Brunswick, N.J.: Rutgers University Press.

Mintz, Sidney. 1987. The Historical Sociology of Jamaican Villages. *In* Charles V. Carnegie, ed., *Afro-Caribbean Villages in Historical Perspective,* Research Review No. 2. Kingston: African-Caribbean Institute of Jamaica, pp. 1–19.

———. 1986. *Sweetness and Power: The Place of Sugar in Modern History.* New York: Penguin Books.

———. 1974. *Caribbean Transformations.* Chicago: Aldine Publications.

Mitchell, Faith. 1983. Popular Medical Concepts in Jamaica and Their Impact on Drug Use. *The Western Journal of Medicine* 139:841–47.

Montgomery, Rita E. 1974. A Cross-cultural Study of Menstruation, Menstrual Taboos, and Related Social Variables. *Ethos* 2:137–70.

National Family Planning Board (Jamaica). 1988. Family Planning Acceptors on the Increase. *Family Planning and Population News Magazine* 2(1):2.

Newman, Lucile F. 1985. Context Variables in Fertility Regulation. *In* Lucile F. Newman, ed., *Women's Medicine: A Cross-Cultural Study of Indigenous Fertility Regulation.* New Brunswick, N.J.: Rutgers University Press, pp. 179–91.

Nichter, Mark, and Mimi Nichter. 1987. Cultural Notions of Fertility in South Asia and their Impact on Sri Lankan Family Planning Practices. *Human Organization* 46(1):18–28.

Ots, Thomas. 1990. The Angry Liver, the Anxious Heart, and the Melancholy Spleen: The Phenomenology of Perceptions in Chinese Culture. *Culture, Medicine, and Psychiatry* 14(1):21–58.

Paige, Karen Ericksen, and Jeffery M. Paige. 1981. *The Politics of Reproductive Ritual.* Los Angeles: University of California Press.

Pariser, Harry M. 1985. *Guide to Jamaica,* 2nd ed. Chico, Calif.: Moon Publications.

Patterson, Orlando. 1969 [1967]. *The Sociology of Slavery.* London: MacGibbon and Kee.

Payer, Lynn. 1988. *Medicine and Culture: Varieties of Treatment in the United States, England, West Germany, and France.* New York: Henry Holt and Company.

Phillips, A. S. 1973. *Adolescence in Jamaica.* Kingston: Jamaica Publishing House.

Powell, Dorian, Linda Hewitt, and Prudence Wooming. 1978. *Contraceptive Use in Jamaica.* Mona (Jamaica): Institute of Social and Economic Research, University of the West Indies.

Powell, Dorian, and Jean Jackson, eds. 1988. *Young Adult Reproductive Survey*. Kingston: National Family Planning Board.

Robertson, Diane. 1982. *Jamaican Herbs*. Montego Bay (Jamaica): DeSola Pinto Associates.

Rodman, Hyman. 1966. Illegitimacy in the Caribbean Social Structure: A Reconsideration. *American Sociological Review* 31(5):673–83.

Ross-Frankson, Joan. 1987. The Economic Crisis and Prostitution in Jamaica: A Preliminary Study. Kingston: Sistren Theatre Collective.

Rubin, Vera, and Lambros Comitas. 1975. *Ganja in Jamaica*. Paris: Mouton and Company.

Sargent, Carolyn, and Michael Harris. 1991. Gender, Childbearing, and Child Health in Jamaica. Unpublished paper presented at the 90th Annual Meeting of the American Anthropological Association, Chicago.

Scheper-Hughes, Nancy. 1988. The Madness of Hunger: Sickness, Delirium, and Human Needs. *Culture, Medicine and Psychiatry* 12:1–30.

Schlegel, Alice. 1990. Gender Meanings: General and Specific. *In* P. R. Sanday and R. G. Goodenough, eds., *Beyond the Second Sex: New Directions in the Anthropology of Gender*. Philadelphia: University of Pennsylvania Press, pp. 21–41.

Seaga, Edward. 1969. Revival Cults in Jamaica. *Jamaica Journal* 3(2):3–15.

Senior, Olive. 1991. *Working Miracles: Women's Lives in the English-Speaking Caribbean*. Bloomington: Indiana University Press.

Simpson, George Eaton. 1970. *Religious Cults of the Caribbean*. Rio Piedras (Puerto Rico): Institute of Caribbean Studies.

Skultans, Vieda. 1988. Menstrual Symbolism in South Wales. *In* Thomas Buckley and Alma Gottlieb, eds., *Blood Magic.* Los Angeles: University of California Press, pp. 137–60.

Smith, Honor Ford, ed., 1986. *Lionheart Gal: Life Stories of Jamaican Women.* London: The Women's Press.

Smith, Karl A., and Raymond L. Johnson. 1978. Physician, Nurse, and Midwife Opinion in Jamaica. *In* Henry P. David, Herbert L. Friedman, Jean van der Tak, and Marylis J. Sevilla, eds., *Abortion in Psychosocial Perspective.* New York: Springer Publishing Company, pp. 241–58.

Smith, M. G. 1989. *Poverty in Jamaica.* Kingston: Institute of Social and Economic Research, University of the West Indies.

———. 1984. *Culture, Race and Class in the Commonwealth Caribbean.* Kingston: Department of Extra-mural Studies, University of the West Indies.

Smith, R. T. 1988. *Kinship and Class in the West Indies.* Cambridge: Cambridge University Press.

———. 1987. Hierarchy and the Dual Marriage System in West Indian Society. *In* Jane Fishburne Collier and Sylvia Junko Yanagisako, eds., *Gender and Kinship: Essays Toward a Unified Analysis.* Stanford, Calif.: Stanford University Press, pp. 163–96.

Snow, L. F. 1974. Folk Medical Beliefs and Their Implications for Care of Patients: A Review Based on Studies among Black Americans. *Annals of Internal Medicine* 81(1):82–96.

STATIN (Statistical Institute of Jamaica). 1989. *Statistical Yearbook of Jamaica 1989.* Kingston: Statistical Institute of Jamaica.

———. 1988a. *Demographic Statistics 1988.* Kingston: Statistical Institute of Jamaica.

———. 1988b. *Pocketbook of Statistics Jamaica 1988.* Kingston: Statistical Institute of Jamaica.

———. 1982. Census. (Unpublished information on Portland Parish, Jamaica, from files of STATIN).

Stephens, William N. 1967. A Cross-Cultural Study of Menstrual Taboos. *In* Clellan S. Ford, ed., *Cross-Cultural Approaches: Readings in Comparative Research*. New Haven, Conn.: Human Relations Area Files Press, pp. 67–94.

Taylor, Christopher. 1988. The Concept of Flow in Rwandan Popular Medicine. *Social Science and Medicine* 27(12): 1343–48.

Turner, Victor. 1979 [1968]. Divination as a Phase in a Social Process. *In* William A. Lessa and Evon Z. Vogt, eds., *Reader in Comparative Religion*. San Francisco: Harper and Row, pp. 373–78.

Wedenoja, William. 1989. Mothering and the Practice of 'Balm' in Jamaica. *In* Carol Shepherd McClain, ed., *Women as Healers: Cross-Cultural Perspectives*. New Brunswick, N.J.: Rutgers University Press, pp. 76–97.

———. 1988. The Origins of Revival, a Creole Religion in Jamaica. *In* G. Saunders, ed., *Culture and Christianity*. Westport, Conn.: Greenwood.

———. 1980. The Psychiatric Patient in Rural Jamaica. Unpublished paper presented at the 79th Annual Meeting of the American Anthropological Association, Washington, D.C.

Weekend Enquirer (Kingston, Jamaica). 1989a (5–7 May). Oversize "Dick" Sues the *Enquirer*, p. 38.

———. 1989b (5–7 May). Spread yu legs, mek a si if yu hide anyt'ing up de!! p. 7.

———. 1989c (12–14 May). How Ginny Lost her Punnany.

Weigle, Marta. 1989. *Creation and Procreation*. Philadelphia: University of Pennsylvania Press.

Wilson, Peter J. 1973. *Crab Antics.* New Haven, Conn.: Yale University Press.

Wright, Anne. 1982. Attitudes Toward Childbearing and Menstruation among the Navajo. *In* Margarita Artschwager Kay, ed., *Anthropology of Human Birth.* Philadelphia: F. A. Davis Company, pp. 377–94.

Young, Frank, and Albert Bacdayan. 1965. Menstrual Taboos and Social Rigidity. *Ethnology* 4:225–41.

Index